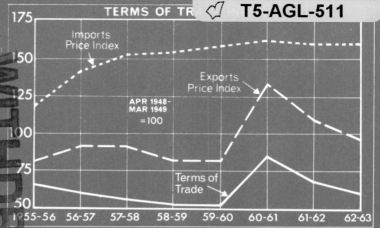

TERMS OF TRADE

APR 1948–
MAR 1949
=100

Imports
Price Index

Exports
Price Index

Terms of
Trade

175
150
125
100
75
50

1955-56   56-57   57-58   58-59   59-60   60-61   61-62   62-63

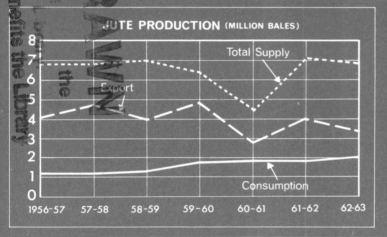

JUTE PRODUCTION (MILLION BALES)

Total Supply

Export

Consumption

8
7
6
5
4
3
2
1
0

1956-57   57-58   58-59   59-60   60-61   61-62   62-63

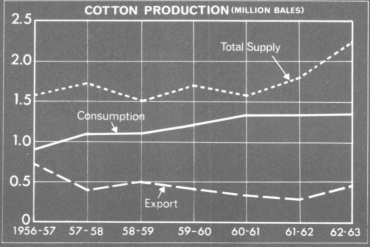

COTTON PRODUCTION (MILLION BALES)

Total Supply

Consumption

Export

2.5
2.0
1.5
1.0
0.5
0

1956-57   57-58   58-59   59-60   60-61   61-62   62-63

We are indebted to the State Bank of Pakistan for supplying these charts and figures.

*Trade, Finance and
Development in Pakistan*

Trade, Finance and Development in Pakistan

J. RUSSELL ANDRUS, PH.D.

AZIZALI F. MOHAMMED, PH.D.

STANFORD UNIVERSITY PRESS
Stanford, California
1966

Stanford University Press
Stanford, California

© Oxford University Press 1966

Printed in Great Britain
by Ebenezer Baylis & Son Ltd.
The Trinity Press, Worcester, and London
L.C. 64–12076

PREFACE

THIS work started as a revised edition of *The Economy of Pakistan*.[1] However, it soon became evident that a mere revision would not suffice. When the earlier book went to press, the First Five Year Plan was just getting under way. As this is written, the Second Plan is nearing completion and a Perspective Plan for the next twenty years is in an advanced stage of preparation. The entire pattern of foreign trade has changed drastically, as Pakistan has become completely or nearly self-sufficient in textiles and several other products which previously figured heavily in imports while at the same time it has become a net importer of food-grains. The business and financial structure has developed a new sophistication. Pakistan, like many other nations in Asia, has acquired through experience a great deal of useful new knowledge as to how to prepare a sound development plan and how to make it work.

For these reasons, only an occasional sentence or paragraph of the earlier work remains, and only the latter part of the *The Economy of Pakistan* is covered in this study, namely the part that is most out of date. Thus a new title is essential, and by narrowing the coverage of the book a more detailed study of the financial and commercial aspects most closely involved in development has been possible.

The present book, therefore, assumes knowledge of the geographical background, vital statistics and basic structure of the Pakistan economy. It focuses on the commercial and financial arrangements in both their external and internal aspects and their relation to the country's programmes of economic development.

This book deals with a number of controversial subjects, on which there are certain to be differences of opinion among competent authorities. We are of course alone responsible for our views, and the International Monetary Fund, the State Bank of Pakistan, the Department of State and the Agency for International Development with which one or the other author has been or is associated bear no responsibility for the views expressed herein.

[1] Oxford University Press, 1958.

Finally, we would like to express our thanks to AFM's colleagues in the State Bank of Pakistan for all their kindness in supplying information; any mistakes in facts or their use are ours. As with the earlier book, Mrs. Sakin Mohammed worked with patience and fortitude typing several drafts. Thanks are also due to Mrs. Lillian H. Cooley, Mrs. Josephine Khan and Miss Marthe M. Ares for wholly unremunerated assistance with the typing of the final manuscript.

JRA
AFM

March 1965

CONTENTS

TABLES

ESSENTIAL STATISTICS

1. Area in Sq. miles

	Area in Sq. miles	Percentages
Pakistan	365,529	100
E. Pakistan	55,126	15·1
W. Pakistan	310,403	84·9

2. Population in millions (1961 Census)

	Population	Percentages
Pakistan	93·8	100
E. Pakistan	50·8	54·2
W. Pakistan	43·0	45·8

3. Population Density per Square mile

East Pakistan (including river areas)	922
West Pakistan	138

4. Rural and Urban Distribution of Population

	Urban	% total population	Rural	% total population
Pakistan	12·3 million	13·1%	81·5 million	86·9%
East Pakistan	2·6 million	5·2%	48·2 million	94·8%
West Pakistan	9·7 million	22·5%	33·2 million	77·5%

5. Annual percentage rate of Population increase (1951–61)

Pakistan	2·1%
East Pakistan	1·9%
West Pakistan	2·4%

6. Distribution of Civilian Labour Force

	Total	Agriculture	% total	Non-agriculture	% total
Pakistan	30·2 million	22·4 million	74·30%	7·8 million	25·70%
East Pakistan	17·4 million	14·9 million	85·26%	2·5 million	14·74%
West Pakistan	12·8 million	7·6 million	59·31%	5·2 million	40·69%

7. Distribution of Manufacturing Labour Force: (numbers in thousands)

	PAKISTAN		E. PAKISTAN		W. PAKISTAN	
	Urban	Rural	Urban	Rural	Urban	Rural
Large-scale Manufacturing	530	—	167	—	363	—
Small-scale Industry	78	1,552	19	631	59	921

8. Gross National Product of Pakistan at Factors Cost
(Base 1959–60) for 1962–63 (Rs. in crores):

Gross Domestic Product	East Pakistan	West Pakistan
(a)	(a)	(a)
3,600·5	1,630·8	1,858·5

9. Per capita Income for 1962–63 (In Rupees):

Pakistan	East Pakistan	West Pakistan
336	280	382

10. Origin of Domestic Product—1962–63:
(percentages)

	PAKISTAN	EAST PAKISTAN	WEST PAKISTAN
Agriculture including Forestry and Fishing	50·7	59·1	46·7
Manufacturing and Mining	10·6	7·6	13·9
Other Economic Activities	34·6	31·7	36·9
Public Administration of Defence	4·6	1·6	2·5
Total:	100·0	100·0	100·0

(a) Provincial totals will not add up national totals because of unallocated items i.e. Central Government, Banking and Insurance and Pakistan International Airlines.

I

PRODUCTION AND MARKETING
OF EXPORT CROPS

OF the major cash crops in Pakistan, jute, cotton, wool, hides and skins, tea and certain varieties of rice are exported. Cash crops for which there is no exportable surplus are sugar-cane, tobacco, oilseeds and betel-nuts. Table 1 provides data on acreage and production of agricultural cash crops. This chapter discusses production and *internal* marketing arrangements for crops entering the export trade.

Jute is a widely-used fibre in the packaging field, because it is both hard-wearing and cheap. As a yarn it goes into carpets, cables and cordage. As cloth it is sewn into sacks for moving and storing a number of foodstuffs and raw materials, as well as some industrial products like fertilizer and cement. Jute fabric also serves as wrapping material (hessian) and is used in furniture webbing, upholstery, for backing linoleum and in several other applications, especially after treatment against moisture, mildew, rot, insect damage, fire and acid fumes.

East Pakistan produces about 40 per cent. of the total world crop of jute and is almost the sole exporter of unmanufactured jute, with a near monopoly on the finer varieties. Two major types are grown: *corchorus capsularis* (white) and *olitorius* (golden). From two-thirds to three-fourths of the area is under the former, because it withstands adverse weather conditions better, grows on both high- and low-lying lands, is an early maturing crop, and also because it is possible to transplant *aman* or winter rice immediately if harvesting is not delayed beyond early July. The latter variety (locally known as *bogi* or *desi* and internationally as *tossa*) is mainly grown on high lands in the western parts of the province. Its fibre is normally finer, softer and stronger and more lustrous than *capsularis*, and generally commands a price premium in the market. Jute is generally sown from the middle of February to the middle of May, but sowings as late as early June are not uncommon on the higher lands. Harvesting begins in June and may continue to the end of September.

There are two reasons for East Bengal's quasi-monopoly in the cultivation of high-quality raw jute: (1) geographical conditions are appropriate—damp heat, rainfall evenly distributed during the growing period, rich loamy or alluvial soil, and ample supplies of water for washing the crop; (2) jute is a *bast* or inner

TABLE 1

ACREAGE AND PRODUCTION OF PRINCIPAL CASH CROPS

Crop	10 Year Average Ended 1956–57	1958 –59	1959 –60	1960 –61	1961 –62	1962 –63	1963 –64
	A: *ACREAGE* (*In thousands of acres*)						
E. Pakistan							
Jute	1,597	1,528	1,375	1,518	2,061	1,723	1,700
Tea	74	76	78	78	79	81	84
Tobacco	126	111	110	102	108	102	101
Sugar-cane	244	244	281	279	286	318	396
Cotton	55	51	52	47	39	40	38
Rape/Mustard	491	554	578	558	577	576	500
Sub-Total	2,584	2,564	2,474	2,582	3,150	2,840	2,769
W. Pakistan							
Cotton	3,118	3,273	3,318	3,195	3,449	3,395	3,634
Tobacco	57	89	95	96	112	117	109
Sugar-cane	587	1,057	980	959	1,003	1,312	1,180
Rape/Mustard	1,176	1,493	1,387	1,233	1,238	1,242	1,173
Sub-Total	4,945	5,912	5,780	5,483	5,777	6,066	6,096
Total—Pakistan	7,529	8,476	8,254	8,065	8,927	8,906	8,865
	B: *PRODUCTION* (*In thousands of tons*)						
E. Pakistan							
Jute[1]	968	1,125	964	803	1,244	1,125	1,049
Tea[2]	20	24	25	19	26	23	25
Tobacco	45	42	27	25	31	29	28
Sugar-cane (raw)	3,576	3,834	3,611	3,955	4,418	4,749	5,363
Cotton (lint)	3	3	3	3	3	3	7
Rape/Mustard	94	105	83	97	103	104	89
Sub-Total	4,706	5,079	4,741	5,103	5,835	6,033	6,561
W. Pakistan							
Cotton (lint)	251	268	288	297	319	376	415
Tobacco	35	56	61	59	69	71	74
Sugar-cane (raw)	7,284	12,292	10,494	11,457	14,130	18,148	15,885
Rape/Mustard	184	268	235	211	202	257	208
Sub-Total	7,754	12,884	11,078	12,024	14,720	18,852	16,582
Total—Pakistan	12,460	17,963	15,819	17,127	20,555	24,885	23,143

[1] One ton = 5·6 bales of 400 lbs. each.   [2] One ton = 2,240 lbs.
Source: Central Statistical Office *Monthly Bulletin*, except for jute and cotton production data, which are trade estimates.

bark fibre, and to separate it from its outer sheath the stem of the jute plant is 'retted' to soften tissues, so that the fibre can be readily stripped. The quality of the fibre depends largely on the skill exercised in the highly labour-intensive processes of retting, stripping and washing. It is because wage rates are low and labourers endowed with the traditional skills for jute culture and processing are readily available that the Bengal region of the subcontinent has remained almost the sole producer of raw jute.[1]

The normal yield of white jute is $17\frac{1}{4}$ maunds and of *tossa* about 19 maunds per acre. Yields vary from year to year but by a lesser margin than the variations in acreage. Output changes are therefore chiefly attributable to acreage changes which are affected by (1) weather and flooding conditions and (2) the relative advantage of planting jute on the one hand and *aus* (autumn) rice on the other, as reflected in the relationship between jute prices prevailing at the time of sowing and the retail price of rice at that time. If jute prices at the grower level have been particularly low, the grower may respond by reducing the area under jute, unless he comes to accept the prevailing prices as normal. Rice prices are important, because *aus* paddy is an alternative crop in much of the area normally planted to jute, and rice constitutes the largest item of expenditure in the grower's budget. Thus the acreage under *aus* rice increases as the profit differential from jute narrows. A fairly strong correlation between jute and *aus* paddy prices was found by an F.A.O. study in the pre-war period, 1931–2 to 1939–40. A similar nine-year period of the post-Partition years 1947–8 to 1955–6 shows a weaker correlation, due partly to the regulation of the jute area and the greater pull of rice prices in the period of rice shortages in the immediate post-Partition years.[2] The Jute Enquiry Commission (1961) concluded that a ratio of at least 1·6 to 1 was necessary to stimulate *increases* in jute plantings.[3]

This relationship was little impeded by the regulation of the acreage of jute under the Bengal Jute Regulation Act of 1940.

---

[1] *Report*, Jute Enquiry Commission, Government of Pakistan (Ministry of Commerce), Karachi, 1961. *See* also, *Marketing of Jute in East Pakistan* (Dacca University Socio-Economic Research Board), Dacca, 1961.

[2] FAO Commodity Series—*Jute: A Survey of Markets, Manufacturing and Production*; Bulletin No. 28, Rome, 1957, pp. 20–4.

[3] *Report*, Jute Commission, para. 220.

Although the acreage control was expected to hold output in line with (anticipated) changes in demand so as to maintain jute prices at some 'fair' level, the intended effects were rendered inoperative in several ways. The Government's acreage decision was concerned exclusively with jute and not with rice. There need be no change in the 'licensed' area if Government anticipated no change (or need for change) in prices (or stocks) of jute, whereas price relationships might indicate the profitability of a shift away from jute if rice prices were rising. Hence the area planted to jute could fall below the 'licensed' area, thus illustrating a basic limitation of an acreage control that covers only one of the competing crops. At some level of relative prices and acreage, the grower can plant *less* jute than desired by the licensing authority, and the latter has no effective rejoinder. On the other hand, such a policy could ensure that the acreage cropped to jute was no *more* than that licensed only if adequately administered. Given the hundreds of thousands of small plots on which jute is grown a larger crop could be and was cropped when growers considered it in their interest to do so. The willingness to contravene the licensing regulations increased with the favourableness (to jute) of the price ratio. Acreage cropped was higher than that licensed in nine out of thirteen years since Independence, and was very much larger in 1958–9 and 1959–60. In the latter years the jute/rice price ratio was moving in favour of jute, owing to supply shortages caused by unseasonable weather, illustrating another limitation of acreage control, *viz.* the yield per acre was entirely beyond executive regulation.

For the 1960–61 season, acreage restrictions were relaxed, except in border areas, and the ban imposed on the growing of inferior varieties of jute (*mesta*) was lifted. Despite a rise in area, output was curtailed by severe drought and prices rose to unprecedented levels. In 1961–2 all restrictions on jute cultivation were lifted, and official policy has apparently moved firmly away from acreage controls. It has been recognized that even if licensing controls can be enforced, the effect on the variable which it is meant to control—the price of jute—remains indeterminate unless two conditions are met: (a) the country can exercise a degree of monopolist control over the world market and (b) the demand for jute is largely price-inelastic. The first condition was greatly undermined by the rapid increase in jute output in

India after Independence, which culminated in 1958-9 in a crop large enough to supply all needs of India's mills (except the small imports from Pakistan) and also to permit India's entry as a marginal supplier of raw jute in the world market. Neither of these conditions is met in actual fact. Pakistan cannot control the effective world supply of the fibre because India, with a little over half of the world jute loomage, is largely independent of Pakistan for its raw material. Nor is the non-Indian demand for jute prices inelastic. The pre-eminence of jute as a packaging material is predicated on its relative cheapness. Attempts to hold up prices through output-restrictions encourage both substitute fibres and alternative methods of storing and moving commodities, thus shifting the demand curve for Pakistan jute gradually to the left and perhaps flattening out its slope within the price ranges at which new substitutes or alternatives become successively profitable to adopt.

The growers retain some jute for domestic and other cottage industry uses like making ropes, mats, string and crude sacking material. The local retention is estimated at 300,000 bales and the rest comes to market. Two considerations arise in marketing at the grower level: (a) the time of sale, and (b) the place of sale. The grower would gain from withholding his crop for a while because prices tend to be lowest at harvest time. However, his holding power is limited by inadequate credit facilities, by insufficient storage capacity in the village and by difficulties of transport once the floods begin to recede in October, leaving most rural areas without boat routes to the larger market centres. Moreover, the average cultivator does not grow more than 20 maunds or so, and since harvesting is intermittent, he does not have much fibre available at any time. He therefore sells at his doorstep to peripatetic *farias*, or in the local village *hat* (primary market) to *beparis*. The jute is sold in unassorted condition and the grower suffers both from under-estimation of quality and by under-weighing which is facilitated by a 'bewildering diversity of weights'. Nor are conditions likely to be much better for the individual grower in the larger or secondary markets. He is confronted with a series of discounts and charges for moisture, for anticipated loss in weight and quality ('*dhatia*'), for weighing ('*koyali*'), buyer's office expenses ('*khatia*' and '*kabari*'). The brokers (*dalals*) may not be strictly impartial as between the two

2

parties, as the buyers have greater bargaining power. It is therefore not surprising that as much as 90 per cent. of jute is sold by
growers either in the village or the *hat* to *farias* and *beparis*,
another 4 per cent. to *aretdars*, 5 per cent. to *katcha* balers and
one per cent. to *pucca* balers, shippers and mills.[4]

From the *hats* the jute moves to the baling centres where most
of the *katcha* (manually operated) baling presses and a few *pucca*
(hydraulic pressure) presses are located. The chief buyers are the
balers, while sellers are either the large *beparis* or the *aretdars*.
The latter is a middleman of great importance at this stage; he
performs not only brokerage and assemblage functions like other
dealers in jute, but may also finance many of the *beparis* at the
grower level, and some *aretdars* have their own godowns to store
the fibre. Up to this point the jute has been handled unassorted
and unbaled. In the secondary markets it goes through its first
processing, namely *katcha* baling, the jute being compressed after
being sorted into its commercial grades.[5] Among the *katcha*
balers again, there are three types: representatives of jute mills,
large baling firms with head offices at Narayanganj, Khulna or
Chittagong and buying out-agencies at small secondary or even
primary markets and finally, small concerns of essentially local
importance, with an individual turnover not exceeding 8,000
bales annually. The *katcha* bale comes in sizes varying from 1½ to
4 maunds, with an average of 328 lbs. There were 1,303 *katcha*
baling presses in 1959–60 but many have been idle since the
cessation of *katcha* bale exports to India in 1954. Moreover, jute
mills as well as *pucca* balers often buy loose jute or *katcha* bales
through presses affiliated to them, so that a number of smaller,
independent presses have been eliminated from the trade.

The *pucca* bale is pressed to a uniform weight of 400 lbs. and
measures 10½ cu. ft. At the time of Partition there were 32 *pucca*
presses, located mainly in Narayanganj, Chittagong and Mymensingh districts with a nominal baling capacity of 2·83 million
annually. Following the trade deadlock with India, the capacity
was rapidly increased and by the middle of 1960 there were 88
presses with an effective monthly capacity of 843,500 bales.
However, there is an undue concentration of presses in some
areas and a corresponding shortage in other important centres,

---

[4] *Report*, Jute Commission, para. 238.
[5] See Appendix Note to this chapter on grading of jute.

resulting in uneconomic movements of jute for baling before the jute moves into the shipping terminal stations of Chittagong and Chalna. This movement is mainly by railway or on inland water transport (I.W.T.) flats, with recourse to independently operated large-size boats where other facilities are unavailable. I.W.T. freights tend to be higher than railway freights but the service is generally considered more satisfactory.[6]

At the time of Independence, Calcutta was much the largest terminal market for jute from East Bengal. This was disrupted abruptly in September 1949, because of the exchange rate dispute. To arrest the dangerous fall in jute prices, the Central Government acquired powers under the Jute Ordinance 1949 (replaced by the Act of 1956) to fix minimum support prices, to appoint agents and brokers to purchase, store and sell jute on its behalf and to fix baling and other charges. A Jute Board was created to administer the law. The Provincial Government promulgated an Ordinance to register all dealers in jute. The Ordinance required all dealers, occupiers of jute godowns and *katcha* and *pucca* balers to register and obtain a licence, subject to renewal each year. Minimum prices were fixed for loose jute and 159 agents were appointed who were prepared to 'associate themselves' with the Jute Board in buying at the minimum prices. These agents purchased 850,000 maunds of jute valued at Rs. 20 million with the help of special banking facilities provided by the newly organized National Bank of Pakistan. After the Korean War interlude there was a sharp break in prices early in 1952 and the Jute Board again fixed minimum prices. By June 1952 the Board had purchased 6·9 million maunds at a cost of Rs. 165 million. Prices continued to decline in the face of a bumper 1952–3 crop and minimum prices had to be reduced so that the Board ended up with a loss of roughly Rs. 90 million. Its effective intervention, however, helped to stabilize trading conditions, saved new entrants from bankruptcy and relieved the National Bank of two million maunds of jute with which it was left when borrowers defaulted.

In later years (i.e. up to the end of the 1961–2 season) the Jute Board refrained from supporting internal prices directly, confining itself to fixing minimum prices for exports. An export price check was operated by the State Bank to ensure that export

[6] See discussion in *Report*, Jute Commission, paras. 272–4 and 290–4.

commitments were not made below these levels and that they otherwise reflected current prices.[7]

In 1957 the Provincial Government established a Jute Marketing Corporation with a paid-up capital of Rs. 20 million, for the purchase of jute with a view to ensuring a fair price to the grower, assisting in promoting co-operative societies, establishing regulated markets and standard grades and buying jute in the border areas. During the first season of its operation, the Corporation was given a procurement monopoly in the border areas and collected about a million maunds of jute. However, it incurred a loss of Rs. 638,000 because of a fall in the market and high initial expenditures. In 1958–9 its functions were allocated to two separate committees for purchase and sale of jute respectively. A little over 1·1 million maunds were lifted but sold at a loss of Rs. 1·99 million. In 1959–60 a new management was inducted and under its revitalized leadership the Corporation has gradually come to acquire a position of strength in jute marketing, all the way from purchasing from growers to selling abroad under its own well-established 'export' mark. By 1961–2 the Corporation had about 70 buying centres throughout the province, including over a dozen growers' centres where purchases were made directly from growers at premium prices. The Corporation has acquired its own pressing facilities and its activities have afforded indirect support to the market when prices were tending to fall.

Despite the improvements in the jute trade in the past 15 years, in particular, the elimination of foreign dominance and the achievement of national banking, baling, shipping and manufacturing capacity, there have been persistent complaints that the existing marketing arrangements do not ensure a 'fair' return to the grower of jute. In some respects, his position may have deteriorated as the eclipse of foreign trading elements reduced the number of buyers operating in the market.

A Jute Enquiry Commission was appointed in 1959 with wide-ranging terms of reference including, among others, the suggestion of measures 'to ensure stable price levels and a fair return to the grower, *aretdar* and baler'. The Commission sought to determine a 'fair return' by relating the price of jute at grower level to

---

[7] The EPC procedure was temporarily suspended in the later part of the 1961–2 season, but restored in the 1962–3 season.

(i) the jute-paddy ratio; (ii) the cost of production of jute; (iii) the export prices of raw jute and (iv) the price of jute goods. As for (i) the critical price ratio at which the grower was just induced to grow jute was 1·6:1 at prevailing costs of production and yields per acre, and on the basis of a support price of Rs. 12 per maund of paddy at which Government has undertaken to purchase paddy wherever offered, the 'distress' price for jute was found to be Rs. 19·2 per maund. Assuming the cost of production to be Rs. 16 per maund on the average, the Commission suggested a minimum margin of Rs. 5 to the grower, or a price of Rs. 21 per maund in respect of (ii).[8] For basis (iii) the Commission assumed an export price of raw jute of £100 per ton for Export Firsts and £40 per ton for Cuttings, and calculating marketing costs, including middlemen's profits, to be Rs. 19·4 per maund, a minimum price of Rs. 21 for loose unassorted jute was indicated. For basis (iv) the price of jute goods was assumed to be Rs. 110 for sacking (B-Twills per 100 bags) and Rs. 42 for hessian (40 × 10 oz. per 100 yards) and with conversion costs of raw jute taken at Rs. 665 and Rs. 370 per ton respectively for sacking and hessian, the price that could be paid to the grower worked out at Rs. 25½ per maund F.O.B. baling centres and Rs. 22 per maund at the grower level. Finally, taking into account the cost of maintaining his family, the 'physical strain on the jute grower, the risks of cultivation, harvesting, storage, marketing and price fluctuations', the Commission concluded that the grower would secure a fair return at an average price of Rs. 25 per maund for unassorted jute.

To ensure this price it was necessary to undertake buffer stock operations through an organization which would be empowered to buy jute from growers at minimum prices, store it if necessary and sell it at predetermined maximum prices. It was felt a single authority should be responsible for jute, although actual price stabilization operations could be conducted by other agencies under its direction. The Authority was expected to adopt a

[8] The cost of production has been calculated more recently at Rs. 19·99 per maund for white and Rs. 19·35 per maund for *tossa* jute on an average-size holding of 5·71 acres, of which roughly one-fourth was planted to jute. The cost presumably relates to land obtained on cash rent, as more than 88 per cent. of holdings surveyed were worked on that basis; share-cropping accounted for 10·4 per cent. and only 1·4 per cent. were on a lease basis. Cf. Central Jute Committee: 'Report on Cost of Production of Jute', 1962.

series of interlocking measures for improving the marketing, baling, transport and storage of jute.

To implement these recommendations, a Jute Ordinance was issued in 1962 'for regulating and promoting the internal and international trade in jute and jute manufactures'. The new law replaced both the Central Jute Act of 1956 and the Provincial Jute Dealers' Registration Law of 1949. A single authority—the Jute Board—is entrusted with the problems of jute, including the licensing of the jute trade. The Central Government was empowered to fix minimum prices below which and maximum prices above which jute or jute manufactures of various grades may not be sold or purchased, either for domestic use or export. Following a sharp break in jute prices in September 1962, minimum prices for assorted and unassorted white and *tossa* jute were fixed at grower level by the Jute Board. For the first time, minimum prices were fixed differently in the various zones, i.e. at Rs. 24 in Jat, Rs. 23 in District and Rs. 22 in Northern zones, with a premium of two rupees in all zones for *tossa* jute. As for assorted jute, the price of White Jat B-Bottoms loose was fixed at Rs. 27½ per maund with a grade premium of two rupees respectively for each higher grade. These prices were for the *first* transaction in the internal market with scope left for the trade to add its normal establishment, transport and other costs, plus usual trade profits. While any sales/purchases below these minimum prices are now a penal offence punishable with fine, imprisonment or both, in addition to confiscation of the jute, it was recognized that no enforcement machinery can really be expected to oversee the myriad transactions taking place. To make the prices effective, purchases at minimum prices by the Jute Marketing Corporation were authorized. A revolving fund of Rs. 80 million has been set up to finance purchases through JMC centres as well as through other purchasing agencies. It remains to be seen whether this scheme will prove any more effective than the earlier ones in protecting the interests of the grower while maintaining the supply of raw jute to the world market at competitive prices.

Equally useful results will probably come through raising yields per acre so as to reduce unit costs of production. This will require a concerted effort to improve cultural practices (e.g. through irrigation and better ploughing) to provide supplies of improved seed, implements and fertilizers to the grower at prices he can afford, and to control pests and plant diseases. At the present time the production and distribution of superior nucleus and improved seed by the Pakistan Central Jute Committee and the Agriculture Department fall far short of need. It is hoped, by the end of the Second Plan period, to place 2,500 acres under nucleus seed and then to multiply them through Government farms and registered growers so as to meet the entire need for improved seeds in a five-year period. Arrangements for distribution of the improved seeds, fertilizers and implements as well as pesticides are being made by the supply wing of the Agricultural Development Corporation, recently established in the province. A Jute Research Institute at Tejgaon is doing research on the breeding of improved strains of jute.

Cotton is a West Pakistan crop[9] which according to international standards is classified as medium-staple, American Upland type except for about one-tenth of the output which is Asiatic short-staple *Desi* cotton. The staple ranges between $1\frac{1}{16}''$ (for newer selections of 289F) to $\frac{3}{4}''-\frac{7}{8}''$ (4F), with intermediate staples of $\frac{15}{16}''$ to $1''$ (N.T. Sind) $\frac{27}{32}''-\frac{15}{16}''$ (L.S.S.). The first American strains were introduced in 1914 and gradually replaced *desi* cotton ($\frac{1}{3}''-\frac{5}{8}''$) which grew in the Indus Basin for centuries. There was a tendency to move progressively to longer staples; L.S.S. steadily replaced 4F in the mid-thirties, and in turn yielded ground to the 289F varieties in the former Punjab (124F and 199F) and N.T. in the former Sind (M-4). Finer selections of 289F known as *Lassani* ($1\frac{1}{32}''-1\frac{1}{16}''$) and other longer staples are now developed.

Cotton is a summer crop and is extensively grown on irrigated lands. Sowing starts by the beginning of May in the south and may continue till July in the north. Picking commences by the end of July and may continue up to the middle of January. Planting is mostly 'broadcast' and little manure is applied, although the use of chemical fertilizers is spreading. Variations in yield are accounted for mainly by weather conditions, although immediately after Partition, the inexperience of refugees in cotton farming on irrigated lands reduced output. Both acreage

[9] There is a small crop of 10 to 55,000 bales in East Pakistan known as *Comilla*. It 'is the best harsh short-staple grown anywhere in the world, and commands a premium in price over all comparable varieties'. (SFYP, p. 135.)

and production increased after 1950–51, as conditions returned to normal. In 1952–3, the crop reached a peak of 1·8 million bales. The food shortages that emerged in 1953–4 led to an official discouragement of cotton growing in favour of summer grains. The growth of the textile industry led to a sharp increase in domestic consumption and, in order to maintain the exportable surplus, a grow-more-cotton campaign was launched with the 1955–6 crop. The campaign proved largely ineffective. Against a First Plan target of 2¼ million bales, production stagnated in the range 1·5 to 1·7 million bales as yields were almost stationary at 189 lbs. per acre. Recurring weather difficulties, insect damage and water shortages in the canals were held responsible in earlier years. Later, there was increasing recognition that the causes of stagnation lay deeper. Low applications of irrigation water, the accumulation of salts in the soil, unreliable seeds, inadequate plant protection and uneven cover of plants have combined to keep yields low. Market incentives have also worked against cotton. Sugar-cane has proved more profitable, encouraging the diversion from cotton not of land as such but of precious irrigation supplies and peasant energy. The return from cotton has been depressed by export duties on cotton and by price controls on cotton manufactures enforced at various times (though not now) in behalf of the domestic consumers. Prices of cotton-seed (which constitute two-thirds of the weight of *kapas*) have similarly been kept down by price controls on oil products and by growing imports of edible oils under Public Law 480.

The Second Plan reaffirms a target of 2·3 million bales. The present requirements of the cotton textile industry are 1·4 million bales and are expected to rise by the end of the Second Plan period. This would mean the complete absorption of American growths by the textile industry (unless output can be increased to Plan targets) with exports confined to the short-staple cotton not used by the textile mills. The Plan expects the larger output to be obtained mainly by greater use of fertilizer and improved seed, modernization of ginning equipment and adoption of better cultivation practices. Acreage is to be expanded by 9 per cent. On the side of incentives, the lifting of price controls on cotton textiles in January 1961 may have helped but it remains to be seen whether additional market inducements will be necessary to overcome the attractiveness of other crops. Without these inducements, there can be no assurance that improved methods will actually be applied by the grower.[10]

Studies on cotton are conducted under the aegis of the Central Cotton Committee (established in 1949) and financed through a cess of Rs. 0·25 per bale on ginned cotton plus grants from Government. The Committee seeks to improve yields through research and extension work. It has set up an Institute of Cotton Research and Technology at Karachi, with testing and laboratory facilities, to advise cotton breeders and textile mills on technological and spinning properties of various cottons. The number of research stations has increased to 17 and the number of schemes assisted by the Committee is over 30 at the present time.

Cotton is a cross-pollinated plant and care must be exercised to prevent admixture of different seeds. A Cotton Control Act was passed in the Punjab in 1949 (later extended to Bahawalpur) providing for the cultivation of specified staples in specified zones. The control is being extended to the whole of West Pakistan under new legislation, which also provides for stricter supervision at the ginneries. Effective enforcement is essential if seed improvements are to be successful.

The average cultivator does not grow more than a few hundred pounds of *kapas* (unginned cotton) and retains a little for hand-spinning and other domestic uses. He may sell his produce either in the nearest *mandy* (market-place) or ginning factory or at his doorstep to itinerant dealers, agents or brokers representing ginners. Sometimes sales are made on a forward basis and in return the grower may obtain an advance of a few rupees per maund of *phutti* (bundles of *kapas*) contracted. Forward sales are made with or without fixation of prices. Sometimes, even ready sales may be made on an 'unfixed-price' basis.

The responsibility for transporting *kapas* to the ginnery rests on the grower, even when the sale is ex-village. Where communications are good, he uses his own *gaddy* (bullock-cart). Alternatively, a small discount in the price is conceded and then the ginner or dealer arranges for transport through contractors operating with strings of camels in areas where communications

[10] The rise in production since 1962–3 raises hopes that a breakthrough may have occurred in cotton farming (see next chapter).

are primitive or with carts and lorries where roads are better. In parts of Hyderabad Division, *kapas* is brought to the factories by rail.

Cotton thus finds its way to the ginning factory or the *mandy*. The *mandy* system is well established in the Canal Colonies, with the exception of parts of Multan Division. There are over 160 *mandies* in this region, an average *mandy* servicing fifty to sixty villages. No *mandies* dealing in cotton are found in Hyderabad or Khairpur Divisions. Ginning factories are generally situated near the *mandies*. The most important functionary in the *mandy* is the commission agent (*arhatiya*). Strictly speaking, he is a middleman between the grower and the ginner, though working on behalf of the grower. The agent receives for his services (and for other incidental charges incurred such as shortage and weighing) a varying charge, generally not exceeding Rs. 1·56 per maund of *kapas* in most of the 'regulated' *mandies*. He also performs this service for the small dealer and sometimes may even finance him. In non-*mandy* areas, the broker acting on behalf of the ginner generally takes the place of the commission agent.

The price received by the grower for his *kapas* is closely related to the price of lint cotton of the same staple in the Karachi market, and the ginning output of *kapas*, which varies between 28 and 35 per cent., but is taken on the average at 33 per cent. (i.e. three maunds of *kapas* equal one maund of lint plus two maunds of cotton-seed). The grower is also paid for the cotton-seed at the prevailing market prices. Payment is made by the ginner directly (or through the commission agent), either immediately on weighing or after a lapse of time, according to the usage of the area; the normal wait is three days after weighment.

The ginning process is done mostly on roller gins though the vogue of saw gins is gradually spreading. There are 807 ginning and pressing units in West Pakistan of which 450 are small units with only one or two gins. The equipment of the industry is largely outdated and it has been poorly maintained, as many of the factories were until recently evacuee property operated by 'allottees' on annual leases. This factor coupled with the non-issuance of import licences for modernizing equipment accounted for the almost total failure to spend the First Plan provision of Rs. 68 million for the industry. Another allocation of Rs. 16 million for PIDC participation with private capital in setting up seven model ginning units was partially spent, with four units completed. In the Second Plan period a loan of U.S. $6·4 million was secured for ginning machinery and distributed through the Industrial Development Bank in 1962.

After cotton is ginned, much of the American type is sold to textile mills, some of whom have their own ginneries. Large Karachi export houses may also own ginning factories or buy from up-country ginneries through agents who may actually supervise the ginning. The rest is consigned to commission houses in Karachi, the ginner receiving some advance payment when the cotton is dispatched and final payment when it is sold. The commission houses are able to obtain the business of many ginners because they own huge storage yards (plinths) where cotton is kept prior to sale and shipment. The transactions between the selling groups (commission houses) and the buying groups (export houses and mills) at Karachi are mediated by brokers appointed by the Karachi Cotton Association which has also operated a 'futures' market since 1955. The latter has enabled growers, ginners, merchants and the textile industry to protect themselves against market fluctuations by 'hedging' their commitments in the 'futures' market.

Finally, cotton in the hands of export houses is sold to foreign importers. In the absence of established grades, the basis of sale is types evolved by the export houses over a period. A type usually represents a standard cotton with a specific colour, cleanliness, and consistent spinning performance. It is a blend based on a very detailed knowledge of the properties of cotton in different tracts and the varying reactions to moisture and climatic changes. Within the cotton-growing area of the country, the variations in quality and staple are known to be enormous.[11]

There was official intervention in the marketing mechanism in the early fifties. Many firms in the trade had little experience since they were introduced deliberately into the trade after Partition, through the official export licensing policy. There was a crisis late in 1950 due to widespread non-fulfilment of contracts following a sharp rise in price in the wake of the Korean War and a short crop in the U.S.A. Export duties had to be raised from Rs. 60 to Rs. 300 per bale in November 1950 to depress internal

[11] The description of the marketing process is drawn mainly from *Marketing and Financing of Cotton in Pakistan* (State Bank of Pakistan, 1953).

market prices and thereby enable export commitments to be met. To prevent a recurrence, legislation was enacted[12] giving Government powers to fix minimum prices for cotton, to regulate ginning and pressing charges, to compel ginners to buy cotton and pay not less than the minimum prices fixed, to deal in cotton and to register and regulate the trading and movement of cotton. A Cotton Board was created to administer the legislation. The Board was also charged with the scrutiny of trading practices concerning marketing, forward transactions, insurance, storage, etc. Government intervention through the Board became necessary late in February 1952 when prices collapsed following a textile recession. A price support scheme fixed floor prices for cotton at Karachi on the basis of Rs. 90 per maund for 289F, roller-ginned, with appropriate differentials on the basis of types, staples and qualities. The Cotton Board undertook to purchase cotton at the support price. By the end of the 1951–2 season, the Board had purchased about 450,000 bales which were later sold to foreign buyers, in some cases at lower prices. The Board also subsidized the sale of cotton by export houses at prices below the support levels. These operations led to a loss of about Rs. 40 million. The remaining stocks were bartered against 48,814 bales of cotton yarn.

Although price supports were not continued in the 1952–3 season, minimum export prices were fixed, as in the case of jute. An export-price check operated by the State Bank to safeguard against under-invoicing of cotton exports was employed for the purpose of ensuring that contracts below the minimum fixed prices were not approved. In recent years, the growth of the domestic textile industry in the face of stagnating cotton production has gradually transformed the market; external forces except in the case of *desi* varieties have lost strength as rising domestic absorption has cut into the exportable surplus. Factors affecting sales of cotton manufactures, the imposition or removal of price or distribution controls on yarn and cloth at various times are now more important in the cotton market.

Wool production is estimated at 30 to 32 million lb. annually. Local utilization is about 8 million lb. and the rest is exported. The former Punjab produces slightly more than half of the total

---

[12] Cotton Ordinance (December 1950) replaced by the Pakistan Cotton Act (April 1951).

output though the best wool comes from the north-western and Baluchistan regions. About nine-tenths of the output is shorn wool, the rest being pulled from the skins of slaughtered animals or dead animals. There are two clippings, one in February-March and the second in September-October. The average annual yield of wool per sheep is somewhat less than four lbs. on an average (as against ten lbs. in Australia).

Pakistan wool is classed as 'carpet wool' (below 46S) as it comes from fleece which is light, coarse, uneven, and kempy, suitable for the manufacture of low count yarns, used in the weaving of carpets, rough blankets, etc. However, with improvements in trading and marketing arrangements, some of Pakistan's wool could be used for medium-grade serges, tweeds, rugs, hosiery, and other fabrics or for mixing with finer wools. Proper grading is impeded by failure of shepherds to separate wool clipped from different parts of sheep. The neglect is sometimes compounded by middlemen who mix adulterants for weight. Some exporters do what they can to clean and standardize the product but by the time it reaches them, the wool is usually classed as one of several varieties of 'carpet type'.

The marketing process starts with itinerant small merchants moving into the villages ahead of the shearing season and making purchases from shepherds on the basis of expected yield. A cash advance is often made. Sometimes village shopkeepers lend money against promise of delivery later. A large part of the output being thus sold in advance, the producer loses interest in the quality of the fleece, for his contract makes no stipulation about quality. Shearing is ordinarily done on dirty ground with primitive shears and the sheep are rarely washed. Sometimes colours are sorted out, but not always.

The small merchants transport the wool to wholesale merchants and commission agents in the town markets. These dealers are usually concerned with preparing wool for the market except for some who are also exporters. In the past, there was much 'quality-mixing' by exporters in order to evolve special blends or standards. With the compulsory application of a Wool Grading Scheme in September 1954, the number of grades was reduced to three, corresponding to the broad classifications generally prevalent in the trade.

The sale of wool to foreign customers is arranged in two ways:

by consignment to the Liverpool Auctions or sale on direct c.i.f. basis. In the past, the greater part of Pakistan's wool was sold in the former manner. Sales were conducted by four firms of brokers dealing only with a few Pakistan export houses, mostly foreign, which in turn had no direct dealings with local merchants. With the improvement in standards enforced by the Grading Scheme, overseas buyers have relaxed their insistence on visual inspection at the Liverpool auctions. Larger quantities are sold directly on the basis of certificates issued by the Wool Test House at Karachi. The only intermediary is the broker in the foreign country. This is a less expensive alternative (commissions on Liverpool sales totalled 9 per cent.) and avoids the 'gambling' feature of the consignment sales which were often consummated four to six months after consignment by the local exporter. Many local exporters assert, however, that they can obtain better prices through the Liverpool Auctions.

The breeding of animals with a heavier and finer fleece is under way through the crossing of local with imported breeds (e.g., Rambouillet and Corridale) and through selection amongst local breeds (e.g., Tirshi, Kaghani and Harnai). Mention may be made of the Commonwealth Livestock Farm in the Thal established under the Colombo Plan, where scientific sheep rearing and management techniques are being used. The Second Plan provides for the improvement of six existing sheep breeding farms and the setting up of five new farms, with emphasis on ram multiplication and their distribution to private breeders. Modern shearing units are being established in the grazing areas. It is proposed to extend the operation of the Grading Scheme to assure proper grading and baling of wool in up-country markets.

Tea is the only crop grown in the country on a plantation basis in East Pakistan. Production has risen from 617,000 lbs. grown on 4,865 acres in 1882 to 55–60 million lbs. grown on 70–78,000 acres in recent years. Immediately after Partition, output tended to be depressed by the disruption of traditional channels of supply of seed, tea-chests, fuel and building material, the abandonment or neglect of several Indian-owned estates, transport difficulties, especially at Chittagong port, and finally, by the curtailment of credit facilities by Indian banks which had been active in tea finance before 1949. Yields began to rise after 1951–2, owing mainly to the continuity of management on the European-owned estates.[13] A statutory body, the Pakistan Tea Board, was established in 1950 to attend to problems of the industry and some funds sanctioned to facilitate movement from the gardens to the port. A special release of foreign exchange of Rs. 3 million in 1955 permitted imports of machinery for modernizing the processing of tea. Two factories with a combined annual output of 550,000 units have been established for the manufacture of tea-chests but these are said to be costlier than the imported items. The use of fertilizer is being extended, although the supply in the past has been high-priced and often untimely.

Acreage has remained more or less stationary, at an average figure of 77,000 acres.[14] Yields after improving from 4·9 maunds per acre in 1947–8 to 8·7 maunds in 1956–7 have tended to stagnate in more recent years. Domestic consumption has meanwhile grown rapidly, partly through the substitution of the local commodity for previously imported teas, and the lack of response in tea output had led as in the case of cotton to a progressive decline in the export surplus. In 1951, domestic consumption was 10 million lbs. and exports were 47 million lbs. In 1961, exports virtually disappeared as the crop fell to 42·5 million lbs. owing to drought. In 1962–3, domestic consumption was running near 50 million lbs.

Confronted with this situation a number of steps have been taken to raise output. Gardens owned by Pakistanis have suffered from a severe lack of working capital. Some medium-term loans have been advanced by the Agricultural Development Bank against the hypothecation of crops. Without assurance of regular supplies of food-grains for feeding the large complement of workers and their families, most tea gardens have earmarked for growing cereals lands which could have been more rationally utilized in planting tea. While powers have been recently taken to enforce the expansion of tea cultivation *on a compulsory basis*, more promising results are likely to result from decisions to release an additional area of 8,500 acres for tea cultivation in Sylhet and by the supply of subsidized fertilizer to the estates.

[13] Of 124 estates in 1959, 70 per cent. were European-owned, 19 per cent. Pakistani and the rest were Indian-owned.

[14] This figure is well below the maximum of 83,756 acres permitted to Pakistan under the International Tea Agreement in 1950; this acreage can be extended by 5 per cent. and now lands can be planted up to another 10 per cent. in replacement of old areas.

Some changes in the marketing mechanism in recent years may well have impaired incentives for expansion. In the early years, the export market was the main outlet for tea, with the United Kingdom as the largest customer. Formerly tea was sent to the U.K. under a bulk purchase agreement with the Ministry of Food. After its termination, tea was shipped to London on a consignment basis for sale in the auctions. A small quantity was exported direct on a c.i.f. basis. After Partition, auctions were started in Chittagong, the first public sale taking place in July 1949. Transactions in these auctions tended to be confined to local traders buying for the West Pakistan markets. In 1958, it was decided to impose restrictions on the export of tea on a consignment basis so as to conserve foreign exchange spent on brokerage, warehousing and handling in London. A more radical intervention in the normal marketing machinery was the fixation in 1959 of a minimum export quota of 12 million lbs. The overall quota was distributed among the gardens in proportion to their average production in the preceding three seasons (with small gardens being exempt). A separate set of Export Auctions were established at Chittagong where each garden would sell tea up to its annual allotment. In the 1959–60 season, the compulsory export quota was raised to 20 million lbs. It had to be suspended in January 1960 after only 5 million lbs. had been contracted for export in order to feed the domestic market where prices were rising sharply under the stimulus of a larger offtake. The excise duty on tea was raised from Re. 0·125 in April 1959 to Re. 0·361 and again to Re. 0·625 in April 1960. In 1961, the export duty was cut from Re. 0·38 per lb. to Re. 0·25 and abolished in 1963. While this should render exports more profitable relatively to the domestic market, it remains to be seen whether a policy of maintaining exports through compulsory quotas and of holding down profits in the domestic market through price-controls can provide the incentives necessary for the expansion of tea output. A long term target of 80 million pounds was laid down by Government in 1957. The Second Plan proposes a partial movement to 64 million lbs. by 1964–5. Since the tea bush comes into bearing four or five years after planting, any significant expansion in tea production will probably appear only in subsequent Plan periods.

Hides and Skins. The country produces roughly 15 million pieces of hides and skins per year, over 60 per cent. in West

Pakistan. The main components are kips or the hides of oxen (4·5 million), buffs or the hides of buffalo (0·9 million), goatskins (5·5 million), sheepskins (2·2 million), lamb and kid skins (1·2 million) and fancy skins (0·9 million). East Pakistan contributes over two-thirds of kips, less than one-third of goatskins and almost the entire supply of fancy skins, while fur skins (lamb and kid) are exclusive to the western wing. About 80 per cent. of the buffs are also supplied by West Pakistan. It is estimated that over 40 per cent. of the kips and 30 per cent. of the buffs are obtained from slaughtered animals, with the percentages much higher for skins.

The country consumes about 4·2 million hides leaving 1·2 million hides and almost the entire supply of skins for export. In recent years, exports of hides have tended to decline, reflecting in part the decline of the cattle population through indiscriminate slaughter for meat and in part the larger offtake of the tanning industry. There would appear to have been some substitution of exports of leather and leather manufactures for raw hides.

The marketing process for hides and skins usually involves peripatetic dealers operating at village level and moving their purchases to bigger traders in collecting areas where transport and assembling facilities exist. While export markets are well-established and the quality tends to be fairly satisfactory, damage is often caused by improper flaying, curing and marketing procedures. Dealers in some areas are known to beat skins in order to stretch them; poor storage leads to damage by mite and warble fly. Transport bottlenecks on the railways lead to delays in booking or transhipment and since facilities for storage are largely non-existent at booking stations, there is deterioration, especially in the rainy seasons. Some attention is presently being given to educating butchers, flayers and curers in desirable procedures and drying sheds and model curing yards are being planned for important collecting centres. Research on methods of exterminating the warble fly is a high priority item, as this insect punctures hides and reduces quality. A grading scheme for hides and skins, on the lines of wool, has been sanctioned by Government, although implementation has been slow owing to trade resistance.

3

APPENDIX NOTE: JUTE GRADING

Jute is classified according to (1) zone, (2) colour, (3) *Katcha* assortment grades and (4) *Pucca* grades.

Zones: There are 3 growing zones:
  (a) Jat: Districts of Dacca, Mymensingh and Tippera.
  (b) District: Districts of Pabna, Faridpur, Kushtia, Jessore, Khulna, Barisal, Sylhet, Chittagong and Noakhali.
  (c) Northern: Districts of Rangpur, Dinajpur, Bogra and Rajshahi.

Jat is the finest quality jute, with firm and well-defined fibre, even strands, good lustre, colour and length. District jute is close to Jat in quality but the fibre is not uniform in texture and strands; its colour varies from light cream to dull grey and its length is shorter. Northern jute is of somewhat inferior quality; the fibre is dull-coloured, fluffy, hairy and barky, generally of medium length and relatively weak.

Colour: There are two colours—white and golden brown to red, corresponding to the main varieties *capsularis* and *olitorius*.

Katcha Grades: These represent rough assortments and are based mainly on the percentage of roots (or cuttings) in the fibre. Specifications are laid down by the Pakistan Jute Association as follows:

Grade	Description	% of cuttings not to exceed White	% of cuttings not to exceed Tossa
Top	Very strong fibre, excellent colour and lustre, good length, free from all blemish	15	10
Middle	Strong fibre, fair length, average colour of district in which grown, free from *shamla*, speck runners and harsh crop ends	15	10
Bottom	Sound fibre, fair length, average colour (except grey), weak fibre, speck and runners	20	15
B—Bottom	Sound fibre of any colour free from hard-centred jute and runners	30	20
C—Bottom	Fibre of medium strength of any colour, free from runners and heavy crop ends	35	25
X—Bottom	Weak, hard-centred jute of any length, free from tangled and ravelled jute and stick or hunka	40	30
Habi Jabi	Tangled and ravelled jute of any description, free from dust and hunka and stick	—	—
Cuttings	Barky or hard portions of jute cut from the bottom or top of stems	—	—

Pucca Grades: The export trade operates on the basis of standard grades recognized by the London Jute Association. There are 22 grades for long jute and their correspondence to *Katcha* PJA grades is roughly as follows:

White Jute	*Pucca* Grades	
Top	Dundee Firsts, with some Dundee Lightnings	
Middle	Dundee Lightnings with some Dundee Hearts	
Bottom	Dundee Hearts and Mill Firsts	
B—Bottom	Export Firsts/Mill Lightnings	
C—Bottom	Export Lightnings/Mill Hearts	
X—Bottom	Export Hearts	

Tossa Jute	Jat	District
Top	Dacca Tossa 2/3	Crack Tossa 2/3
Middle	Dacca Tossa 4	Crack Tossa 4
Bottom	Dacca Tossa 5	Dundee Tossa 2/3
5—Bottom	Dacca Tossa 6	Dunda Rossa 4
C—Bottom	Outport Tossa 2/3	Outport Tossa 2/3
X—Bottom	Outport Tossa 4	Outport Tossa 4

In addition, there are 6 standard grades for cuttings.

Note: Against each standard grade, there are a number of private 'marks' which represent variations within each grade range. There are about 2,000 private marks as each export firm seeks to develop a 'differentiated product'.

Source: Report, Jute Enquiry Commission, Ch. IX.

II

FOREIGN TRADE

THE pattern of Pakistan's foreign trade, in the first decade of the country's existence, was similar to that of many other relatively underdeveloped countries. Two raw material products—cotton and jute—provided over three-fourths of total exports. When raw wool, tea, hides and skins were added, the figure for major raw material exports amounted to over 90 per cent. Imports consisted chiefly of manufactured consumer goods, with textile manufactures accounting for over 30 per cent. of the total in the early years.

A drastic change has taken place in both imports and exports in the past few years. Pakistan now has a large net export of jute and cotton goods, while the share of all raw materials has fallen to 63 per cent. by 1962–3. It produces many of the consumer goods which constituted its leading imports. Machinery and transportation equipment have been imported in ever-increasing quantities. Petroleum and iron and steel are other major import categories, the growth of which emphasizes the developing nature of Pakistan's economy.

A much less welcome change has been the emergence of very large imports of wheat and rice (about 15 per cent. of imports) which now take second place, after machinery and millwork. This factor lends significance to the Second Five Year Plan's emphasis on agriculture. Another important aspect of recent trade statistics is the high proportion (one-third to one-half) of imports financed by foreign aid. Much of this consists of loans, which can eventually be paid off only by the emergence of a pronounced and sustained excess of exports and service receipts over imports and invisible payments.

The circumstances of Pakistan's emergence as an independent nation in 1947 led to a sudden and drastic interruption of long-established channels of 'domestic' trade within undivided India, and Pakistan turned quickly to the establishment of new trade connexions. Most large-scale foreign and domestic trade had been in the hands of non-Muslims in the areas which became Pakistan, and new trading firms and patterns had to be established simultaneously. India's devaluation of the rupee in 1949 was followed by a trade deadlock which led to a great increase in trade with other foreign countries, in some cases involving the export to distant markets of commodities sorely needed in India, and the import from far-off countries of commodities which would ordinarily have been purchased from India. By 1960–61 India was purchasing no more than 5 per cent. of Pakistan's exports, and furnishing a little less than 5 per cent. of Pakistan's imports.

The Korean War caused a tremendous upsurge in world demand for Pakistan's exports, with a resultant rise in export earnings. In June 1950 a large number of items were placed on Open General Licence (O.G.L.) i.e. these could be imported without licensing restrictions. In July 1951 import policy was further liberalized and almost 85 per cent. of total private imports by value were permitted without licence. This action, coinciding with adverse movements in terms of trade, resulted in a rapid loss of foreign exchange reserves. Declining commodity prices caused earnings from exports to fall below payments for imports, so that all invisible payments plus Government payments not included in imports had to be met by drawing on foreign exchange reserves.

To protect reserves, credits for import financing were restricted in June 1952; but this proved insufficient to stop the drain, and the O.G.L. was completely suspended in November of that year. The struggle to maintain a liberal import policy had ended. (For subsequent developments *see* later section on Import Policy.)

Table 2 gives available figures[1] for Pakistan's foreign trade since 1 July 1948.

It is evident that the balance of trade has shown large deficits since 1956–7, reflecting in part the gradual decline in export earnings to the low level of Rs. 1325·3 million in 1958–9 and the gradual increase in aid-financed imports:

---

[1] Complete figures for Pakistan's foreign trade are unavailable, especially in the earlier years, owing to the absence of published data on (a) imports of defence stores (b) land-borne imports on Government account. Land trade data are included from July 1949. Export figures include re-exports.

TABLE 2

FOREIGN TRADE BY PROVINCE

(In millions of rupees)

Trade Year	Exports			Imports		
	East Pak.	W. Pak.	Total	East Pak.	W. Pak.	Total
1949–50	628·9	565·2	1,194·1	384·8	912·2	1,297·1
1950–51	1,211·1	1,342·5	2,553·5	452·9	1,167·1	1,620·0
1951–52	1,086·6	921·9	2,008·6	763·4	1,473·9	2,237·3
1952–53	642·5	867·4	1,509·9	366·4	1,017·3	1,383·6
1953–54	645·1	641·0	1,286·0	293·8	824·2	1,118·0
1954–55	731·6	491·4	1,223·0	320·2	783·0	1,103·3
1955–56	1,041·3	742·4	1,783·7	360·7	964·4	1,325·1
1956–57	909·4	698·2	1,607·6	818·5	1,516·1	2,334·6
1957–58	988·1	433·6	1,421·7	735·6	1,314·3	2,050·0
1958–59	880·9	444·4	1,325·3	553·8	1,024·6	1,578·4
1959–60	1,079·6	763·1	1,842·7	655·3	1,805·7	2,461·0
1960–61	1,259·0	540·2	1,799·4	1,014·4	2,173·3	3,187·6
1961–62	1,300·6	542·9	1,843·0	872·8	2,236·2	3,109·0
1962–63	1,249·2	784·5	2,033·7	1,018·7	2,800·1	3,818·8
1963–64	1,208·0[1]	835·0[1]	2,043·0[1]	1,449·0	2,981·0	4,430·0

Source: Central Statistical Office, *Bulletin.*
[1] Provisional.

The preceding table brings out clearly the striking divergence in the foreign trade balance of the country's two provinces. While East Pakistan has consistently shown a trade surplus, West Pakistan has registered a deficit (except in 1950–51). On a rough basis, the former has contributed two-thirds of total exports and absorbed one-third of total imports. Foreign trade balances, however, tell only part of the story. In the coastal trade between the two wings, East Pakistan has consistently been in deficit, although through 1955–6 this deficit was smaller than the surplus on foreign trade, so that the province had an over-all 'global' surplus in trade (though not necessarily in its 'global' balance of payments, especially if account is taken of clandestine capital movements to India). After that year, there have been over-all deficits in the province, with the exception of 1959–60, reflecting the large receipt of foreign aid goods by both provinces and the growing ability of the faster-developing industries of West Pakistan to meet many of the consumer needs of the eastern wing. There remains, however, an open question on the terms of trade, for while East Pakistan sells the greater part of its 'global' exports on the world market, it now buys a third to a half of its 'global' imports from the highly protected industries of West Pakistan. However, rice from West Pakistan is available at prices lower than the world market.[2] The following analysis of exports and imports relates to items moving in foreign trade only.

1. EXPORTS[3]

(1) *Raw jute* is Pakistan's most important export. It has thus far produced approximately half of total export earnings. However, this proportion is diminishing, for whereas nearly all jute was exported in the early years, domestic manufacturing capacity now absorbs nearly one-third of the crop and by 1964–5, when 12,000 looms may be working, mill consumption is expected to reach 2·7 million bales[4] or around 40 per cent. of total production. The share of raw jute in export earnings is thus bound to decline further, both because there will be less jute to export, and because of the steady and continued increase in exports of many different types of manufactured commodities, including jute manufactures.

Since Partition, the jute export trade has passed through some major vicissitudes. India was at the outset by far the most important consumer, taking 5·3 million bales as against 0·8 million by the rest of the world in 1947–8.[5] In 1948–9 Indian purchases were at the more normal level of 3·9 million bales, exports to other countries increasing to 1·8 million bales. By 1950–51 two-thirds of Pakistan's exports of jute were absorbed by countries other than India, chiefly the U.S.A., the U.K., France, West Germany and Belgium. Thereafter Indian purchases declined progressively as Indian domestic production of raw jute rose from 1·7 million bales in 1947–8 to about 6·3 million bales in 1961–2,[6] and Indian imports of raw jute from Pakistan were under 0·4 million bales in the latter year. India has thus achieved its goal of virtual self-sufficiency in raw jute, and will import only minor quantities hereafter, perhaps no more than 0·3 to 0·5 million bales in years

[2] *See* N. Islam, 'Some Aspects of Inter-wing Trade and Terms of Trade in Pakistan', *The Pakistan Development Review*, Vol. III, No. 1.

[3] *See* Table 3 for details respecting exports of the ten principal commodities.

[4] *Report*, Jute Enquiry Commission, Government of Pakistan, 1961, p. 22.

[5] However, some of the raw jute exported to India may have been re-exported by that country on its own account. *See* Chapter I for further details as to the jute trade. One long ton of jute equals 5·6 bales.

[6] In addition, India produced *mesta* fibre or *kenaf*—the crop being 1·7 million bales in 1961–2, giving a combined jute/*mesta* crop of 8 million bales.

TABLE 3

Principal Exports

1948–49/1963–64

A: *VALUE (In millions of rupees)*

	Jute		Cotton		Wool	Hides	Skins	Tea	Fish	Rice	Sports Goods	Misc.	Total
	Raw	Manuf.	Raw	Manuf.									
1948–49	1,195·6	—	364·7	—	31·0	28·3	20·2	42·4	—	8·4	n.a.	n.a.	957·6[1]
1949–50	525·8	—	397·6	—	35·1	13·2	16·4	45·6	—	7·4	n.a.	153·0	1,194·1
1950–51	1,098·4	—	987·5	—	79·8	40·2	24·8	29·1	9·7	4·5	n.a.	289·2	2,553·5
1951–52	996·1	—	777·5	—	31·2	16·8	19·3	42·5	12·5	33·3	n.a.	85·2	2,008·6
1952–53	566·4	—	694·0	—	57·8	15·0	19·8	30·8	17·3	3·7	5·1	102·7	1,509·6
1953–54	556·4	—	497·4	—	46·9	8·6	22·2	31·9	26·3	1·7	5·6	91·7	1,286·1
1954–55	598·2	23·1	296·5	1·3	50·0	10·9	19·3	55·8	28·8	74·4	5·9	63·6	1,223·0
1955–56	828·6	105·7	462·1	35·7	68·3	11·5	27·7	34·3	25·9	43·5	9·5	128·6	1,783·7
1956–57	705·8	91·0	352·4	92·6	98·6	5·0	32·3	51·4	20·2	19·2	14·0	113·9	1,607·6
1957–58	853·5	90·8	214·0	33·4	66·7	10·6	28·0	19·3	32·2	—	11·5	79·3	1,421·7
1958–59	654·8	155·2	192·1	53·8	65·3	15·3	39·7	27·9	46·7	18·1	9·7	65·9	1,325·3
1959–60	729·1	227·1	188·8	231·4	75·4	8·7	67·6	35·5	56·9	68·0	11·8	146·0	1,842·7
1960–61	848·1	313·8	137·6	118·2	70·9	7·7	44·5	1·1	72·1	48·9	11·5	139·3	1,799·5
1961–62	850·0	325·0	125·0	38·4	70·0	9·4	55·6	20·5	104·8	86·5	11·7	187·5	1,850·0
1962–63	792·7	306·8	264·0	66·0	68·5	9·0	39·6	6·4	87·0	149·8	15·4	210·3	2,033·7
1963–64*	745·0	320·0	400·0	98·0	51·0		36·0	—		13·0	77·0	207·0	2,043·0

B: VOLUME

	1,000 bales	1,000 tons	1,000 bales	mill. lbs.[2]	mill. lbs.	mill. pcs.	mill. pcs.	mill. lbs.	1,000 cwts.	1,000 tons
1948–49	6,049	—	805	—	22·55	1·91	7·96	31·29	—	
1949–50	3,459	—	961	—	25·98	2·60	8·99	30·79	—	
1950–51	6,654	—	1,372	—	31·33	3·83	11·18	23·62	—	
1951–52	4,885	—	1,095	—	18·54	1·52	7·16	34·13	n.a.	84·9
1952–53	5,275	1	1,507	—	29·28	2·00	8·18	24·22	n.a.	8·5
1953–54	5,124	10	1,171	—	22·23	1·80	8·37	23·33	n.a.	3·7
1954–55	5,142	14	713	0·40	24·42	1·28	7·22	26·03	n.a.	204·9
1955–56	5,684	88	948	17·84	28·61	1·51	8·87	14·08	143	143·3
1956–57	4,067	72	664	43·22	34·62	1·49	9·80	21·03	514	58·5
1957–58	4,880	69	447	28·10	27·17	0·52	7·84	8·36	470	—
1958–59	4,086	133	461	77·18	30·77	1·12	10·58	10·58	475	24·1
1959–60	4,817	203	449	429·90	31·03	1·23	11·70	15·76	595	86·7
1960–61	2,950	—	293	281·97	28·55	1·66	—	0·49	574	69·7
1961–62	4,028	215	273	177·65	28·56	n.a.	n.a.	11·36	638	101·8
1962–63	4,337	218	622	345·44	27·73	n.a.	n.a.	3·12	921	168·9
1963–64*	4,270	n.a.	850	332·00	19·00	n.a.	n.a.	—	695	n.a.

Source: Central Statistical Office

[1] Sea-borne exports only.

[2] Volume in million lbs. of yarn with cotton fabrics converted at 1 square yard = 4 lbs. yarn in the following years: 1957–58: 3·16 m.yds.; 1958–59: 12·78 m.yds.; 1959–60: 79·52 m.yds.; 1960–61: 60·73 m.yds.; 1961–62: 43·17 m.yds.; 1962–63: 84·24 m.yds.

* Figures are provisional.

of normal crop. A part of this loss to Pakistan's exports is being absorbed by increasing manufacturing capacity, and around 1·7 million bales of low quality jute and cuttings, for which India was hitherto the only foreign market, are being consumed by local mills annually. This may increase to 3 million bales by 1964–5. Prospects for jute sales to countries other than India are difficult to forecast. If past trends continue, they may stabilize around 4 to 4·5 million bales yearly. Much will depend on competition from substitutes, like paper containers or cotton bags, and from alternatives such as the mechanical or bulk handling of produce. Another uncertain factor is the future competition from new sources of supply such as Thailand or even India.[7] The demand for raw jute has proved elastic beyond a certain price range and only so long as jute is a reasonably *cheap* packing material, in adequate and regular supply, will it be used in preference to substitutes or alternatives. The Second Five Year Plan estimated annual export earnings conservatively at Rs. 800 million—not much below the receipts of recent years.

(2) *Jute manufactures* have steadily climbed in importance and in 1961–62 replaced cotton as the second largest export, with a value of Rs. 325 million or 17·5 per cent. of total exports in that year. The Second Five Year Plan provides for an increase in jute looms from 8,000 to 12,000, giving a production of over 400,000 tons. With domestic consumption of jute goods estimated at around 90,000 tons in 1964–5, there should be an exportable surplus of 310,000 to 345,000 tons which can be marketed without difficulty if the present trend of increase of world consumption of jute and allied fibres at 5 per cent. per annum is maintained. Export receipts from jute goods should therefore rise by a third or more in the next few years.

(3) *Raw cotton* has been second or third in importance among exports in most years, although in 1959–60 it fell behind cotton manufactures. The growth of the domestic industry, plus a virtually stagnant production of cotton, combined to reduce the share of cotton from 20·4 per cent. of total exports in 1948–9 and 47·5 per cent in 1950–51 to 6·6 per cent. in 1961–2. However, the Second Five Year Plan target production of 2,292,000 bales was

---

[7] The export duty on raw jute in Pakistan has 'protected' jute growing in these countries; the duty was Rs. 20 per bale on long jute and Rs. 10 on cuttings until June 1964 when it was cut by 50 per cent.

attained in 1963–64, averting a threat that increased processing would lead to virtual elimination of medium-staple cotton from the export trade. Already more than 40 per cent. of the quantity exported consists of short-staple *desi* cottons, domestic consumption of this grade being negligible. However, this is an unstable commodity in the export trade because there has been increasing substitution in favour of rayon and various synthetics in the traditional markets for harsh, short-staple cotton. For instance, there is the growing trend towards foam rubber in automobile upholstery and mattresses, while plastics have been impinging upon the market for cotton in respect of certain medicinal products. While there will probably always be a certain minimum demand in specialized uses, such as for absorbent cotton, mixing with wool in blanket manufacture, and for the production of very coarse yarns up to 10s count, world exports have shown a declining trend with the lowest sales reached in 1959–60 at 330,000 bales (400 lbs.). India and Pakistan are almost the only exporters of *desi* cotton, with roughly equal quantities exported. While the export duty on *desi* cotton has been progressively cut, it has been removed altogether from East Bengal Comillas. Exports have stabilized at 150,000 bales a year recently with Japan absorbing nearly 70 per cent. Exports of staple varieties fell to the low level of 165,000 bales in 1960–61 but recovered to 734,000 bales in 1962–3 following increased production and a sharp reduction in export duty from Rs. 75 to Rs. 25 per bale late in 1962. With a still larger crop in 1963–4, the duty was lowered to Rs. 10 in 1964. Hong Kong, Japan and China, the major outlets, absorb roughly 70 per cent. of staple exports. India's offtake has shrunk as domestic output has risen and U.S. cotton has been available against payment in Indian rupees. When cotton was included in a bilateral rupee agreement with India in 1960, sales rose to 114,000 bales in 1961–62. With the lapse of this arrangement in 1963, Indian purchases declined.

(4) *Cotton manufactures* were not exported in significant quantity until 1955–6, when cotton twist and yarn first appeared as important exports. In 1957–8 cotton cloth was exported for the first time. With the introduction of the Bonus Scheme[8] in January 1959, both items rose sharply. Cotton yarn sales rose from 3,066 metric tons in 1958 to 37,434 tons in calendar 1959,

---

[8] *See* discussion of that Scheme on pp. 36–43 *infra*.

while cloth sales rose from 4,049,000 yards to 42,003,000 yards. In 1960, yarn exports increased further to 41,046 metric tons, despite the reduction of the bonus entitlement on yarn from 20 to 10 per cent. of export receipts. In January 1961 yarn was removed altogether from the Bonus Scheme and while there were exports of 5,565 tons in the first half of the year, presumably by way of fulfilment of export commitments entered into during the preceding year, a collapse of exports ensued thereafter. In 1961–2 exports were no more than 2,250 metric tons (roughly 4½ million lbs. as against 110 million lbs. in 1959–60) valued at Rs. 8·2 million only. This indicated that without the artificial stimulus of a special export rate, the home market demand was sufficiently strong to leave very little for export. However, a part of the decline under cotton yarn was apparently due to the fact that cotton cloth remained on the Bonus Scheme list throughout, so it was more profitable to manufacture the yarn into cloth, where feasible. Even in the case of cotton cloth, however, there was a decline after reaching a peak of 80 million yards in 1959–60 to half that figure in 1961–2. Cloth earned Rs. 30 million in 1961–2 and total cotton manufactures earned Rs. 38·4 million, against a peak of Rs. 231·4 million in 1959–60. With the restoration of a 10 per cent. bonus entitlement on cotton yarn in August 1962 and the fixation of a compulsory minimum export quota of 80 million yards of cotton cloth per year, the export performance of the textile industry improved to Rs. 66 million in 1962–3. The bonus on yarn was raised to 15 per cent. and the cloth quota to 150 million yards in 1964. Prospects of access to the United Kingdom market, the largest outlet for Pakistan's grey cloth, are clouded by limitations governing entry of cotton goods into that market, such as unilateral quotas.[9] The home market is another limiting factor, given the high income-elasticity of demand for cotton cloth in the country. It is doubtful whether the Second Plan's target for export of cotton and its manufactures, viz. 800,000 bales equivalent, will be realized by 1964–5, even with the increase in spindles and loomage now under way.

(5) *Raw wool* exports have been at a level of approximately 30 million lbs. annually, and earnings have averaged around 60 to 70 million rupees, although in exceptional years, receipts have reached as high as Rs. 98·6 million, as in 1956–7. The lower grade

[9] *See* further discussion in the concluding section of this chapter.

carpet wool, which is sent mostly to the U.S.A. and the U.K., accounts for about 90 per cent. of sales. Various factors, some of which are indicated in Chapter I, operate against Pakistan wool in export markets, but since the adoption of the Wool Grading and Marketing Rules, 1953, there has been a significant increase in the application of recognized and consistent grading standards, with consequent benefit for the entire wool export trade. Prospects seem to indicate a continuation of exports at about their present level, although the Second Plan estimates average earnings at the rather optimistic level of Rs. 80 million per year.

(6) *Hides and Skins* have ordinarily ranked next after raw wool, although they fell behind fish in 1960–61. In 1959–60 they reached a high level of Rs. 82·9 million or 4·5 per cent. of total exports, but average earnings have been in the range of Rs. 50 to Rs. 60 million in recent years. Of a production of from 10 to 20 million pieces, approximately 60 per cent. are exported. Half of the total consists of goatskins, for which the U.S.A. and the U.K. are the chief customers. Exports of cow and buffalo hides have declined, as the domestic industry now consumes 70 to 80 per cent. of production. Internal consumption of hides is increasing with the growth of the domestic leather industry. Pakistan now faces increased competition from hides originating in Africa, where great improvements have apparently been achieved in curing. Prospects are for a continuation of exports at about the present rate, and the Second Plan estimate of earnings of Rs. 42 million per year appears conservative in the light of actual receipts in the first two years of the Plan.

(7) *Fish* exports, mostly to India and Ceylon, have risen rapidly in recent years, amounting to over 921,077 cwt. in 1962–3, valued at about Rs. 105 million. The Second Plan provides for a 25 per cent. increase in production of fisheries and recent successful efforts to introduce modern methods of fishing give prospects of export of a part of the increased output. The Plan estimate of Rs. 50 million as annual earnings will be exceeded substantially.

(8) *Rice* together with other cereals was exported on Government account exclusively in earlier years of good crops. The rice trade was returned to private hands only in 1959–60 but the internal procurement of food-grains continues to be handled

by the Government. Such exports have been possible only in years of good rice crops in East Pakistan, for otherwise the normal surplus of West Pakistan is pre-empted for consumption in the other province. There were large exports in some of the earlier years (69,300 tons in 1948, 206,500 tons in 1951, 137,900 tons in 1954 and 146,400 tons in 1955). Thereafter exports were virtually eliminated by the difficult food situation. They were revived in 1959 following Government's decision to reserve certain superior varieties exclusively for the export market (e.g. Basmati, Parmal). Export earnings in 1959–60 were Rs. 68·0 million and increased to Rs. 86·5 million in 1961–2. With the excellent rice harvest of the latter year, it became possible to release some of the medium varieties grown in West Pakistan (e.g. Sind Kangni and Joshi) for export. It was also realized that these varieties would earn more foreign exchange than would have to be paid for equivalent quantities of lower quality Burmese rice which has quite a vogue in the eastern wing. Export receipts therefore rose to around Rs. 150 million in 1962–3. Production of superior varieties is increasing perceptibly in West Pakistan and there are reasonable prospects that the Second Plan target of 70,000 to 95,000 tons of export of superior varieties can be realized, following the excellent harvests in 1963–64.

(9) *Tea* was a significant item of export until 1956–7 with average earnings of Rs. 40 million annually. As in the case of raw cotton, growing domestic consumption in the face of unchanging output cut into exports and in 1960–61, when the crop was unusually low, tea was virtually eliminated as an export. Domestic offtake is being curbed (or at least discouraged) by increased excise taxes, while export duties have been progressively lowered. In 1961–2 it was possible to sell 11·2 million lbs. abroad. With home offtake rising steadily (estimated at 47 million lbs. in 1962–3), the Second Plan's expectation of exports of 22 million lbs. from a higher crop of 64 million lbs. in 1964–5 appears unattainable.

Other items of export mentioned in the Second Plan are newsprint (11,000 to 12,000 tons a year), mechanical paper (8,000 to 9,000 tons), refined petroleum products and petro-chemicals, sports goods (at Rs. 10 million a year), shoes, pottery goods and metal products. The item of petroleum products and petrochemicals will be significant only after the Karachi Refinery and allied chemical plants come into operation, at which time exports may hopefully reach Rs. 90 million per year. The Second Plan's estimate for all the items mentioned in this paragraph plus rice and fish totals Rs. 214 million per year but actual exports may well reach twice this figure.

The decline in earnings from the major export staples may not be reversible. Therefore there seems to be no practical alternative to the vigorous promotion of efficient production and export of a wide variety of manufactured goods. Since many of these products have a market at home, the promotion of exports requires not merely the adoption or continuation of suitable commercial policies, but also the pursuit of appropriate exchange rate, monetary and fiscal policies to ensure that export surpluses are generated and that market incentives operate to direct these surpluses to outlets abroad. The next section examines the commercial policies directed to export promotion in Pakistan.

The earliest instrumentality for promoting exports was the bilateral trade agreement. In many agreements, jute and cotton appeared prominently on the export list, although a major objective always was the introduction of relatively lesser known exports to foreign markets. These arrangements were permissive in that the agreements incorporated target quantities to be licensed with no guarantee that the same would in fact be shipped. Quite often there was a wide margin between targets prescribed and actual trading performance. With the inauguration of import restrictions after 1952, there appeared a tendency to use the licensing weapon for obtaining assurances of guaranteed offtake of the country's exports; such terms were included in agreements with Japan and France, and latterly with India. A policy of barter was adopted for the first time in October 1952 in an agreement with the U.S.S.R. for the exchange of wheat against cotton and jute, and later with Japan and India for wheat against rice. In 1953 a barter of old crop cotton against cotton yarn was used to clear stocks. A similar policy was adopted in 1954 for disposal of lower quality rice stocks. Another innovation was the inclusion of a payments clause in trade agreements with France from 1955, whereby cotton exports would initially be paid for into a French franc account, and specified imports from France would initially be paid for from this special account, with outstanding balances being settled in sterling. Gradually there has been a shift away from agreements involving firm and binding commitments, as the disadvantages of bilateralism have been realized. *Ad hoc* deals for the exchange of some Pakistani products for cement, coal or miscellaneous imports continue, especially with Communist countries, but such bilateral trading does not cover more than 2 per cent. of the country's foreign trade at this time. At the end of 1962 trade agreements were operative with 23 countries,[10] of which only the agreement with India provides for quotas and only the ones with Nepal and Yugoslavia require settlements through bilateral payments accounts.

Several measures have been taken in recent years to stimulate the export of minor products by grading and standardization, reduction in postal and freight rates, publicity through participation in foreign expositions and exhibitions, and also through 'international' fairs at home, as well as by strengthening commercial representation abroad. As industrialization proceeded, measures were taken to introduce manufactured goods into the export trade. An Export Licensing Scheme selected industries for their export potential and established procedures for licensing their requirements of imported spares and equipment. In order to reduce the cost of production of export articles, rebates were allowed on import duty paid on raw materials used in manufacture. An Export Incentive Scheme was introduced in July 1954 under which exporters of selected commodities were entitled to receive from 15 to 40 per cent. of their earnings for importing essential consumer goods (presumably for sale at the high prices prevailing in the internal market). Finally, the export control was steadily relaxed. The number of freely exportable items increased from 38 at the end of 1952 to 357 at the end of 1956. In January 1959 the export control was lifted altogether, except for 18 items of essential consumption, the export of which was prohibited.

The *Export Bonus Scheme* was introduced in January 1959 and replaced all previous devices for stimulating exports. Excluding the country's major raw materials, viz., jute, cotton, wool, tea, hides and skins and certain varieties of rice, exporters of all other

---

[10] Austria, Belgium, Bulgaria, Burma, Ceylon, China, Czechoslovakia, Greece, Hungary, India, Indonesia, Iran, Iraq, Italy, Morocco, Nepal, Norway, Philippines, Poland, Portugal, U.A.R., U.S.S.R., and Yugoslavia. There are treaties of friendship and commerce with the U.S.A., Japan and Malaya.

items were issued negotiable import bonus vouchers for specified percentages of the F.O.B. value of items exported by them. Voucher holders were given the right to apply within one month for import licences for any of more than 219 items (since raised to 269). To start with, there were two bonus percentages. For commodities in their natural state, *plus* jute and cotton manufactures, the rate was 20 per cent., i.e. for every Rs. 500 of export receipts the exporter was given Rs. 100 of bonus vouchers which he could either sell in the market or use to acquire permitted imports by paying for them at the official exchange rate. For all manufactured items (other than jute and cotton goods), the bonus percentage was 40 per cent. The 20 per cent. rate was also applied to net earnings from certain service industries: aircraft repairs, salvage operations, ship repairs, shipping and (later) the hotel industry. A third percentage was introduced in January 1960 when the bonus admissible on cotton yarn was reduced to 10 per cent., and in January 1961 this item was removed from the Bonus Scheme, only to be restored in August 1962 at the 10 per cent. rate. In December 1961 half the bonus vouchers generated by exports of jute manufactures were restricted to the import of spare parts, machinery and other requirements of industry in East Pakistan.[11]

From the inception of the Scheme, bonus vouchers have sold at a substantial 'premium'. Expressing the market price as a percentage of 'face value', quotations have ranged, except for short periods, above 100, and have been as high as 190. The payment of such high 'premiums' stemmed from the fact that the vouchers could be exchanged for import licences to buy foreign goods (at the official rate of exchange) which were scarce in the economy and could therefore be sold at high profits. The Scheme thus exploited the profits of the import trade for the benefit of the export sector. The extent to which exports were thereby stimulated depended only on the price of the bonus vouchers; other factors were the relative strengths of the home versus foreign market demands for exportable products, the ease or

---

[11] The entitlement rate for cotton yarn was raised to 15 per cent. in 1963. Several other percentages were introduced, e.g., 30 per cent. for tobacco, rice and certain invisibles, 35 per cent. for fruit and potatoes and 10 per cent. for shrimps. In June 1964, the various rates were reduced to two: 20 per cent. for all items previously at or below that level and 30 per cent. for items at or above that level.

4

difficulty of increasing the supply of exportables and the effect of increased supply on domestic and foreign prices respectively.[12] Nor can the *net* increment to the country's foreign exchange receipts attributable to the Scheme be determined unequivocally.

The value of exports covered by the Scheme was Rs. 565·7 million in 1959, rose to Rs. 695 million in 1960 and appeared to level off in 1961–2 but rise to Rs. 891 million in 1963. The figures are only a starting point for estimating the contribution of the Scheme to raising export earnings. For one thing, the rise in exports of processed goods was at the expense of raw materials that would otherwise have been exported. In fact, this type of offset can be generalized: to the extent that diversion of certain goods from the home to the foreign market releases domestic purchasing power for spending on other goods which could have been exported, there is a presumed loss of earnings. Secondly, allowance must be made for a trend factor, i.e. for any rise in exports which might have been expected had there been no Bonus Scheme. Thirdly, to the extent that processed items took the place of raw material exports, there would be foreign exchange inputs of processing (fuels, imported raw materials, spares, depreciation on machinery, etc.) which must be subtracted from the earnings attributable to the Scheme. Finally, the entire 'value added' by processing need not be reflected in equivalent exchange receipts. The exporter calculates his return in rupees but in so doing he may act in a manner which does not maximize the country's foreign exchange earnings. Confronted by a negatively inclined demand curve in the foreign market, the exporter may find it rational to price his exportables below cost of production in the expectation that the loss sustained thereby would be recouped from the sale of bonus vouchers earned by him. If the price to the foreign buyer is even lower than the cost of domestic raw material embodied in the exported article, the country earns less foreign exchange from the processed commo-

---

[12] In more rigorous language, given an unchanged price for bonus vouchers, the increase in exports will be greater, *the more elastic* is (1) the marginal cost curve (2) the domestic demand curve (3) the export demand curve and (4) the more slowly these elasticities fall as the quantities produced and the quantities sold in each market change. (Cf. Bruton and Bose, 'The Export Bonus Scheme: A Preliminary Report', *The Pakistan Development Review*, Karachi, Vol. II, No. 2, p. 236.)

dity than if the raw material had been exported instead. This is not an empty theoretical construction: there is reason to believe that during the period when cotton yarn attracted a 20 per cent. bonus, the export earnings from it were no larger and might well have been lower than would have been secured by exporting raw cotton. Another kind of perverse result has also been in evidence: it was more profitable at certain times to export yarn at the expense of cloth even though foreign exchange earnings may have been greater had cloth been exported.

A study by the Institute of Development Economics, Karachi, has attempted to measure the *net* contribution of the Scheme to earnings from cotton and jute manufactures, which together constitute over 60 per cent. of total exports under the Scheme. The entire exercise requires a series of assumptions, more or less arbitrary, and depends on data which is avowedly deficient. Its conclusions are useful in suggesting orders of magnitude and within the limitations imposed by data, its procedures are scientific. Making allowance for trend factors in respect of raw jute and raw cotton on the one hand and hessian, sacking, cotton yarn and cloth on the other, it finds that over the three-year period 1959–61 inclusive, the Scheme yielded *gross* additional earnings of possibly Rs. 350 million from jute manufactures and Rs. 150 million from cotton manufactures. It is estimated that in the absence of these exports there would have been larger earnings from raw jute of Rs. 44–84 million[13] and from raw cotton of Rs. 86–99 million,[14] so that the *net* increase in earnings is reduced to Rs. 320–370 million in all, or Rs. 105–123 million per annum. As an essentially short-period analysis, the exercise ignores both the foreign exchange inputs of larger exports of manufactures and the possibility of retaliation by competing suppliers, especially India. The three-year period under study also coincided with strong textile markets abroad, and especially in the case of jute textiles there was an increase in the rate of

[13] The lower estimate proceeds from the assumption that larger raw jute exports in 1959 and 1960 could not have been marketed except through a 2 per cent. reduction in export price in 1959 and 2½ per cent. in 1960. The assumption implies 'a price-elasticity of demand higher than seems warranted' (op. cit., p. 247).

[14] This loss is partly offset by larger exports of cotton waste, valued at Rs. 21·8 million. There is some evidence, however, that staple cotton was to some extent exported *mala fide* as cotton waste.

growth of world demand which may not be sustainable. The sharp decline in profits from sale of bonus vouchers consequent upon the decision taken in July 1961 to make 50 per cent. of the vouchers earned by the jute industry non-usable for general imports makes it less likely that jute goods exports will grow much above trend values. In the case of cotton manufactures, the actual level of cotton production effectively governs the stimulus to exports. The high income-elasticity of demand for cotton goods and the low price-elasticity of domestic demand, coupled with the negatively sloping foreign demand curve confronting textile exporters has meant that the play of relative price incentives has been weak and tends to grow weaker. This is perhaps best illustrated by Government's decision early in 1962 to fix compulsory export quotas for the cotton textile industry.

Turning to other exports under the Scheme, there is a perceptible improvement over 1958–9 in the last few years. The value of residual exports was Rs. 267·8 million in 1959–60 compared with Rs. 130 million in the preceding year and Rs. 480·2 million in 1962–3. A major factor in the improvement, however, was the emergence of rice exports from 1959 onwards after their virtual absence in the preceding two years. This reflected the disposal of increasing surpluses from growing domestic output rather than any immediate stimulus of the Scheme to agriculture. Excluding rice, the increase over 1958–9 was still Rs. 218 million by 1962–3. The most substantial improvement was in the case of fish exports which rose from Rs. 32 million in the base year to over Rs. 104 million in 1962–3. Another factor was the rise in exports of cotton waste, which was a by-product of the larger utilization of cotton by the domestic industry. The stimulus of the Scheme could also be seen in rising exports of oilcakes, spices, leather manufactures, manures, gums and resins, molasses, etc. Finally, unclassified exports rose from about Rs. 40 million to over Rs. 120 million in the course of five years. The actual contribution of the Bonus Scheme to these increases in exports cannot be determined as it is virtually impossible to hypothesize how much would have been earned from these commodities in the absence of the Scheme. Nevertheless, there is little doubt that by making the foreign market more attractive relative to the domestic market, the Scheme created export consciousness in the business community and introduced many new items in the export trade for the first time. The Scheme in its present form is expected to continue through the end of the Second Plan period, but could be extended after some modifications.

The significance of the Scheme on the import side is not adequately measured by the value of bonus vouchers issued under it. The amounts were Rs. 95·8 million in 1959, Rs. 138·0 million in 1960, Rs. 151·2 million in 1961, Rs. 175·3 million in 1962 and Rs. 196·6 million in 1963. No more than 10 per cent. of imports on private accounts have come under the Scheme; in relation to *total* imports the percentage has ranged between 4·4 and 5·1 per cent. Through June 1963 consumer goods accounted for only 19·6 per cent. of 'bonus' imports, the most important items being sugar, art-silk fabrics, second-hand clothing, clocks and watches, earthenware (including china), motor-cars and automotive conveyances, electrical instruments, appliances and accessories, haberdashery, playing-cards and other previously restricted goods. Raw materials, spares and transport requirements accounted for another 34·1 per cent. and included dyes and chemicals, paper and pasteboard, commercial vehicles and marine craft, nylon, silk and art-silk yarn and thread, iron, steel and hardware, thermo-plastic moulding compounds, asphalt, pitch and tar. Another 32·4 per cent. of imports consisted of machinery, tools and workshop equipment with jute and other textile industries accounting for over 70 per cent. of imports in this category.[15] Since these industries were also the main earners of bonus imports, it can be presumed that vouchers were utilized, perhaps to the extent of one-third or more, by their original holders. The vouchers that were sold have made it possible to restore a degree of freedom to the import trade which was missing ever since the suspension of the Open General Licence in November 1952. Market preferences have been allowed to determine the composition of imports—albeit in a marginal sector, but enough to demonstrate that it may be feasible to substitute for quantitative restrictions a realistic pricing of foreign exchange. The distribution of 'bonus' imports has shown no lop-sided emphasis on consumer goods and

[15] About 12½ per cent. of imports under the Scheme are not classified.

this fact has abated somewhat the fear that any lessening of licensing controls would result in loss of scarce foreign exchange on low priority consumption goods. The grip of 'category holders' on the import trade has slightly relaxed since licences under the Scheme can be issued to anybody who presents vouchers to the licensing authority. By making the issuance of licences virtually automatic, the Scheme circumvented the delays endemic to the bureaucratic review process. When import policy was still highly restrictive, this simplification of licensing procedure contributed to a more effective utilization of industrial capacity, not so much by enlarging as by quickening the flow of spares, raw materials and other industrial requirements. With the introduction of the automatic licensing procedure in respect of many items of industrial use, the application of the 'Request Basis' procedure whereby licences are issued to industries based on their own estimates of need (now applicable to 173 of the country's 230 industries) and the extension of the open general licensing procedure to as many as 51 items, the significance of the Scheme on the import side has tended to diminish.

On the export side, Government policy also appears to be moving away from exclusive reliance on the Scheme as an instrument of export promotion. The *de facto* compulsory fixation of export quotas for the cotton textile industry has been noted earlier. A group of 12 industries having export potentialities has been singled out for the grant of special import licences to modernize their plant facilities. The import policy since January–June 1962 import period links industry licensing with export performance. Over forty industries on the 'Request' procedure are issued initial licences only to the extent of 80 per cent. of the value of licences issued to them in the preceding licensing period, with the promise that if their actual exports exceed this 80 per cent. figure, they would receive additional licences equal to the F.O.B. value of that excess. (Failing to reach this export goal, their residual needs could only be met through purchase of bonus vouchers.) Finally, an Export Credit Guarantee Scheme was introduced in March 1962. It underwrites the exporter's financial risks to the extent of 75 per cent. of loss sustained on commercial risks and 85 per cent. on political risks. These risks are not covered by normal insurance guarantees and hence the security provided by the Scheme will encourage exporters to explore new markets.[16]

2. IMPORTS

An analysis of trends in Pakistan's imports is greatly handicapped by the lack of published data on the composition of Government imports up to 1957. Table 4 shows the content of imports on private account up to 1956–7 and provides a more detailed breakdown of private plus Government imports (excluding defence stores) for subsequent years. The analysis in the following paragraphs relates to the latter period.

(1) *Machinery and Millwork* has normally ranked first among imports, accounting for almost one-fifth to one-sixth of total imports. A great variety of items are included, and for the most part they are being used in the construction of new factories or additions to existing factories. A considerable proportion of such imports depends directly on foreign aid and the imports come, for the most part, from the countries making the loans and grants. As the Second Five Year Plan is successfully implemented, there will be further substantial increases in this import item.

(2) *Cereals and Cereal Preparations* have ranked a close second among imports and have even moved into first place in 1957–8, 1958–9 and 1960–61, accounting for 29·0, 20·9 and 17·3 per cent. respectively of imports in those years. Their volume and value depended on the excess of local demand for foodstuffs over domestic production plus the commitments for purchase under the U.S. surplus disposal programme (Public Law 480). Following excellent crops in 1960 and 1961 it was possible to reduce P.L. 480 imports in 1961–2. Despite the decision to reduce the sale price of imported grains in mid-1962, imports did not increase. However, if the higher food production of the last few years is adversely affected by natural factors or by damage to price incentives, while population continues to grow at its present high rate, imports of grain may again rise.

(3) *Metals, Ores and Manufactures* constitute a varied assortment, with iron and steel included along with non-ferrous metals. Their growth has been rapid and reflects the rising capacity of

[16] For a critical evaluation of the exchange rate problems occasioned by the Export Bonus Scheme, see Chapter III, 'Balance of Payments', pp. 76–81.

TABLE 4

Principal Imports

(In millions of rupees)

A:	1948–49	1949–50	1950–51	1951–52	1952–53	1953–54	1954–55	1955–56	1956–57
I. *Private Account*	1,258·1	1,132·0	1,430·3	1,962·8	936·2	735·1	922·2	989·8	1,019·4
Chemicals, drugs and medicines	47·2	39·9	43·5	64·0	42·5	45·2	48·4	75·4	80·8
Machinery and millwork instruments, apparatus and appliances	90·8	100·4	144·1	217·4	136·8	190·3	338·6	181·9	268·6
Metals and ores	42·3	57·4	70·2	183·2	82·8	76·9	80·2	131·8	197·0
Mineral oils	27·2	35·3	62·9	97·7	89·1	94·6	108·2	114·2	102·4
Cotton manufactures	502·0	369·5	536·0	626·3	149·5	67·4	65·0	78·5	20·1
Vehicles	58·1	58·0	65·5	93·0	41·9	27·0	44·8	58·4	91·2
II. *Government Account*	201·0	16·50	189·7	274·6	447·4	382·9	181·1	353·3	1,315·1
Food-grains	49·5	23·1	26·2	10·6	308·0	153·0	—	63·1	638·5
Sugar	47·8	42·8	67·2	120·7	24·1	20·0	29·8	51·6	60·6
III. *Total*	1,459·1	1,297·0	1,620·0	2,237·4	1,383·6	1,118·0	1,103·3	1,325·1	2,334·5

B:	1957-58	1958-59	1959-60	1960-61	1961-62	1962-63	1963-64
Grain, pulses and flour	594·5	329·4	361·8	552·9	413·0	387·6	573·0
Machinery and millwork	304·7	324·9	551·1	485·8	595·0	826·0	808·0
Electrical goods and apparatus	61·0	37·0	74·2	90·9	95·0	262·8	255·0
Petroleum products	94·7	109·3	238·2	311·1	250·0	244·7	243·0
Base metals	} 277·8	} 192·3	} 257·6	433·8	460·5	460·0	618·0
Manufactures of metals, n.e.s.				89·3	102·9	126·8	130·0
Transport equipment	139·7	98·8	152·8	254·5	250·0	340·0	479·0
Chemicals	48·4	34·2	61·0	67·1	55·7	58·0	94·0
Drugs and medicines	45·1	42·2	80·3	90·3	90·0	73·3	104·0
Dyes and colours	35·9	27·5	43·7	57·1	62·4	58·2	75·0
Coal	66·9	65·1	47·5	52·1	50·0	47·3	50·0
Non-metallic mineral products	31·2	21·6	52·7	56·4	63·6	57·5	127·0
Vegetable and animal oils and fats—edible	13·2	18·0	74·5	102·8	100·0	208·0	165·0
Cotton manufactures	8·7	2·6	12·9	24·3	18·2	13·1	65·0
Crude materials—inedible	92·2	82·2	136·6	128·5	150·0	176·3	180·0
Sugar and sugar products	50·8	19·0	—	1·2	52·5	43·4	2·0
Cutlery, hardware and instruments	31·2	25·7	51·8	36·2	37·6	47·3	36·0
TOTAL	2,049·9	1,578·4	2,460·9	3,187·6	3,069·5	3,818·8	4,430·0
I. Private Account	939·7	839·7	1,682·0	2,120·8	2,120·0	2,870·7	3,191·0
II. Government Account	1,110·3	738·7	778·9	1,066·8	949·5	948·1	1,239·0

Source: Central Statistical Office.

Pakistan industry to absorb items requiring considerable fabrication. In the past five years their share has ranged between 10·5 per cent. and 18·4 per cent. of total exports and is slated to increase in importance under the Second Plan.

(4) *Petroleum and Petroleum Products* have increased by nearly ten times since the early years of independence and now account for almost 10 per cent. of total imports. As this item includes essentials like kerosene, motor spirits, diesel and furnace oils and aviation spirits, there is bound to be an increase in consumption, although the establishment of the Karachi Refinery will save almost Rs. 35–40 million a year in imports and will earn some foreign exchange from the export of refined items surplus to the home market. Petroleum products and coal together constitute about 12 per cent. of imports.

(5) *Transport Equipment* imports have greatly increased in importance, chiefly as a result of economic development, and partly as a result of urbanization, with imports now running at 8 per cent. of the total. Given the Second Plan's emphasis on road transportation, and the wide-spread and growing determination of individuals to avail themselves of modern means of transportation, this item may well grow unless assembling facilities now under construction can use a great deal more of locally made parts.

(6) *Instruments, Apparatus and Appliances* cover a wide range of electrical and non-electrical items, largely used in production, but in some cases devoted to direct consumer uses. These range between 3 and 5 per cent. of total imports. Items (1), (5) and (6) can be classified as capital goods.

The six categories of imports just listed constituted from 50 to 60 per cent. of imports in the six years ending 1962–3. The remainder consists substantially of industrial requirements which, though not identifiable individually, combine to make a formidable figure. Consumer goods (excluding food-grains) have gradually shrunk in importance, the most dramatic case being the decline of cotton manufactures from one-fourth to one-third of total imports prior to 1951–2 (when peak imports were Rs. 626·3 million) to virtually nothing since 1956–7. Sugar is another consumer item which has declined from a peak of Rs. 120·7 million in 1951–2 to Rs. 23 million in 1962–3. The main consumer goods imports now needed (apart from food-grains) are drugs and medicines, kerosene, motor vehicles, second-hand clothing and spices. The changing trend of the three main categories of imports is shown in Table 5.

TABLE 5
COMMODITY PATTERN OF IMPORT TRADE[1]
(percentages)

	Capital Goods	Industrial Materials	Consumer Goods
1952	9·98	30·43	59·59
1953	19·00	28·39	52·61
1954	30·26	24·62	45·12
1955	26·67	24·49	48·84
1956	18·60	28·38	53·02
1957	15·18	21·92	62·90
1958	16·63	26·12	57·25
1959	20·10	22·74	57·16
1960	20·39	21·86	57·75
1961	20·65	39·83	39·52
1962	31·67	35·51	32·82
1963	26·94	33·46	39·60
1964[2]	29·00	25·00	46·00

[1] *Source: Economic Survey of Pakistan*, 1963–64, Table 39.
[2] Provisional.

Import Policy

The most widely discussed issue in import policy since 1951 is the changing degree of its restrictiveness. In the first place, the main criticisms were that a liberal import policy was continued well after export earnings had begun to decline; that when restrictions appeared inevitable, weaker methods of credit control were employed, instead of quantitative cuts, so that valuable foreign exchange reserves were lost. It is argued that a liberal import policy could have been justified to some extent if the rising flow of imported goods had consisted of developmental materials. Instead, substantial quantities of textiles were imported. In some cases, e.g. drugs and medicines, excess imports were smuggled to neighbouring countries. On the other hand, the liberal import policy was defended on the grounds that (a) it was an effective anti-inflationary device; (b) it helped to increase exports to 'treaty' countries; and (c) it provided a major support to the country's finances by sustaining customs revenues at high levels. In retrospect it is difficult to avoid the conclusion that, despite any incidental advantages, the liberal import policy represented a miscalculation of the gravest proportions. With foreign exchange reserves reduced to dangerous levels, Pakistan was exposed to instability emanating from its external markets and was forced to seek external assistance for meeting its food shortages and for sustaining imports at the barest level of subsistence.

Import policy became restrictive after 1953 and in this phase was criticized for its severity, and for imposing hardship on consumers. More than 70 per cent. of exchange available for commercial imports was reserved for industrial requirements. While new industrial units were being imported, existing units were unable to work to capacity, owing to inadequate licences. Finally, it was during this period that the import trade was preserved for 'category holders'. Licensing was, for the most part, restricted to traders who could establish that they had imported an item or items during the five half-yearly periods from July 1950 to 1952. The average value of imports for one licensing period was designated as the trader's 'category' and depending upon the foreign exchange situation, licences were issued automatically, the 'basis for licensing' being expressed as a percentage of the 'category'. Given the quantitative restrictions of this phase, ruling market prices reflected acute scarcity conditions and bore little or no relation to the landed cost of imports. These excessive profits attracted a degree of political interference as attempts were made to redistribute the rewards of a system based on a fortuitous measure of performance.

With the home market so completely protected from outside competition, the restrictive import policy did bring about a remarkable rate of industrial growth. The new industries, however, demanded direct access to imports of their requirements. Official estimates were made of the capacity of each enterprise and licences were issued accordingly. Finally, licences for new capacity were issued on an *ad hoc* basis as deferred payment credits were negotiated in 1954 and 1955 and later as foreign aid became available to the country.

Beginning in 1955, non-project commodity aid from the U.S. became available. As existing foreign exchange budgetary procedures tended to treat the private sector as a residual claimant, commodity aid was deliberately directed to enlarging the flow of imports to that sector.[17] The formalities involved in the

---

[17] The aid was financed in large part from Mutual Security Programme appropriations as 'Defence Support'. In addition, non-cereal items under

utilization of commodity aid were found to be rather cumbersome and even onerous for small importers. These included price-checks against over-invoicing of imports, obtaining shipping space on U.S. flag vessels or of waiver to this stipulation, securing clearance from Washington for particular items, procedures for stamping of aid-imports to show origin, regulations governing negotiation of documents through 'designated' banks, etc. There were considerable delays in the utilization of commodity aid in the earlier stages. In 1956 and 1957, a part of commodity aid (amounting to $17 million) was programmed through triangular trade arrangements, i.e. proceeds of sales of U.S. surplus agricultural commodities to Austria, Germany and Italy were made available to Pakistan. As these countries were not traditional suppliers for many commodities, there were difficulties both in finding eligible commodities to be imported and importers willing to apply for the licences. Eventually it was recognized that the procedural burden of administering commodity aid through the private sector was rather excessive. It was also attended with irregularities of a political character, e.g. a special allocation of $10 million for machinery imports in 1957 had to be re-programmed for state trading items like sugar and coal.[18] There followed a gradual shift of commodity aid to a few 'bulk' items like iron and steel. Simultaneously, Government has proceeded to allot larger funds out of Pakistan's own foreign exchange, i.e. by way of 'cash' licensing.

A stocktaking of the foreign exchange position was undertaken by the new regime in 1958. All unutilized import licences were frozen as of 31 December 1958 and released only gradually, while new licensing remained almost at a standstill. In the second half of 1959 licensing was resumed at the preceding year's restrictive levels, but the Bonus Scheme helped to supply imports of sorely needed spare parts, raw materials and consumer goods, although at relatively high cost. In 1960 a process of relaxing quantitative restrictions began. The licensing of drugs and medicines was placed on an 'automatic approval' system which entitled an importer to another licence as soon as he had exhausted the previous

Title I, Public Law 480, and surplus agricultural disposals under Section 402 were also channelled through the private sector. Cereal imports were exclusively on Government account.

[18] Report to Congress: 'Economic and Technical Assistance Program for Pakistan', Comptroller General of the U.S., Washington, 1959.

one. By the first half of 1961 automatic licensing facilities were available to 118 industries and another 51 were licensed on the basis of 100 per cent. of their assessed single-shift capacity. In March 1961 11 items were placed on a 'regulated' open general licence. This involves the issue of licences for stated amounts (usually Rs. 10,000 to 50,000 at a time) to registered commercial importers—(other than established importers holding 'categories' of Rs. 1,000 or above). Repeat licences were issued on proof that the major part of earlier licences had been utilized. An effort has also been made to introduce new firms into the import trade. With such import staples as iron and steel, dyes and chemicals, cement, office equipment and motor-car spares placed on the free list (now covering 51 items) there has been a substantial *de facto* liberalization of commercial imports. In the case of industrial consumers, in addition to the automatic licensing procedure applicable to 62 items, a 'request' procedure was introduced in the second half of 1961. Licensing to industry had thus far been based on official assessment of capacity. It was realized that such estimates became quickly out of date. Manufacturing units in most industries were given the privilege of estimating their own import needs and licences are issued on that basis, with the facility of repeating them against bills of entry with few exceptions. Finally, a group of 12 industries were singled out for issue of special import licences to develop their export potential.

The semi-annual import programming since 1962 has introduced a degree of selectivity by linking the level of licensing in over 40 industries with their export performance.

The grant of licences under the various procedures has been simplified and the over-all liberalization of imports has restored a considerable measure of freedom to the economy. It is estimated that more than four-fifths of all industrial units in Pakistan now operate at full single-shift capacity as against 30 per cent. in 1959. There has been a decline in prices of certain imported goods. Many newcomers have entered the trade and the hold of 'category' importers has been loosened, thus making for healthier distribution arrangements. A tendency to over-import has been in evidence, but this is perhaps inevitable, as there has been a long period of restriction when stocks were run down to the point of virtual exhaustion. The using of foreign exchange reserves for liberalizing imports has its counterpart in accumulating inventories of imported goods, preventing localized shortages and facilitating a smoother flow of production.

Commonwealth Preferences

One of the more controversial issues in Pakistan's commercial policy relates to preferences introduced in 1932 within the Commonwealth and the possible ending of this system if the U.K. were ever to enter the Common Market established under the Treaty of Rome (1956). The preferences involve the admission of commodities from the U.K. (and a few other Commonwealth countries) at much lower rates of duty than the standard rates applied to other countries. In return, similar tariff concessions or other forms of preference are granted to Pakistan's exports.

After Independence, the preferences were insistently challenged on the score that there was no *quid pro quo*. It was argued that the U.K. had offered concessions on items it would have had to buy in any case from Pakistan (e.g. raw jute) or for which the possibilities of export promotion were limited (e.g. coir mats, tanned sheepskins). For an important item like raw cotton, on which a tariff preference would have been meaningful, only oral promises of encouraging consumption in British factories were made. In return, specific advantages were obtained by the U.K. on a wide variety of articles imported by Pakistan. Nor did the lower duty on 'preferred' commodities help the consumer, since U.K. supplies did not fully meet the total market demand and hence prices on British goods were generally no lower than for comparable goods from non-preferred sources. In effect, Pakistan was deprived of customs revenue to the extent that goods were diverted from the higher to the lower duty, i.e. British industry was subsidized by the Pakistani tax-payer.

Consultation with the U.K. led to a re-negotiation of preferences under the Financial Agreement of 1951. Tariff concessions on over thirty U.K. items were abolished (e.g. bicycles, chemicals, etc.) and the margin of preference on most other items was reduced (e.g. the tariff on cotton piece-goods was cut from 18 to 15 per cent. on printed and from 16 to 6 per cent. on grey textiles). A few items were introduced to the preferential list by Pakistan for the first time, including rayon piece-goods, mixed fabrics and iron manufactures. The U.K. continued existing concessions in favour of Pakistan and extended preferences on additional items such as sports goods. The Agreement also provided for most-favoured Commonwealth-nation treatment in that products not included in the Agreement would obtain the same preferences as were granted by the U.K. to any other Commonwealth country. The Agreement appears to have gone far to redress the balance of advantage and brought into bolder relief the benefits of the preference system to Pakistan, viz. the lower rates of duty (or free admission) for many of Pakistan's raw materials and a few of its newly-developed manufactures did help producers and exporters in Pakistan to operate successfully in the U.K., their single most important market.

This market was threatened when Britain, in 1958, organized a free-trade zone composed of the seven countries remaining outside the Common Market (EEC). Pakistan and other Commonwealth countries lost their preferences with Britain, as the European Free Trade Area (EFTA) reduced barriers among members. This loss was more potential than immediate, however, as the other EFTA members were not suppliers of the few manufactured goods which Pakistan's nascent industries had begun to export to the U.K.

Britain's negotiations with the Common Market created a more serious threat to Pakistan's trade, although in these negotiations Britain made every effort to minimize the damage to Commonwealth countries. While the Common Market's external tariff on Pakistan's two major raw material exports is zero, damage would arise in the case of manufactures, where the external tariff ranges between 18 and 32 per cent., and cotton textiles, sporting goods, cutlery, surgical instruments, hand-knotted carpets, handloom products and leather goods would be hard hit.

The Common Market countries have granted 'Associated' Status to many of their formerly colonial territories, permitting goods from those states to enter the Common Market free of duty. There is no likelihood that Britain, if it ever enters, can secure similar privileges for Commonwealth countries, with their much larger trade.

Again, the closer linking of Britain to the Common Market would involve redirection of British investment and development activities from the Commonwealth to the associated territories inside the Common Market. These dangers have receded in the wake of the failure of British negotiations early in 1963 but there persists considerable disquiet with quota and other non-tariff restraints on the entry of Pakistan manufactures into the U.K. market. This is exemplified in the decision since 1963 to hold exports of cotton manufactures from Pakistan to 42·4 million yards of cloth and 0·6 million pounds of yarn representing actual exports in 1961. Pakistan's plea that its textile industry is still in the process of developing overseas markets, that 1961 yarn exports were the lowest in years and cannot serve as a benchmark and that commitments had already been made for much larger shipments in 1963 were turned away on the ground that it would reopen the question of quotas established for and accepted by other Commonwealth sources of cheap textiles, viz. India and Hong Kong. The problem is not confined to the United Kingdom. The U.S.A. has imposed similar restrictions on certain varieties of cloth on the ground of 'market disruption'.

III

BALANCE OF PAYMENTS

THE balance of payments is a systematic account of the economic transactions of the residents of a country with the rest of the world. It covers the exchange of goods with other countries (the balance of trade) as well as services rendered *to* or *by* foreigners, including freight and insurance, travel, agency services and income from investment. The balance of goods and services, supplemented by *private* unilateral transfers or donations, is defined as 'the current account' in this chapter. A deficit on current account is financed by private capital inflow or by borrowing abroad or by foreign aid. The residual deficit/surplus is reflected in movements of the country's foreign exchange reserves. Table 6 gives annual figures for the balance of payments of Pakistan from 1956–7 to 1963–4 (July/June).[1]

The country has incurred deficits on current account in all years except 1950–51. The balance of visible trade, which covers exports and imports *on private account* shows a surplus in all years so that Government account expenditures and net transactions on services are 'responsible' for the current account deficits.[2] It must be emphasized that 'deficits' are not necessarily undesirable,

[1] The statistics are based on Exchange Control records. As there was no Exchange Control with India until 27 February 1951 and with Nepal and Tibet until 16 March 1951, transactions with these countries are not covered prior to these dates. Transactions with Afghanistan are excluded throughout. The figures of merchandise trade in the balance of payments tables differ from the trade statistics collected through the Customs in respect of (i) valuation, (ii) timing, and (iii) coverage. Some transactions are not covered by exchange control, e.g., gifts not involving monetary payments or receipts, reinvested earnings of foreign concerns, foreign investment in the shape of imported plant and equipment financed through inter-company adjustments. Data on foreign aid are not derived from exchange control sources. Credits repayable in rupees have been included with official donations instead of with official loans and long-term obligations. Purchases of U.S. surplus agricultural commodities against payment in rupees are also included under official donations instead of short-term liabilities owed to foreigners.

[2] However, a part of U.S. commodity aid is handled through and meant for the private sector. If separate figures were available, the balance of trade *on private account* would probably show a deficit as well.

54

in the sense of being unwanted or unplanned; the country can only 'absorb' capital inflows by running a current account deficit. The aim of balance of payments policy in a country like Pakistan which is developing with substantial external assistance is (a) to hold the deficit within the limits of expected capital inflow, and (b) to develop and allocate the country's resources so as to progressively reduce, and eventually terminate, its dependence on foreign aid.

Pakistan has experienced balance of payments difficulties from the outset. Deficits emerged after the middle of 1948 as traders rebuilt stocks under a liberal import licensing policy and large quantities of defence and other stores were purchased by Government agencies. The recorded deficit of Rs. 455·4 million in 1948–9 was partly offset by a surplus with India as reflected in the working of the special payments arrangements with that country.[3] Under these arrangements, the respective central banks would freely buy and sell each other's currency; balances would be held to the extent of Rs. 150 million, beyond which the holding central bank would be paid in 'free' sterling.[4] The maximum transfer in free sterling was fixed at Rs. 100 million (raised to Rs. 200 million in the 1949–50 agreement); settlement of excess balances would take place in blocked sterling.[5] (Identifiable capital transfers would be similarly paid for.) Under the Agreement, Pakistan accumulated balances in its favour. The first year's results yielded a surplus of Rs. 247 million. By 18 September 1949, the rupee balances held in India had increased to Rs. 257·8 million. With only a small part of the accumulating Indian rupees converted into free sterling (Rs. 23 million), and with the rest paid for either in blocked sterling (Rs. 96 million) or in non-convertible Indian rupee balances, the surpluses with India were not wholly available for meeting deficits elsewhere.

In 1949–50, the deficit was smaller owing to the restriction of

[3] The position for India remained indeterminate in the first year after Partition when a considerable number of transactions were financed with bank-notes which circulated freely in both countries. In the absence of exchange control no record was maintained of movements in the accounts of Indian residents with Pakistan banks and in the accounts of Pakistan residents with banks in India.

[4] Free sterling could be spent without special release by the U.K.

[5] Blocked sterling could be spent only after release by the U.K. It was placed in a separate account with the Bank of England, the 'No. 2 Account' as distinct from free sterling lodged in the 'No. 1 Account'.

TABLE 6

BALANCE OF PAYMENTS

1956–57/1963–64

(July/June Year)

(In millions of rupees)

A. CURRENT ACCOUNT

		1956–57	1957–58	1958–59	1959–60	1960–61	1961–62	1962–63	1963–64
1.	Merchandise	+820·5	+587·6	+745·4	+851·1	+691·1	+593·3	+919·7	+433·3
1.1	Exports F.O.B.	1,621·4	1,425·3	1,440·5	1,759·4	1,877·4	1,919·6	2,215·6	2,215·1
1.2	Imports on private account[1]	800·9	837·7	695·1	908·3	1,186·3	1,326·3	1,295·9	1,781·8
2.	Imports and other payments on Government account (net)[2]	−1,597·6	−1,954·4	−1,329·4	−1,532·1	−1,833·9	−1,321·1	−2,293·9	−1,945·4
3.	Foreign travel	−71·5	−56·7	−23·2	−25·0	−31·9	−30·5	−34·6	−46·0
3.1	Credit	3·1	2·6	4·2	4·3	6·2	8·9	9·0	8·0
3.2	Debit	74·6	59·3	27·4	29·3	37·9	39·4	43·6	54·0
4.	Transportation and insurance	−87·4	−84·0	−73·2	−132·1	−176·0	−206·2	−218·5	−276·9
4.1	Credit	67·2	65·6	71·1	80·9	79·7	84·3	72·2	107·3
4.2	Debit	154·6	149·6	144·3	213·0	255·7	290·5	290·8	384·2
5.	Investment income	−31·1	−6·9	−19·3	−31·7	−32·3	−37·0	−78·1	−114·9
5.1	Credit	44·4	31·3	27·6	34·8	44·4	47·4	36·3	36·1
5.2	Debit	75·5	38·2	46·9	66·5	76·7	84·3	114·5	151·0
6.	Miscellaneous[3]	+4·8	−5·0	+72·8	+50·4	+26·0	+67·5	+118·7	+80·2
6.1	Credit	82·4	83·6	143·2	138·0	148·9	166·2	215·1	199·2
6.2	Debit	77·6	88·6	70·4	87·6	123·0	98·7	96·3	119·0
7.	Mon-monetary gold (net)[4]	—	+2·0	+5·4	+12·9	+2·7	+0·7	—	+1·5
8.	Goods and services account	−962·1	−1,517·2	−621·5	−806·4	−1,354·1	−933·4	−1,586·1	−1,872·0
8.1	Credit	1,855·1	1,647·9	1,752·8	2,098·1	2,255·8	2,227·1	2,710·8	2,674·9
8.2	Debit	2,817·2	3,165·1	2,374·3	2,904·5	3,610·1	3,260·5	4,297·0	4,546·9
9.	Private remittances and migrants' transfers	−13·0	−12·9	−·2	−6·0	−5·4	+1·6	+4·0	+80·6
10.	Current account	−975·1	−1,530·1	−621·7	−812·4	−1,359·5	−931·8	−1,582·1	−1,791·4

B. CAPITAL ACCOUNT

11.	Private capital movements	+35.9	+22.5	+1.4	+7.2	+18.8	+1.8	−3.1	−16.0
11.1	Direct investment and other long-term capital[5]	+21.2	+28.3	+10.7	+14.1	+25.4	+1.5	+9.0	+9.0
11.2	Short-term (net)[6]	+14.7	−5.8	−9.3	−6.9	−6.6	+0.2	−12.1	−25.0
12.	Official grants and loans	+729.7	+1,224.2	+765.0	+969.6	+1,363.9	+922.2	+1,904.9	+1,855.0
12.1	Donations—official[7]	+706.0	+1,194.4	+656.7	+940.8	+1,303.9	+830.5	+1,494.5	+875.9
12.2	Loans and long-term obligations	+56.7	+62.1	+153.5	+69.9	+113.0	+145.9	+520.7	+1,072.8
12.3	Contractual repayments	−33.0	−32.4	−44.2	−41.1	−53.0	−64.2	−110.3	−93.7
13.	Short-term liabilities[8]	−.5	−3.8	+2.5	+1.7	+14.0	+6.4	+9.9	+5.0
14.	Reserve/monetary movements	+228.8	+289.3	−118.0	−204.5	+16.3	+102.7	−314.0	+121.2
14.1	Foreign securities	−64.2	+119.0	−49.3	−122.6	−145.3	+141.4	+6.7	−105.7
14.2	Short-term claims	+293.0	+172.3	−63.3	−9.5	+107.8	−38.0	−320.7	+287.9
14.3	Monetary gold		−2.0	−5.4	−12.9	−2.7	−0.7		−1.5
14.4	Net IMF position[9]				−59.5	+59.5	+91.4	−15.5	−59.5
15.	Suspense accounts[10]	−18.8	−2.0	−30.2	−39.6	−56.5	−91.4		−173.7
16.	Capital account	+975.1	+1,530.1	+621.7	+812.4	+1,359.5	+931.8	+1,582.1	+1,791.4

Source: State Bank of Pakistan

[1] Includes Government imports through normal banking channels prior to July 1953.
[2] Includes all aid-financed imports, whether for private sector or Government sector.
[3] Credit entries cover receipts for agency services, refunds and rebates etc.; debit entries cover corresponding payments under the same heads, film rentals, royalties, expenses for education, etc.
[4] Value of confiscated gold acquired by State Bank of Pakistan from customs authorities.
[5] Covers only amounts of cash brought into the country by foreigners for investment.
[6] Changes in inter-company accounts of foreign companies and repayments of private short-term debt to foreigners.
[7] Includes *grants* from U.S.A., Colombo Plan, UN Agencies, loans repayable in local currency and U.S. *sales* of surplus commodities against payment in rupees.
[8] Covers changes in non-resident accounts of foreign banks, governments, central banks and international agencies but excludes portion of capital subscriptions to IMF and IBRD paid in special rupee certificates.
[9] Covers payment of subscription to IMF in gold (debit) and a drawing on the Fund (credit).
[10] Suspense items result from leads and lags in reporting of transactions to Exchange control and are in the nature of short-term banking assets.

imports in the uncertain period following Pakistan's decision not to devalue its currency in September 1949.[6] By the first half of 1950–51, the deficit had been largely eliminated and by a sharp improvement in earnings from raw cotton was transformed into a massive surplus of Rs. 577·6 million for the year, as export prices rose after the outbreak of the Korean War. The situation relapsed with the weakening of commodity markets while imports rose rapidly under the stimulus of incomes swollen by the preceding boom. A deficit re-emerged in 1951–2 and grew larger in 1952–3 as earnings declined faster than payments. Imports were curtailed by the contraction of export incomes just as sharply as they had risen in the preceding year and a half, illustrating the working out of the income adjustment process in the balance of payments.[7] The process was speeded up by the suspension of the open general licence for imports in the latter half of 1952. The decline in receipts also showed up for the first time the serious contraction of the country's jute market in India.

In the next two years, the pressure on the balance of payments intensified as export earnings continued to decline. Two factors contributed to the pressures in this period. The capacity to import declined more than the fall in export volume because of a deterioration in the country's terms of trade. Secondly, the difficulties in the external sector were intensified by the emergence of food deficits after 1952. The country had been more or less self-sufficient in its food supply in earlier years. While the shortages were met in part from foreign loans and aid, the country incurred a substantial expenditure of Rs. 258 million out of its own resources in the two years ending 1953–4. The only offset to these pressures came from the industrial growth stimulated by the import restrictions on consumer goods. The import substitution was not without its cost to the balance of payments. The rapid expansion of the cotton textile industry reduced the exportable surplus of raw cotton substantially. Some of the industrial development was probably unsound and even the sound projects created import needs for fuel, raw materials and spare parts.

---

[6] See section on 'Exchange Rate Policies' *infra* pp. 77.

[7] It may be noted that taking 1950–51 and 1951–2 together the balance on goods and services account showed a surplus of only 135·5 million, indicating the quick absorption of the high level of earnings by the expansion in imports.

With the devaluation of the Pakistan rupee in July 1955 (discussed later), the balance of payments improved. The value of exports rose by 10 per cent. (in foreign exchange terms), while payments on private imports declined, but the improvement proved short-lived. The declining trend was resumed in 1956–7 and intensified in 1957–8. The pressures during this period were derived from somewhat different sources than in the three years preceding 1955–6. While the terms of trade continued to deteriorate, the forces responsible for the trend changed. A recession of export prices predominated in the earlier period while rising import prices were prominent in the later phase. Secondly, deficit-financing by the Government in the face of stagnating agricultural output and a slowing down of industrial expansion led to mounting inflationary pressures.[8] Given the high income-elasticity of demand for food in a poor country, the rise in credit-financed spending was substantially directed towards food-grains. In the rural areas there also appears to have been a shift in consumption from coarse grains to wheat and rice, thus reducing the marketable surplus of these staples. This was partly due to the restriction of imports of semi-luxuries like art-silk fabrics; deprived of their 'inducement goods' the farmers may have responded by consuming more of their output instead of bringing it to market. Next, the industrial growth of earlier years aggravated the effect of internal inflationary pressures on the balance of payments by 'permitting a much greater substitution between export goods and home goods in excess demand conditions'.[9] This was particularly true of raw cotton where there was a growing absorption in domestic industry without a corresponding increase in the export of cotton manufactures. Inflation also made for higher costs in the new industries and reduced their competitiveness in export markets, apart from the fact that the booming home market left little or no incentive, at the unchanged exchange rate, to export at all. Finally, a part of

[8] While deficit financing had begun as early as 1952, it was not unduly inflationary so long as it could be offset by running down foreign exchange reserves. There was some rise in liquidity as money balances were built up in anticipation of improved availabilities. In so far as this happened, inflation was suppressed and pressure on the balance of payments postponed. (*See* Parvez Hasan, 'Balance of Payments Problems of Pakistan', *The Pakistan Development Review*, Vol. I, No. 2, for a competent review of balance of payments developments in 1948–60.)

[9] Hasan, *ibid.*

the increased liquidity accumulated during this period may have leaked away into balances held abroad through evasion of exchange control regulations.[10]

The payments pressures reached a peak in the third quarter of 1958 and foreign exchange reserves were reduced to as low as Rs. 726 million at the end of September 1958. A new phase commenced with the assumption of power by a new government in October 1958. The monetary expansion, which was a dominant cause of payment difficulties in the preceding few years, was terminated. The Export Bonus Scheme was introduced. (*See* preceding chapter and last section of this chapter.) There was no immediate response on the side of earnings and the rise in reserves in 1958–9 was attributable to lower imports out of the country's own resources. A liberal import policy was inaugurated in mid-1959 and has since been progressively extended. Large imports of industrial requirements helped to raise industrial output of which a part has been exported. In 1959–60 earnings from cotton manufactures more than tripled and rose one-half in the case of jute manufactures compared to the preceding year. However, the year's experience pointed up sharply the fundamental conflict between domestic requirements and exports. Widespread shortages of cotton yarn in the home market forced Government to curtail its exports. Despite the halving of earnings from cotton manufactures in 1960–61, total receipts rose owing entirely to a rise in raw jute prices due to a short crop. Imports in this year rose very sharply as licences for the private sector were freely issued and the over-all deficit reached a figure of Rs. 1,359·5 million. In 1961–2, the deficit was lower at Rs. 931·8 million as export earnings improved slightly while cereals imports fell substantially. The prospects for the rest of the Plan period are discussed later.

The means for financing the current account deficits are shown in lines 11 to 15 of Table 6. It is evident that the reserves, both inherited and accumulated during the Korean War boom, provided the greater part of the financing for current account deficits up to 1952–3. In the earlier years, the deficits were to some extent restricted to the releases allowed by U.K. out of the sterling

[10] When an amnesty was granted by the new régime for declarations of foreign assets illegally held by Pakistani residents, an amount of Rs. 82·8 million was declared.

balances inherited by the country.[11] A release of £16 million was made in February 1948. Thereafter, annual agreements provided for ordinary releases of £10 million, £17 million, and £15 million respectively and the 1950–51 agreement also regularized an over-drawing of £14 million by Pakistan following non-receipt of sterling from India under the Payments Agreement. By the middle of June 1951 the blocked sterling balances were reduced to £57 million and were finally disposed of under a six-year agreement which provided for an immediate transfer of £30 million to the No. 1 Account on the understanding that it would normally be held as currency reserve but could be drawn in consultation with the U.K. The remainder, after deducting £4

TABLE 7
GOLD, DOLLAR, AND STERLING RESERVES
(In millions of rupees)

Year	At the end of			
	March	June	September	December
1951	1,381·6	1,513·1	1,490·0	1,481·1
1952	1,344·9	1,045·7	662.3	606·1
1953	674.8	668.8	669·4	688·9
1954	719·6	630·5	560·6	631·0
1955	677·1	696·4	1,000·5[1]	1,156·2
1956	1,348·1	1,394·6	1,271·3	1,262·9
1957	1,257·0	1,200·5	1,092·4	1,021·4
1958	956·3	880·5	726·2	765·8
1959	908·4	1,043·2	1,121·2	1,227·2
1960	1,321·5	1,169·6	1,180·2	1,294·0
1961	1,430·0	1,225·1	1,092·6	1,133·0
1962	1,148·6	1,128·1	1,049·6	1,183·8
1963	1,328·5	1,436·1	1,384·2	1,328·0
1964	1,408·1	1,235·3	1,176·6	1,042·8

Source: State Bank of Pakistan
[1] Including appreciation of Rs. 296·6 million due to the devaluation of rupee in August, 1955.

[11] These reserves were derived in the first instance, from the division of assets of the Issue and Banking Departments of the Reserve Bank of India. Gold valued at Rs. 89·1 million and sterling securities valued at Rs. 671·2 million from the Issue Department of the Reserve Bank were received or were held pending transfer and are shown as part of the foreign exchange reserves. Government of India securities, though technically foreign assets, are not included for various reasons. Foreign exchange assets also accrued from the division of assets and liabilities in the Banking Department of the Reserve Bank. Amounts standing to the credit of the Central and Provincial Governments and scheduled banks in Pakistan as on 30 June 1948 were paid over mainly by transfer from the Reserve Bank's Sterling Account No. 2 with the Bank of England, Pakistan's share amounting to £147 million.

million for purchase of gold for Pakistan's reserve, was released in equal instalments over six years commencing July 1951. In effect, after July 1951, virtually no limitations remained and the total foreign exchange assets—whether currently earned or inherited at Partition—were available for use; their movement is indicated in Table 7.

By September 1954, reserves were reduced to a level below which they were not allowed to decline and in later years their use as a financing item has been residual. In some years capital inflows, including foreign aid, have been large enough to allow some rebuilding of reserves despite deficits in the current account.

The figures of private foreign investment as recorded by exchange control are relatively modest, averaging Rs. 15 million per year. The statistics under-estimate the inflow, being restricted to rupees purchased by foreigners for investment. Capital goods supplied by parent companies abroad from their own resources and reinvested earnings are not included. According to Plan documents, the actual inflow was Rs. 425 million in the First Plan period as against the recorded inflow of Rs. 82·7 million.

Official loans and long-term obligations cover disbursements of credit repayable in *foreign exchange*. In the years prior to 1956–7, the *net* financing provided by this item was substantial. Therefore, repayments have gradually risen to Rs. 45 million. With the current account deficits running at an average annual rate of over Rs. 1,000 million, the brunt of financing was until 1961 carried by foreign aid, i.e., grants, loans repayable in rupees and sales of surplus agricultural commodities against payment in rupees. With the shift in U.S. assistance from grants to long-term loans from fiscal 1962, the latter item has become quite substantial in later years. The remaining items in the capital account, viz., short-term private capital, short-term liabilities and suspense items exhibit no discernible pattern, offsetting the current account in some years and adding to it in others. The items reflect, in the main, leads and lags in receipts and payments and tend to be self-reversing over time.

From small beginnings, the scale and diversity of non-military assistance has expanded year after year. The data in Table 8 relate to aid *commitments* while line 12.1 of Table 6 records its utilization, the difference between the two sets of figures providing a rough measure of changes in the aid-pipeline from year to year. The commitment data indicate the content of aid to be of five types:

(a) *technical* assistance, involving the provision of experts, consultant services, training for nationals and equipment for training institutions; (b) *project* aid, covering capital goods, other materials and services for specific development projects; (c) non-project commodity shipments of raw materials, fuels, spares and other essential supplies; (d) food-grains and (e) emergency aid, such as flood relief. The content of aid provides some clue to the purposes for which it is intended, e.g., (a) and (b) would presumably be for investment while (c) and (d) would be designed to meet the normal 'maintenance' needs of the economy. However, (c) consists in part of intermediate goods like iron and steel which contribute to investment activities.[12]

In the earliest years, U.S. and Colombo Plan commitments were almost exclusively for technical and project assistance. When the harvests failed in 1951 and 1953, Pakistan appealed for and received emergency wheat shipments from the U.S.A., Canada and Australia. After the signing of a military alliance in 1954, there was a perceptible rise in U.S. commitments. Non-project assistance was extended for the first time in 1954-5 and surplus agricultural commodities provided under the Agricultural Trade Development and Assistance Act of 1954 (Public Law 480). As food deficits grew in subsequent years, the scale of assistance under the latter legislation was expanded. The rate of utilization of aid relative to commitments has tended to rise as the country's absorptive capacity for developmental purposes has improved and as the 'commodity-mix' of aid appropriations has shifted to fast moving cereal and other general items.

In appraising the prospects for the balance of payments in the next few years, it is important to recognize how great has become

---

[12] Apart from this problem of classification a more fundamental difficulty in relating the content of aid to its end results lies in the substitutability of resources. So long as the aid-receiving government has the power to substitute between *aid* and its *own* resources in alternative uses, it can reduce its *own* resources in the sector for which aid is received and by shifting them elsewhere realize the 'additive' contribution of aid in a completely unrelated sector. For a systematic analysis of this problem and its application to Pakistan cf. A. F. Mohammed, 'Some Aspects of the Impact of Foreign Aid on an Under-developed Country: The Case of Pakistan' (unpublished Ph.D. thesis, The George Washington University) 1958.

TABLE 8

Non-Military Foreign Aid[1]

(Grants, Loans repayable in Rupees and Sales against Rupees)

(Year ending June)

(In millions of U.S. dollars)

	1952	1953	1954	1955	1956	1957	1958	1959	1960	1961	1962	1963
1. USA	10·6	42·2	91·2	107·5	176·1	170·4	149·0	272·3	264·6	170·0	206·2	200·2
1.1 Technical co-operation	10·6	12·0	8·2	5·3	8·7	6·0	5·6	5·8	7·1	7·5	8·0	9·0
1.2 Project aid	—	—	14·4	20·4	29·7	27·9	−0·7	−2·3	−0·4	—	—	—
1.3 DLF/AID project loan	—	—	—	—	—	—	4·0	86·4	40·8	22·3	5·6	—
1.4 Non-project aid												
1.4.1 General commodities	—	—	—	36·8	68·1	45·2	49·2	85·4	84·6	89·4	—	—
1.4.2 Surplus agricultural commodities	—	—	—	—	11·6	16·9	1·5	10·6	6·8	6·2	—	—
1.5 Public Law 480												
1.5.1 Title I	—	—	—	29·4	16·9	74·4	65·4	86·0	114·6	45·2	168·0[4]	155·4[4]
1.5.2 Title II	—	—	—	9·5	31·1	—	8·0	—	—	—	—	35·5
1.6 Regional activities	—	—	—	—	—	—	15·6	0·4	11·1	—	25·0	0·3
1.7 Relief and others	—	—	68·6	6·1	10·0	—	0·4	—	—	—	—	—
2. Canada	10·0	9·1	14·5	10·1	9·0	10·4	14·4	13·0	15·0	15·0	15·0	12·1
2.1 Project aid	10·0	9·1	9·5	10·1	9·0	8·9	12·4	6·2	4·6	6·9	5·4	5·1
2.2 Commodity assistance	—	—	5·0	—	—	1·5	2·0	6·8	10·4	8·1	9·5	7·0
3. Australia	4·5	4·1	9·0	7·2	1·6	0·4	0·2	0·7	0·6	1·5	1·4	1·1
4. New Zealand	0·7	0·7	0·7	1·0	0·8	0·8	1·2	—	0·6	—	0·3	0·2
5. Council for Technical Co-operation[2]	0·2	0·4	0·8	1·1	1·3	1·3	1·5	1·5	1·3	1·5	2·8	3·1
6. United Nations[3]	1·3	0·9	—	1·1	1·1	1·5	3·3	2·4	0·9	4·5	4·5	4·5
7. Ford Foundation	—	—	—	—	—	2·7	—	2·2	3·0	2·5	4·4	2·9
8. Other sources	1·6	1·3	0·7	0·7	2·2	1·1	—	—	—	1·0	1·0	1·0
Total	28·9	58·7	117·6	128·7	192·1	188·6	169·7	291·1	286·0	196·0	235·6	225·1

[1] Does not include commitments for Indus Waters Settlement Plan.

[2] Figures refer to actual expenditures for technical assistance provided under the Colombo Plan and are estimates only prior to 1957–8.

[3] Annual distribution is estimated and includes commitments by U.N. Special Fund since 1961.

[4] Pro-rating of multi-year Agreement signed in October 1961 for U.S. $621 million.

Sources: AID Operations Reports/Colombo Plan Reports/Economic Survey 1963–64, Govt. of Pakistan.

the dependence of the Pakistan economy on foreign aid and loans. Table 9 estimates aid requirements during the Second Plan.

The average payments bill of Rs. five billion a year is almost double the annual foreign exchange earnings. This is not a fair measure of the underlying imbalance as it includes expenditures on the Indus Basin Settlement Works which are of a wholly exceptional character and are reimbursable under international agreement administered by the World Bank. Foreign exchange spending on the Indus Works during the Second Plan period is estimated at Rs. 1·4 billion.[13] There is also some question whether the entire programme of P.L. 480 imports represents present consumption requirements of the economy. A part of the commodities to be supplied under the four-year agreement for $621 million (signed in October 1961) is for building emergency food stocks, a procedure no different analytically from the use of aid for accumulating foreign exchange reserves. Another portion of the grain shipments is used for financing local currency outlays connected with rural works projects. These imports in a sense are meant to meet an additional demand for food arising from the additional income generated by projects which would not have been undertaken but for the enlarged availability of P.L. 480 food-grains.[14] According to the original version of the Five Year Plan there was a deficit even in respect of non-development payments while the entire requirements of the Second Plan for imported capital goods remained uncovered. Under a recent reclassification of imports the foreign exchange requirements for the Second Plan have been revised upwards by

[13] The amount reimbursable to Pakistan is somewhat larger. The original Agreement had provided for the sale of some 'free' foreign exchange to the State Bank on the assumption that local spending on the Indus Basin Works would generate demand for consumer items (other than food-grains covered by P.L. 480 shipments) which must be imported. Certain amounts were received in 1961 and 1962 and are included in the figure for the country's own earnings. Under the Agreement, as amended, the provision of 'free' foreign exchange is discontinued because of the sharp increase in the direct foreign exchange cost of the Works.

[14] On the other hand, the per capita intake of food-grains may rise irreversibly to the extent that the introduction of P.L. 480 imports lowers prices for food-grains. At the same time, domestic production may be discouraged by the overhang of P.L. 480 reserve stocks and by releases from these stocks whenever prices tend to rise, i.e., whenever market incentives tend to move in favour of the farmer.

TABLE 9

AID REQUIREMENTS IN SECOND PLAN

(Year ending June)

(In millions of rupees)

	1961	1962	1963	1964	1965	Total
					Estimates	
1. Exports and invisible receipts	2,286	2,384	2,748	2,785	3,050	13,253
2. Non-development payments						
2.1 Consumer goods	570	547	563	598	645	2,923
2.2 Raw materials for consumer goods	317	334	306	339	585	1,881
2.3 Freight/Insurance	67	92	93	95	134	481
2.4 Debt Service (inc. repayments)	100	120	188	243	300	951
2.5 Other invisible expenditure	328	331	352	357	370	1,738
3. P.L. 480	503	323	691	832	740	3,089
4. Development payments						
4.1 Capital goods	1,116	1,410	1,690	2,019	2,450	8,735
4.2 Raw materials for capital goods	549	459	415	652	870	2,945
4.3 Freight/Insurance	127	209	220	270	348	1,174
4.4 Technical assistance	63	64	97	128	100	432
5. Indus Basin	60	170	300	400	450	1,380
6. Total Payments (2+3+4+5)	3,850	4,059	4,895	5,933	6,992	25,729
7. Over-all deficit (6−1)	1,564	1,675	2,147	3,148	3,942	12,476
8. Private foreign investment	−90	−90	−81	−90	−100	−451
9. Change in foreign exchange reserves and other short-term capital movements	23	−17	319	47	−250	122
10. Deficit to be covered by external resources (7−8+9)	1,497	1,568	2,385	3,105	3,592	12,147

Source: The Third Five Year Plan (1965–70), Annex 1, Chapter VI.

taking account of both the capital goods component of Plan outlays and the requirements in the form of raw materials chiefly employed in the manufacture of capital goods. While this has raised the over-all foreign exchange requirements of the Second Plan, there has been a corresponding reduction in non-development payments and there is no longer any deficit on this score. Moreover, the country's foreign exchange earnings are expected to be roughly 17 per cent. higher than the original Plan estimates, leaving a surplus of roughly Rs. one billion a year which is available for meeting investment requirements. The remaining requirements constitute a minimum measure of the deficit, roughly Rs. 1·6 billion a year plus that portion of P.L. 480 shipments which represents the 'normal' deficit in grains at the present time. As far as the Second Plan period is concerned, the deficit will be wholly covered by foreign assistance pledged by friendly countries both within a consortium organized by the International Bank and from other sources. There was at the commencement of the Plan, a pipeline (i.e., aid committed less disbursed) of about $300 million. The amount of the assistance pledged by the Consortium is $1·8 billion while another $310 million was pledged by the same countries outside the Consortium. Another $120 million is pledged by other countries giving a grand total of $2·5 billion. Disbursements against these commitments are expected to be about $1·5 billion, leaving an aid-pipeline of almost $1 billion at the start of the Third Plan.

While the magnitude of foreign assistance that the country has already been able to attract gives reasonable hope that it will continue to be forthcoming in future years, serious questions arise as to the country's ability to service the rising external debt. There has been a gradual hardening of the terms on which foreign assistance has been available. To take the U.S.A., the largest aid-giving country, as an illustration, its aid in the earlier years was almost entirely on a grant basis. After 1957 project aid was gradually shifted to loans repayable in rupees. Since 1962 project as a non-project aid (other than P.L. 480 sales against rupees) has been in the form of loans repayable in foreign exchange, albeit mostly on 'soft' terms, i.e., at rates of interest not exceeding 3/4ths to two per cent. and with repayments spread over 40 years. Other countries have lent mostly on conventional terms, i.e., at 5 to 6 per cent. interest, with repayments in 10–20 years. The external debt has been rising sharply and at the end of 1963, the amount outstanding (i.e., loans committed less undisbursed less repaid) was Rs. 2,525 million; including loans undisbursed, the debt level was Rs. 5830 million, as shown in the following table:

TABLE 10

OFFICIAL AND OTHER EXTERNAL DEBT
(In millions of rupees)
(As of 31 December 1963)

	Committed	Undisbursed	Outstanding
IBRD/IDA/IFC	1,865·0	1,041·5	621·7
U.S.A.	2,049·2	984·8	1,048·6
U.K.	493·1	187·1	268·0
W. Germany	630·2	375·6	254·2
Japan	514·1	360·8	153·3
Canada	28·1	3·3	24·8
France	25·2	25·2	—
Italy	28·6	28·6	—
U.S.S.R.	142·8	112·3	30·5
Yugoslavia	47·6	47·6	—
Privately-placed[1]	261·8	138·0	123·8

[1] Includes suppliers' credits, loans sold by IBRD/US–ExIM Bank to private banks and direct loans by banks.
Source: IBRD/Colombo Plan Reports and estimates by authors.

The present level of debt raises a servicing problem which will become more difficult as initial grace periods on repayment of principal expire. If present trends continue, the gross debt level would be expected to rise by at least Rs. 2·5 billion a year. The debt service on the present debt (including undisbursed) and on a rising debt are estimated in Table 11 during the next 10 years, assuming that the new debt will be on terms roughly similar to that incurred in recent years.

The table illustrates how the debt service burden will rise, assuming that external loans are divided equally between 'hard' and 'soft'. Even with foreign exchange earnings projected to rise by 8 per cent a year, almost one-quarter of these would be absorbed by the debt service by the end of the Fourth Plan period. It is obvious that if the terms of new loans are the same as in recent years, the country's capacity to take on additional debt after 1974–5 will be highly restricted, unless foreign exchange earnings can rise much faster than assumed. The prospects for

TABLE 11

EXTERNAL DEBT SERVICE

(In millions of rupees)

Year	Service		Projected earnings[2]	(3) as % of (4)
	on existing debt	on (2) plus annual rise of Rs. 2,400 m.[1]		
(1)	(2)	(3)	(4)	(5)
1964–65	300	375	3,050	12·3
1965–66	312	460	3,294	13·9
1966–67	336	558	3,558	15·6
1967–68	384	756	3,843	19·6
1968–69	380	900	4,150	21·7
1969–70	363	1,020	4,482	22·7
1970–71	342	1,135	4,840	23·4
1971–72	331	1,256	5,227	24·0
1972–73	320	1,375	5,645	24·3
1973–74	312	1,489	6,097	24·4
1974–75	302	1,626	6,585	24·6

[1] Rs. 1·2 billion at $\frac{3}{4}$ of 1% repayable in 50 years with 10 years grace period; Rs. 1·2 billion at $5\frac{1}{2}$% repayable in 18 years with 3 years grace period.
[2] Earnings based on 8% annual increase from 1964–65.

this are none too bright, at least on the presently known resource base. Jute and cotton, whether in raw or processed form, are likely to remain the hard core of exports and the world market potential for neither fibre is especially promising. Nevertheless the highest priorities will need to be given in the allocation of investment to export industries and domestic policies will have to ensure that the home market does not pre-empt exports.

The amount of investment which can be sustained by any given level of capital inflow is directly related to the foreign exchange component of investment as well as the amount of foreign exchange which can be released from non-development payments. With the increasing level of debt service and the rising import requirements associated with rising income and the changing character of output, the contribution that the country's own foreign exchange earnings can make to the financing of investment depends crucially on the success of import substitution. The main avenue for net import substitution lies in food self-sufficiency. The growth of industries producing steel, cement, fertilizer, artificial fibres and industrial chemicals will reduce

6

import requirements as will petroleum refining and steel-making. Progress is being made in the manufacture of spares and accessories, in the assembly of tractors, and transport equipment and in the production of some capital goods. However, the net foreign exchange saving is likely to be considerably less than the value of the new output. Several of the new industries will depend substantially on raw material imports, e.g., on crude petroleum and iron ore.

The conditions necessary for achieving ultimate viability are not going to be easy to fulfil in Pakistan.[15] As the preceding review has shown, the country has experienced current account deficits throughout its history, with the exception of 1950–51. These have been financed by depletion of sterling balance, received at the time of Partition, the loss of the Korean War boom accumulated reserves and latterly by large infusions of foreign aid. It must be realized that aid performs a dual function in Pakistan: it is an increment to the total resources available to the country for investment and it permits the country to meet its *specific* shortage of foreign exchange. In the former role, it helps the country to achieve a rate of growth higher than that which the domestic economy can generate through domestic savings alone. If the same rate of investment is to be maintained without aid, the rate of domestic savings must rise. Even if the required rate of savings can be achieved in an *ex-ante* sense, it will not be realized if the composition of output is not adapted to the structure of demand—sector by sector. The aid programme in its second aspect, helps to cover the sectoral imbalances in the foreign sector.[16] Pakistan can dispense with foreign aid only if and when its economy can make the necessary 'directional' changes—involving the shift of resources to the production of additional goods for export or for the production of import-substitutes. Resource endowments in Pakistan, at least as presently known, place fairly severe technological limitations on net import-substitution, e.g., absence of good iron ore and petroleum. Hence it is the export sector which must carry the major

---

[15] The discussion of this paragraph is based on A. F. Mohammed's 'Note on the Foreign Exchange Limitation', *Pakistan Economic Journal*, Vol. IX, pp. 83–86.

[16] It really does more than that—because of the highly flexible character of the foreign exchange resource, aid permits the economy to escape from the necessity of achieving *internal* balance in many other sectors.

burden of dispensing with aid. Here another limitation emerges: even if domestic resources can be released for the export sector, through adequate domestic savings, conditions of foreign demand may not permit export earnings to expand correspondingly. The country must then reconcile itself to a lower rate of growth because persisting balance of payments deficits means that the rate of growth is being pushed too fast for the economy to produce the particular kinds of goods and services including exports, which the economy requires to sustain this rate of growth.

APPENDIX I—STERLING AREA MEMBERSHIP

The term 'Sterling Area' refers to a group of countries with closely related foreign exchange systems and held to the pound sterling through certain well-defined arrangements. These arrangements are the gradual, natural outgrowth of the U.K.'s historic role in world trade and finance and its special political relationship with most Sterling Area countries. Membership in the Sterling Area involves certain obligations which are voluntarily assumed, including:

(a) the use of the pound sterling as a common international currency for the settlement of accounts among members.

(b) the acceptance of the pound sterling for any payments surplus with non-members and the willingness to convert and hold their earnings of non-Area currencies in the form of sterling.

(c) the maintenance of a stable, though not unalterable, exchange rate with the pound sterling, and hence with all other countries doing the same through the buying and selling of the pound sterling against local currency at prescribed rates by the monetary authorities of each member country.

(d) the adherence to the terms of any payments arrangements negotiated by the U.K. on behalf of the Sterling Area as a whole with countries outside the Area.

In 1931 a deliberate and conscious decision to accept these practices was faced by several countries when the pound was de-linked from gold and lost its convertibility into that form of international purchasing power at a fixed rate. For most countries in the British Commonwealth and Empire, the decision to follow the pound sterling was a matter of course. On the eve of the outbreak of war in 1939 the Sterling Area acquired statutory definition. Exchange controls were introduced for the purpose of economizing the use of gold and 'hard' currency resources and for applying them to the maximum benefit of the Area. A net of regulations was thrown around the group of countries which continued to adhere to sterling. Free transfers of funds were permitted within the Area and restrictions were placed on the movement of funds, whether in the form of current payments or capital transfers, to the non-sterling countries. The currencies of the non-sterling countries were placed in a common pool, along with exchange and other claims against such countries appropriate for use in a monetary sense. Permission for drawing upon this pool was granted according to the priority needs of each participating country.

After the end of the war and the failure of the experiment in multi-
lateral convertibility of August 1947 the Sterling Area operated within
the framework of payments agreements negotiated by the United Kingdom with all the principal non-sterling countries of the world. The
need for such bilateral agreements came to an end, with few exceptions,
following the establishment of *de facto* convertibility into gold by the
U.K. in December 1958 and of *de jure* convertibility in 1961.[17]

Prior to Independence, undivided India was necessarily a part of
the Sterling Area. Both India and Pakistan have thus far remained within the Area, though after attaining independence they had the right to
withdraw at any time. There have been arguments of a political nature
against Pakistan's continued membership, but such arguments fall
outside the field of this study.

The present-day basis of the nexus with sterling is found in the
trading relationships of Pakistan with the U.K. and with other countries
in the Area. Over the last decade sterling countries have become more
important customers of Pakistan's exports, notwithstanding that their
role as suppliers has tended to diminish as Pakistan's imports from the

TABLE 12

DISTRIBUTION OF RECEIPTS AND PAYMENTS

(percentage of total)

Countries	Receipts		Payments		
	1951–52	1963–64	1951–52	1963–64	
				Incl. Aid	Excl. Aid
1. U.S.A.	3·4	10·8	11·0	38·3	25·2
2. Canada	0·1	0·9	1·2	1·3	0·7
3. U.K.	17·2	22·8	31·5	24·3	29·8
4. India	18·8	3·9	15·3	2·8	3·5
5. Other St. Area	5·1	22·2	6·0	6·7	5·3
Sub-total St. Area (3+4+5)	41·1	48·9	52·8	33·8	38·6
6. Western Europe	24·9	16·3	13·1	16·6	20·6
7. Japan	9·8	4·9	17·0	7·0	8·6
8. Rest of world	20·7	2·8	4·9	1·1	1·4
Total in millions of rupees	2,371·0	2,785·3	2,821·4	4,576·8	3,700·9

Source: State Bank of Pakistan.

[17] It may be noted that the monetary authorities of Sterling Area countries
always had the right of convertibility subject only to mutual understandings with
the U.K. to give due regard to the common interest in making withdrawals.
The protection of this interest is no whit abated and may even have become
more intense with the right now granted to non-Sterling-Area residents to convert sterling acquired by them in current transactions into gold and non-Area
currencies.

U.S. have risen. This is in great part due to receipts of large amounts of 'tied' aid from the U.S. If aid-financed payments are excluded, there is little change from 1951–2 in the percentage share of payments made to sterling countries.

Together with trade come a number of ancillary services—commercial credit, shipping, insurance, commodity brokerage—for which Pakistan also pays in sterling. The London money-market still finances a portion of the country's Sterling Area trade, especially its exports. More significant is the fact that even trade with non-sterling countries is invoiced in sterling and financed by the 'bill on London', although on a gradually diminishing scale. Finally, the U.K. has functioned as a traditional source of private capital, there being no controls on the movement of funds out of London into Sterling Area countries.

It can be argued that while the substantial trade and financial connexions with the Sterling Area make it eminently convenient to hold adequate working balances in sterling, there is no need to keep almost all the country's foreign assets in London, especially since exchange commissions have to be paid to U.K. banks first when converting non-sterling currency receipts into sterling balances and again when non-sterling payments have to be made. Sterling has been subjected to periodic 'crises of confidence' in the post-war world and holding of reserves in that currency, especially as backing for Pakistan's note issue, is hardly designed to inspire confidence. The gold value of these sterling assets can be changed by the U.K. without consultation with other members. The government of the Sterling Area rests exclusively and perhaps inevitably with the British authorities, because the pound sterling is the currency of the United Kingdom. However, another devaluation, not previously agreed upon, or an eventual closer alignment of sterling with Common Market currencies would undermine the Area, since it would entail changes in the framework of other members' external trade relations, without their concurrence.

Finally, there does not appear to be a *quid pro quo* in the matter of capital. The holding of sterling assets in London involves short-term lending to the U.K. but Pakistan has not obtained much private or official capital from the U.K., and the right of privileged access to the London capital market has had little real significance. The white dominions, Rhodesia and Kuwait have absorbed the bulk of British *private* investment in developing countries while the scope of *public* lending has been limited by the difficult balance of payments situation of the U.K.[18] If the U.K. were to join the Common Market it would

[18] See Andrew Schonfield: *The Attack on World Poverty* (London, Chatto and Windus, 1960), pp. 149–153. He argues that 'the Sterling Area, as it now stands, prevents Britain from making as effective a contribution to the underdeveloped countries as would be possible without it.'

remove direct controls on capital movements to countries inside the Market, thus further reducing the trickle of capital now flowing to sterling countries like Pakistan. Indeed, the main source of capital, especially public funds, is now the United States. A substantial part of aid-imports are financed through 'designated' American banks and carried in U.S. flag vessels. The holding of reserves in U.S. dollars would appear to have some, though by no means any overwhelming, justification, for the U.S. dollar has not been without its uncertainties in recent years. There is no assurance that the flow of *private* dollar capital would be increased by leaving the Sterling Area, since the real impediments to foreign investments are found in socio-political conditions and in the restricted resource base of Pakistan. On the other hand, interest rates on short-term dollar claims have been consistently lower than on corresponding sterling claims, so that income from reserve assets would suffer. The income factor would also rule against shifting to larger gold holdings, quite apart from the impracticability of expecting the U.K. to welcome any significant conversion of sterling balances into gold. The last-mentioned factor illustrates the kind of non-economic elements that are involved in the Sterling Area membership, along with considerations of public policy, the forces of institutional inertia and the habits of group action ingrained by decades of belonging to the 'sterling club'. Meanwhile, the world payments system continues to evolve in ways that weaken the strictly economic elements in the Sterling Area membership. The role of sterling in any enlarged European Economic Community, the possibilities for generalizing the reserve currency responsibilities of sterling and the dollar, and the proposals for 'internationalizing' the reserve function by transforming the International Monetary Fund into a truly super-central bank raise questions about the relevance of Sterling Area arrangements which only the future can answer.

APPENDIX II—EXCHANGE RATE PROBLEMS

Pakistan inherited a sterling parity of Re.1 = 1s. 6d. which had applied to the subcontinent's trade with the Sterling Area since 1926. Pakistan decided not to follow other sterling countries when the pound was devalued in September 1949. It was argued that the relatively inelastic supply of most of the country's raw material exports and the apparent lack of sensitivity of foreign offtake to changes in price made it unlikely that the balance of payments would benefit from a lower parity. The decision meant an appreciation of the Pakistan rupee *vis-à-vis* the pound sterling and other devalued currencies. This was expected to be beneficial on the import side as it would leave prices unchanged for imports from non-devaluing countries and lead to lower prices of goods supplied by devaluing countries. To the extent that there was a switch of purchases from non-devaluing to devaluing countries, the country's terms of trade might improve. This outcome would protect Pakistan's newly-started development projects from the burden of higher rupee import costs. The internal price level was expected to decline in line with the lowering of the landed cost of most articles of daily consumption, whereas devaluation would have injected a cost-push into the inflationary environment then prevailing in East Pakistan. As to any disadvantage to exports in sterling markets, it was thought that a modicum of adjustment in internal prices would be sufficient. It was urged by authorities in Pakistan that the decision not to devalue was animated not only by Pakistan's national interest but that of the Sterling Area as a whole. For if a devaluation had failed to increase the physical volume of sales to the dollar area to the extent of the lowering of parity, there would be a net decline in Pakistan's dollar earnings and also in the earnings of the Area.

In the event, the validity of these arguments was never proved. India refused to test the Pakistan exchange rate in normal trade, and this unprecedented reaction on the part of the country's largest trading partner led to changes in trading patterns, the effects of which could not be disentangled from the effects of non-devaluation proper. A sharp rise in cotton prices consequent upon a short crop in the United States helped improve Pakistan's earnings in 1949–50. Next, the Korean War boom led to an exceptional rise in exports. India eventually recognized the Pakistan exchange rate in February 1951.

As commodity prices receded to more normal levels, one fundamental change in Pakistan's export trade became evident. Its market for raw jute in India had shrunk in the aftermath of the trade war, i.e. the price-elasticity of foreign demand for Pakistan's jute turned out to be quite high. As against 4·13 million bales exported to that country in 1948–9, the figure was reduced to 1·23 million bales in 1954–5. While Pakistan's non-devaluation decision cannot be held responsible for India's campaign to attain near self-sufficiency in raw jute, it doubtless intensified a trend that was already under way. On the import side, the lower rupee costs resulting from the cheapening of currencies of major suppliers and a liberal import policy led to heavy imports and accelerated the working out of the income adjustment process in the balance of payments.[19] The exceptional earnings of the Korean boom were quickly absorbed and the economy was saved from the inflationary legacy of a massive surplus in the external accounts. In that sense, the non-devaluation decision was perhaps not unjustified in the light of later events.

However, with the commodity boom reversed, hindsight suggests that it would have been appropriate to have devalued, perhaps in 1952. Instead, import restrictions and exchange controls were gradually tightened to sustain what appears to have been an overvalued exchange rate.

By the middle of 1955 the parity was becoming increasingly difficult to support. Export earnings had declined from Rs 2,137·2 million in 1951–2 to Rs. 1,180·3 million in 1954–5. The major factors in this decline were falling prices in foreign markets and the processing and consumption at home of raw materials like cotton, which were previously exported. Unless the foreign market was made more attractive through a change in relative prices, the home market would continue to pre-empt the supplies which the rapidly developing industrial capacity of the country was producing. Manufactured goods like jute and cotton textiles were faced with direct competition from countries which had devalued in 1949. Finally, it was necessary to offset the pressure of declining external prices on the income of the jute and cotton grower.[20] The Pakistan rupee was devalued by 30 per cent. on 31 July 1955.

The immediate effects were encouraging. Export earnings rose by about 10 per cent. in terms of foreign currencies in 1955–6, as compared to the preceding year. The over-all export price index (based on foreign currency values) actually declined by 13 per cent., so that the

[19] However, the rapid drain of foreign exchange reserves, in consequence, 'showed that a high (overvalued) par value of the currency and a liberalization of trade are incompatible if equilibrium . . . is to be maintained'. Cf. A. F. A. Husain: 'Pakistan's Commercial Policy in the Recession', *Pakistan Economic Journal*, 1954.
[20] To the extent that the overvalued exchange rate reduced growers' incomes while reducing the cost of capital goods, the result was to tax growers in order to subsidize the new industrialists. See further discussion of social welfare implications in Husain's article, *ibid.*, pp. 79–81.

increase in earnings was due to higher quantum. Raw jute exports were 10 per cent. higher by value as against a 12 per cent. decline in export prices. Earnings from cotton rose only 0·4 per cent. in foreign currency but again in the face of a 14 per cent. decline in export price. Increases in the case of wool, hides and skins and some other raw material exports were, however, less than needed to offset the 44 per cent. lowering of the exchange rate. In the case of jute and cotton goods, devaluation was probably a major factor in developing export markets. There was some improvement under 'invisible' receipts, deriving from numerous heads: the 'miscellaneous' group showed a rise of 25 per cent., owing partly to a larger inflow of funds through official channels which would otherwise have been diverted to the black market. Payments on private account, out of the country's own foreign exchange resources, declined in 1955–6. However, this was only partially the price effect of the rise in landed cost in rupee terms following devaluation. The continuance of a restrictive import policy in the immediate post-devaluation period and a substantial shift of private imports from the country's foreign exchange budget to financing through U.S. commodity aid were responsible for the ostensibly lower payments on private account. Imports and other payments on Government account were almost unchanged.

The success of devaluation depended on maintaining the attractiveness of the export market relative to the home market. However, in the following years there was massive deficit financing in the Government sector. Export receipts declined by 22 per cent. in the three years ending 1957–8. In the same period, money supply rose 37 per cent. in the wake of credit creation of Rs. 1,900 million in the Government sector. With foreign exchange reserves virtually exhausted, industrial expansion fettered by shortages of imported requirements and the agricultural sector stagnant, internal inflationary pressure grew in intensity and the home market was successful in securing to itself the export potential which had appeared immediately after devaluation. This was most clearly shown by the decline in the exportable surplus of cotton. Two-thirds of the total decline in earnings was attributable to this commodity, which was increasingly absorbed by the domestic textile industry. By the time a new government came into power late in 1958, the stimulus which the devaluation had provided to exports was well nigh exhausted. However, once the inflationary policies of earlier governments had been halted and even reversed, it was natural that attention should turn again to the exchange rate.

The *Export Bonus Scheme* represents a new phase in the evolution of Pakistan's exchange rate policy. The issue of negotiable bonus vouchers to exporters and their free trading in the market creates a fluctuating multiple rate scheme. The par value of the Pakistan rupee is Rs. 4·76 per U.S. dollar, i.e., an exporter selling goods invoiced for $100.00 receives Rs. 476. In addition, he receives bonus vouchers for (say) 20 per cent. or Rs. 95. Assuming that the prevailing market is 150 per cent. of face value, he can sell the vouchers for Rs. 144. His total receipts from $100.00 of exports are Rs. 620, so that Rs. 6·20 = $1.00 is the effective exchange rate for him in this transaction. It follows that on the export (buying) side there are in addition to the official par value (which applies to exports not included in the bonus scheme) as many effective exchange rates as there are bonus percentages for eligible exports. On the import side there is yet another effective rate. Using the same example, an importer who must buy bonus vouchers for importing something costing Rs. 476 (or $100.00) pays Rs. 714 for the vouchers, or $1\frac{1}{2} \times 476$. He exchanges the vouchers for an import licence at the par value rate. Hence, his actual cost for acquiring $100.00 is Rs. 714 (for the bonus vouchers) plus Rs. 476 (for foreign exchange) or Rs. 1,190. In other words, for him the exchange rate is U.S. $1·00 = Rs. 11·90. Since bonus voucher prices fluctuate, these effective rates keep changing. The following table illustrates this with different voucher prices on the basis of the bonus percentages now prevailing:

TABLE 13

BONUS VOUCHER QUOTATIONS
(percentage of face value)

Effective export (buying rates)	100	120	150	175	200
	In Pakistan Rupees for U.S. Dollar				
Entitlement of:					
20 per cent.	5·71	5·90	6·19	6·43	6·66
30 per cent.	6·18	6·47	6·90	7·26	7·61
Effective import selling rates	9·52	10·47	11·90	13·09	14·28

(Note: Since the start of the Scheme, quotations have fluctuated within a range of 100 to 200 per cent.)

In July 1961, half of the bonus voucher earnings from jute manufactures were reserved for the exclusive use of the jute industry. Subsequently, their use was widened to cover all capital goods needed by industry in East Pakistan (excepting cotton, textile spindles and looms). The effect was to create two more exchange rates. No market quotations for the 'restricted' vouchers are available, but these were officially said to be available in the market at a much lower premium than ordinary bonus vouchers.[21] Assuming the quotations for restricted vouchers to

[21] Press note dated 30 March 1962, Ministry of Industries, Rawalpindi.

be 50 and for ordinary bonus vouchers to be 150, the exporter of jute manufactures obtains an effective rate of Rs. 5·51 per U.S. dollar while the importer of capital goods in East Pakistan obtains an import rate of Rs. 7·12 per dollar. In August 1962 the Scheme was extended to domestic suppliers of specified commodities for use on the Indus Basin works. A bonus voucher entitlement of 40 per cent. was granted for stores supplied by domestic contractors to the extent of the foreign exchange reimbursed by the World Bank *net* of the import content of the supplies made. This type of manipulation of the Bonus Scheme leads to proliferation of multiple rates[22] and is a characteristic weakness of such exchange systems. Pressures are generated for adding to the list of eligible commodities or for adding to the number of bonus entitlement rates or for moving commodities from lower to higher entitlement rates.[23] The public is subjected to continuous rumours of changes and this in turn sets up erratic fluctuations in bonus voucher quotations. There is some evidence of Government desire to moderate fluctuations or at least to support the quotation enough to prevent it from declining much below 100.[24] However, the method adopted for this purpose, namely changes in the items on the 'bonus' import list, unwittingly contributes to greater instability. Trading in bonus vouchers, especially in the forward section, has become one of the more speculative ventures on the country's stock exchanges. Until the decision (taken in June 1961) to extend the Scheme through the end of the Second Plan period, there was a powerful element of uncertainty. Even the present 'guarantee' period may be inadequate for really sound long-term planning of export industries, especially as official declarations emphasize the Scheme's essentially temporary character. Thus, in the short run, the constant fluctuations leave the exporter with no firm or reliable basis for computing his returns for any particular transaction, while in the long run, the uncertainty regarding changes or termination of the Scheme may hold up the growth of appropriate export industries. On the other hand, to the extent that investments do take place, there is a distinct danger of misallocation of resources. The 40 per cent. entitlement rate for processed exports involves an effective exchange so greatly depreciated as to

[22] Several entitlement rates were introduced in 1963–4, e.g. 35 per cent. for fresh fruit and potatoes, 30 per cent. for tobacco, rice, family remittances and certain invisible receipts, 15 per cent. for cotton yarn and 10 per cent. for fresh prawns and shrimps.

[23] Finished textiles, e.g., were moved up from 20 to 40 per cent. and sugar and pickled skins from zero to 20 per cent.

[24] Witness, for example, the decision to introduce 37 new items to the import list in June 1961 as bonus voucher quotations approached 100 for the first time. When this proved insufficient to halt the decline a highly restricted 'nonessential' item, artificial silk yarn, was added in August 1961. When the market again faltered, sugar for general consumption was added.

provide an altogether disproportionate incentive to commit resources which are bound to be wasted if and when the exchange rate system is unified. In fact, this entitlement rate has not applied so far to more than 10 per cent. of the exports covered by the Scheme. Even the lower entitlement rates may encourage the growth of industries which are not really 'economic' in relation to any realistic rate of exchange. The Bonus Scheme encourages industry in two ways: it directly subsidizes most industrial exports from the profits of the import trade, and it protects the home market from the flow of import-substitutes, since items under the bonus enter at effective exchange rates about twice as high as the par value. Without the competition of imports, there is little incentive for many of the industries to operate efficiently or to raise productivity, as internal competition is not yet well developed in many cases. This of course is a well-known consequence of operating *quantitative* import restrictions. It is necessary to emphasize that similar results follow from using *cost* restrictions that are excessive, as under the present Scheme. Some of the drawbacks of the Bonus Scheme were softened by changes introduced in June 1964. The multiplicity of rates that had developed on the export side (there were 7 rates) was reduced by reverting to the original two entitlement rates; all rates below 20 were raised to 20 per cent. and all other rates were consolidated at 30 per cent. With these modifications the Scheme was extended into the Third Plan period but with the caveat that the objective would be to taper off the Scheme as 'our exports become more and more competitive and other measures for helping exports begin to produce results'.[25] This means that the future of the Scheme remains uncertain and the uncertainty increases as time passes, thereby impeding the rational allocation of resources to the export sector. Other drawbacks persist, e.g., an excessively high rate for imports under the Scheme and fluctuating bonus voucher quotations. The multiple rate features of the Scheme inevitably raise questions regarding the viability of the official par value, thereby inhibiting the commitment of capital by foreign investors. The return of the exchange system to a unified and fixed parity would represent a consummation much to be desired.[26]

[25] Speech, Minister of Finance, Government of Pakistan, 1964–5 Budget.
[26] For additional discussion of the Export Bonus Scheme see Chapter II, pp. 35–43.

IV

CENTRAL BANKING

THE State Bank of Pakistan is the chief monetary authority of the country and was established on 1 July 1948. Prior to that date, the Reserve Bank of India discharged all central banking functions. Under the Pakistan Monetary System and Reserve Bank Order, 1947, the Reserve Bank was to operate in Pakistan until 30 September 1948. Late in 1947, differences arose concerning Pakistan's cash balances and it was felt that in disputes between the two Governments, the Reserve Bank could not be expected to preserve an attitude of impartiality, since it was subject to the statutory control of the Government of India. Accordingly, an amending Order was issued on 31 March 1948, enabling Pakistan to take over all central banking functions with effect from 1 July 1948.

The State Bank started operations under an Order issued in May 1948.[1] The Central Government holds 51 per cent. of its share capital of Rs. 30 million and the public has subscribed the remainder. A reserve fund of Rs. 30 million has been contributed by Government. After paying dividends at 4 per cent. per annum, any surplus profits are paid to the Central Government in return for which the Bank is exempted from direct taxation.

A Central Board of Directors is responsible for general direction and supervision and comprises the Governor and Deputy Governors (appointed by Government) and nine Directors of whom six are nominated by the Government (one being a Government official empowered to cast the majority vote) and three elected by the private shareholders, one each by the group of shareholders registered at the three centres of Karachi, Lahore and Dacca. The Government has the right to supersede the entire Board of Directors if it feels that the Board is failing to carry out its duties.

---

[1] The Order was amended from time to time. It was replaced by an Ordinance promulgated in July 1955 and later embodied in the State Bank of Pakistan Act 1956, as amended.

The State Bank has responsibility for protecting the value of the currency, ensuring monetary stability, and 'maintaining conditions most favourable' to the promotion of economic activity on healthy lines. The preamble to the 1956 Act requires the Bank to participate actively in 'fostering the growth of the monetary and credit system in the best national interest' and to assist in the 'fuller utilization of the country's productive capacity' in addition to its task of ensuring monetary stability.

The State Bank has the sole right of note issue. Under a proportional reserve system, the note issue is backed to the extent of at least 30 per cent. of its value by gold, silver and approved foreign exchange, held in a separate Issue Department. The remaining assets may be Pakistan rupee securities, eligible commercial paper and rupee coin. The reserve requirements may be suspended for limited periods by the Central Government.

The Bank enjoys wide powers to influence the availability, cost and use of credit. Commercial banks which accept certain obligations, and have a minimum paid-up capital and reserves of Rs. 500,000 are declared as scheduled banks under Section 37(2) of the State Bank Act.[2] These banks must maintain with the State Bank, a balance not less than 5 per cent. of their demand liabilities and 2 per cent. of their time liabilities in Pakistan. The Government may on the recommendation of the State Bank change the ratio of reserves which the banks must maintain against their deposit-liabilities. By this means any proportion of the commercial banks' lending potential may be frozen by blocking up their deposits. Secondly, the State Bank can vary the bank-rate, i.e. the rate at which it is prepared to discount or re-discount certain types of bills and other commercial paper, and the rates at which it may advance funds against Government securities or other collateral. Thirdly, the Bank may vary the supply and the cost of credit through open-market operations, i.e., by purchase and sale of Government securities and certain types of commercial paper. However, these instruments of control are difficult to employ in the conditions prevailing in an underdeveloped money-market. A part of the economy is not

---

[2] The Act provides that co-operative banks may also be added to the list of scheduled banks and the general proviso that paid-up capital and reserves be not less than Rs. 500,000 may be relaxed at the discretion of the State Bank, provided it is satisfied that their affairs are not being conducted in a manner detrimental to the interests of the depositors.

monetized. The money-market is an 'inter-bank affair' and the security market is confined to a few institutional investors. Open-market operations on a large scale are likely to produce sharp fluctuations in security values.

Under the Banking Companies Ordinance 1962[3] the State Bank has additional powers of selective credit-control. It can give directions to the scheduled banks as to the purpose for which advances may or may not be made, the margins to be maintained against secured advances, and the rates of interest to be charged on advances. It can require a banking company not to enter into a particular transaction or class of transactions.

Under Sections 40 and 41 of the Ordinance (1962), the State Bank can inspect any bank. If the examination of any bank's affairs indicates such a need, the State Bank may issue such directions as it deems fit. Under Section 42(d) it may order changes in the management of a banking company and under certain conditions (laid down in Section 49(3) it may apply to a court of law for an order directing winding up of a banking company. It may also recommend that the Central Government prohibit any bank from accepting fresh deposits. The Bank has continuously improved and extended the inspection machinery in its Banking Control department and a system of periodical examination has been built up. A number of small banks which were found on inspection to be unsatisfactorily run have been 'de-scheduled' or prohibited from accepting fresh deposits. The interests of depositors are also protected by provisions (Section 30) which require banks to maintain daily within Pakistan such percentage of assets against their deposits within the country as the State Bank may prescribe from time to time but not exceeding 85 per cent. At present, this limit is fixed at 80 per cent. They must also maintain (under Section 29) 20 per cent. of their deposits in the form of liquid assets which are defined as cash, gold, and unencumbered approved securities. These provisions enable the State Bank to ensure that funds deposited in the banks are not substantially used outside the country and that a reasonable degree of liquidity is maintained at all times. Finally, new offices of banking companies may not be opened nor the location

---

[3] This Ordinance replaces Part XA of the Companies Act, 1913, the Banking Companies Inspection Ordinance, 1946, the Banking Companies (Restriction of Branches) Act, 1946 and the Banking Companies (Control) Act passed in 1948.

of existing offices changed without its permission under Section 28. This is designed mainly to prevent indiscriminate branch-expansion on the part of the banks. As an integral part of its responsibilities towards the depositor,[4] the State Bank acts as a reservoir of liquidity and provides funds to commercial banks as a lender of last resort.

In 1948, the State Bank faced the task of organizing central banking services quickly and simultaneously undertaking certain duties of an exceptional nature. The dearth of trained and experienced personnel rendered its task difficult as it received only eight experienced officers from the Reserve Bank of India. First, it had to replace pre-Partition currency with its own issues. The operation was highly complex and difficulties of unusual nature required prompt solution to ensure that 'India' notes were retired in the 15-month period provided by the Monetary System Order. The banking system had all but collapsed and the staff working at Government Treasuries was largely untrained. The extensive area of the country, the illiteracy of the rural population and the slow communications, especially in East Pakistan, produced a great strain on the limited number of offices providing exchange facilities. The retirement of 'India' notes was followed by a parallel operation for coinage.

Pakistan established claim to assets of Rs. 1,767·5 million but after the transfer of Rs. 1,276·7 million, India withheld further deliveries of assets on the grounds that in respect of Reserve Bank notes which had entered Pakistan after 1 July 1948, Pakistan was not entitled to any share in assets, because their movement was adjustable under the Payments Agreement. Pakistan pointed out that the possibility of movement of notes across the borders was patent when the arrangements for division of assets were made and that, in any case, such movements were in both directions. The dispute remains unresolved.

A second exceptional task of the State Bank was to assist in the restoration of commercial banking services. This obligation constituted a significant departure from the orthodox practice of central banks in countries with well-developed banking systems. In Pakistan, the central bank had perforce to help create the banks before it could regulate them. Since the shortage of trained

---

[4] Under Section 3 of the Ordinance, 1962, the State Bank has been given powers to inspect and issue directions to co-operative banks. (*See* Ch. 7 *infra*.)

7

personnel was a serious bottleneck, the State Bank immediately organized training courses. The first Officers Training Scheme was started in August 1948 with 100 university graduates placed in training with the few commercial banks then functioning. The courses have since been repeated several times. In September 1951, the State Bank sponsored the setting up of the 'Institute of Bankers in Pakistan' to facilitate studies in banking, to conduct professional examinations, and to safeguard the interest of persons engaged in the profession. By 1953, the need for trained personnel, except at the higher levels, was rather well met.

Simultaneously, the State Bank prepared plans for the setting up of the National Bank of Pakistan as a quasi-public commercial bank to take over the agency functions for conducting Government treasury work and providing remittance facilities then performed by the Imperial Bank of India. The Governor of the State Bank functioned temporarily as first Chairman of the Board of the National Bank during a crucial period of its life.

Meeting the seasonal demand for credit has been the most important of the normal services of the State Bank. Until quite recently, there have been two distinct seasons: the busy season from August/September to April/May and the relatively slack summer season. The major cash crops of the country move during this busy season while the regular demands for import-financing and for marketing food crops remain rather high. The sharp increase in the demand for credit at this period can force up interest rates in the absence of Central Bank accommodation.[5] The State Bank makes loans and advances to scheduled banks repayable on demand or for fixed periods up to 90 days against appropriate security, such as Government bonds. It can also purchase and re-discount eligible commercial paper. A 90-day limit was formerly placed on eligible commercial paper, except for bills and promissory notes issued to finance agricultural operations or the marketing of agricultural crops, in which case the limit was 270 days (raised in 1955 to fifteen months). Since 1956 the Bank has been empowered to make loans to any co-operative bank and to other institutions promoting agricultural and indus-

[5] The seasonal pattern is tending to disappear with the growth of the industrial section. In the three years ending 1958–9, the average busy season expansion was Rs. 322 million and the average slack season retirement was Rs. 246 million. In 1962–3 and 1963–4 there was no net retirement of bank credit.

trial development on 'terms and conditions to be determined by the Central Board'. In emergencies, the Bank may accept commercial paper not endorsed by a scheduled bank and make loans to banks against any collateral it deems satisfactory.

At first, the commercial banks made little use of the re-discount facilities and borrowed exclusively against the collateral of Government securities. This reflected the disuse into which the usance bill had fallen after Partition. The State Bank felt that if the use of these bills could be revived and banks persuaded to obtain seasonal finance by discounting them, their self-liquidating character would facilitate the expansion of central bank credit during the busy season and its direct and automatic contraction during the slack season. It decided to force the pace of development of a bill market by initiating a scheme in 1952 for providing funds to commercial banks against their demand promissory notes if supported by usance bills of their constituents. The banks were encouraged to convert a part of their clients' cash credits— the usual form in which credit was provided—into 90-day usance bills. As an incentive, the lending rate was fixed at $\frac{1}{2}$ per cent. below the bank-rate and the State Bank also agreed to bear half the cost of stamp duty. The concessional rate was later withdrawn as bill discounting became popular. From Rs. 11·4 million in 1952–3, peak borrowing had risen to Rs. 93·2 million in 1963–4. Additional finance was provided against Government securities (Rs. 206·2 million at their peak level in 1963–4). Finally, the State Bank has granted 'counter-finance' facilities to the National Bank and other Pakistani banks to cover their loans to Government departments undertaking substantial activity of a commercial nature.[6] These facilities have lessened the seasonal stringency of funds and helped the country's own banks to develop rapidly despite their lack of access to metropolitan money-markets such as their foreign competitors enjoy.

The State Bank also functions as banker to the Central and Provincial Governments. It has floated a series of central loans, raising the permanent public debt from Rs. 518·3 million in 1948 to Rs. 3,096·9 million in the middle of 1964. It has also floated loans for the provincial governments, their outstanding debt increasing over the same period from Rs. 182·9 million to Rs. 479·7

[6] The implications of the extensive provision of central bank credit for monetary policy are examined in the concluding section of this chapter.

million. It has endeavoured to develop a market for Government securities. Although not required to support Government bond prices at any pre-determined level, its role in the pre-October 1958 period as the residual holder of each year's flotation did result in a stable, if 'administered' market with bond prices frozen at levels dictated by the interest rate which the government of the day was prepared to pay. To popularize sales of 90-day treasury bills, the Bank announced in February 1954 a scheme for re-discounting treasury bills, thus assuring banks that they could buy such bills and then obtain seasonal finance through re-discounting them. As Government banker, the State Bank has furnished 'Ways and Means' advances for periods up to ninety days without limit to the central government. Limits have been fixed for such advances to provincial governments, but they have not always been adhered to.

The State Bank performs various agency functions for Government, the most important being administration of exchange controls. Since these controls are exercised primarily through commercial banks, the State Bank is the natural agency for the purpose. Under the Foreign Exchange Act, 1947, all foreign exchange receipts are surrendered to the State Bank or its authorized dealers. Allocations of foreign exchange are made according to policies laid down by Government. For commercial imports which are licensable import licences must be produced before exchange is released. Payments for invisibles and capital transfers are screened by State Bank officials according to policies set by Government in consultation with the Bank. Strict vigilance is maintained to eliminate leakages of foreign exchange. Such leakages usually arise from non-surrender of foreign exchange earnings and the remittance of exchange for authorized purposes in excess of actual requirements. An 'export-price-check' procedure has been laid down to prevent under-invoicing of the two major exports, jute and cotton, while measures are constantly improved for detecting over-pricing of imports and other practices employed for illicit transfer of funds abroad.

An important source of leakage was formerly the Haj pilgrimage. Intending Hajis carried Pakistani currency notes to the Hedjaz as normal travel credit instruments could not be used in the absence of adequate banking arrangements in that country. To ensure acceptance of the currency notes at par, Government guaranteed their repatriation against sterling. The concession was misused by smugglers who exported large amounts of currency and obtained sterling against them via Saudi Arabian money-changers. To stop the leakage a ban was imposed on the export and import of Pakistani currency (except in restricted amounts) and special Haj notes were issued to pilgrims which were not legal tender in Pakistan. The total sterling liability was thus controlled.

As noted above, the State Bank has helped to revive and expand banking facilities. By and large, the working capital needs of commerce and large-scale industry are now adequately met. The agricultural sector is beginning to draw on institutional sources with substantial State Bank assistance (Chapter VI). Attention has recently turned to the remaining gaps in the credit structure, viz., the need for longer-term loan funds by the industry, mining and transportation sectors, and the lack of credit of all types for small-scale enterprises. The 1956 Act articulated a growing concern over the problems of development finance and provided the State Bank with additional powers to this end. The Bank could make loans for periods up to five years to any scheduled bank or corporation approved by the Government and having as one of its objects the financing of agriculture, or of agricultural and animal produce, or the needs of industry. By an amendment in 1958 the Bank was authorized 'to purchase, hold and sell shares and debentures of any banking company established to promote the economic development of any specific area' or any corporation 'established for the purpose of promoting agricultural or industrial development'.

It was recognized that the normal credit creating powers of the State Bank should not be used for meeting long-term credit needs. Hence the State Bank's role was mainly promotional in the sense of helping to establish new institutions and advisory after they were established.[7] In 1957, it sponsored the Pakistan Industrial Credit and Investment Corporation (*see* Chapter VII). The Bank agreed to provide credit up to Rs. 20 million to the Corporation and while it may have not been needed, it constitutes a reassuring guarantee fund. The State Bank also helped in

---

[7] Its involvement in financing the specialized institutions, two of which are scheduled banks, has actually proved to be for greater than expected. (*See* Chs. VI and VII.)

setting up the Agricultural Bank of Pakistan and its successor, the Agriculture Development Bank. Its contribution has been more substantive in the establishment of the Eastern Mercantile Bank in 1960. Recognizing that banking facilities in East Pakistan were not developing fast enough, the State Bank advocated the setting up of regional banks designed to meet local needs. Private enterprise was not forthcoming, so it participated with two of the leading Pakistani banks in establishing a pilot institution, contributing a third of the share capital. This bank has already established a network of branches in the smaller towns of the province. In material submitted to the Credit Enquiry Commission, the State Bank focused attention on the maldistribution of commercial bank credit (*see* next chapter). The Commission suggested a series of measures for improving the situation. For its part, the State Bank has impressed upon the commercial banks the need to ensure an adequate supply of credit to the small man with results that are not discouraging. It is now working with Government and with banks in developing plans for enlarging the flow of credit to small business interests through specialized institutions providing credit against the security of immovable property for meeting the requirements of middle-class entrants into trade, professional and service industries who may not have other suitable security to offer.

As an integral part of its developmental activity the State Bank, in partnership with commercial banks, is promoting a campaign for inculcating the banking habit among the general population. It is urging the commercial banks to attract primary deposits as an essential prerequisite for credit expansion and has put them on notice that in accommodating their requests for seasonal finance, it would as a matter of policy keep in view the efforts banks make and the success they achieve in attracting fresh deposits.[8]

Finally, we turn to the policies pursued by the State Bank for 'protecting the value of the currency' and 'ensuring monetary stability'. The period since the establishment of the Bank can be

[8] *Speeches*, Governor, State Bank of Pakistan, Annual Meeting (September 1961 and 1962). In a State Bank Report issued in November 1962, it was suggested that the banks be required to pay a penal rate of interest on a graduated scale if their borrowings from the State Bank exceed certain limits. In working out these limits, one purpose would be to relate the size of assistance to a bank's performance in mobilizing deposits (*Dawn*, 24 November 1962).

divided into three parts: (1) from the middle of 1948 to the end of 1952 (2) from 1953 through the end of 1958 and (3) from 1959 to the present time. In the early years, the use of credit policies was directed to defending the external value of the currency. Following Pakistan's decision not to follow sterling in devaluation in September 1949, the import trade became attractive. As import restrictions were relaxed, there was a substantial diversion of funds to that sector. Speculation against the currency led to heavy forward booking of foreign exchange and threatened the country's reserves. In August 1950, the State Bank prohibited the booking of exchange forward unless an irrevocable letter of credit was opened and was supported by a deposit of not less than 35 per cent. of forward cover (later raised to 50 per cent.). The banks were cautioned against committing themselves too heavily in financing the import trade and were warned that sufficient funds should be released for the export trade. To discourage the banks from seeking additional reserves at low cost by pledging Government paper, a differential schedule of lending rates was enforced in October 1950 viz., 3 per cent. or bank-rate for the first week, 4 per cent. for the next two weeks and 5 per cent. thereafter, for advances against Government securities. The State Bank carefully scrutinized the position of banks offering to sell large blocks of Government securities in order to safeguard against any large-scale monetization of the public debt. The sharp upturn in the country's export fortunes in the wake of the Korean War boom led to a lifting of these restrictions.

Another cycle of excessive imports set in soon thereafter and by the middle of 1952 the State Bank had become sufficiently alarmed to reimpose the earlier restrictions with deposit requirements for opening of letters of credits raised to 75 per cent. for imports on the open general licence and 50 per cent. on licensed commodities. To make these measures effective, it was laid down that advances against stocks of imported goods should not exceed 50 per cent. and clean (or unsecured) advances were prohibited. The restrictions apparently failed to stem the rising trend of imports and by triggering expectations that direct restrictions would eventually be imposed may well have produced a perverse effect.[9] The credit restrictions were withdrawn

[9] See note by Mr. Zahid Husain to *Report of Economic Appraisal and Development Enquiry Committee*, 1953.

in March 1953, a few months after the open general licence was suspended and severe quantitative controls on imports were imposed.

The contractionary effects of the post-Korean recession and of the substantial import surplus gradually yielded to the expansionary influences emanating from the large deficits in the Government sector which emerged after 1952–3. For some time, their effect may have been merely to restore the liquidity depleted by earlier external deficits. With the foreign sector forced into balance by 1953–4, the continuance of Government budgetary deficits, financed by the banking system, led to a rapid increase in money-supply. Inflationary pressures developed because the rise in money spending which would have been associated with the growing money-supply[10] was not matched by a corresponding rise in availabilities. This condition prevailed until the closing months of 1958 when a new Government assumed power and decided to abandon the policy of deficit financing. During this period, the State Bank did not find it possible to use its instruments of *general* control, partly on grounds of their limited effectiveness in the prevailing institutional framework and partly by its view of the forces making for inflation, as illustrated by a 'causative' analysis of changes in money supply (Table 14).

The analysis is 'causative' only in the accounting sense that in the consolidated balance-sheet of the monetary system, liabilities that are designated as money, must by definition, equal assets *less* non-monetary liabilities. Hence changes in money-supply can be 'explained' by changes in the offsetting items. As shown in the Monetary Survey, Table 15, the main asset items are 'claims on Government' including provincial governments, 'claims on private sector' and foreign assets of the central bank. Non-money liabilities are Government deposits and deposits in the Postal Saving Bank which are adjusted against claims on Government to 'determine' the gross expansionary effect of that sector; the net effect allows for an adjustment of changes in counterpart funds. Similarly changes in claims on private sector measure its *gross*

---

[10] This assumes a stable functional relationship between the *stock* of money and the *flow* of spending or a constant income-velocity of money. For an interesting analysis casting doubt on the validity of this assumption cf. R. C. Porter, 'Income-velocity and Pakistan's Second Plan', *The Pakistan Development Review*, Vol. I, No. 1.

contribution to changes in money-supply while the *net* effect allows for an adjustment in time-deposits. 'Other Factors' represent the residual obtained by setting Unclassified Assets against Unclassified Liabilities.

TABLE 14

CAUSATIVE ANALYSIS OF MONEY SUPPLY

(In millions of rupees)

Year (ending June)	Increase in Money-supply	Expensionary (+)				Contractionary (−)	
		Government Sector		Private Sector		Foreign Sector	Other Factors
		Gross	Adjustment for Counterpart Funds	Gross	Adjustment for Time-deposits		
1955–56	654	+322	−160	+100	− 44	+444	− 8
1956–57	454	+862	−446	+237	− 5	−217	+ 23
1957–58	351	+715	− 36	+ 42	−132	−282	+ 45
1958–59	198	+217	− 27	− 4	− 53	+222	− 57
1959–60	296	+124	−158	+358	−193	+220	− 55
1960–61	26	+372	−264	+417	−282	−120	− 97
1961–62	227	−114	+404	+600	−280	− 79	−395
1962–63	882	+402	−238	+792	−428	+274	+ 79
1963–64	1,002	+421	+206	+914	−497	−197	+155

Source: Table 15, without items 7 through 10 and excepting 1963–4.

The causative analysis suggests that Government operations exercised by far the largest expansionary effect on money-supply from the middle of 1953 to that of 1959 and this holds true even after credit for the accumulation of counterpart funds is attributed to the public sector. The private sector shows no marked expansion, except for the year 1956–7, when a large expansion was largely attributable to the rise in the value of trade transactions following the devaluation of the previous year. The State Bank introduced a series of selective credit restrictions (*see* discussion below) at the end of that year and the rate of expansion was sharply curtailed. If the domestic sector is given credit for the accumulation of time-deposits its net contribution to the

[11] From 1961–2 operations on the Indus Basin Fund have become a significant component in 'other factors'. In that year, deposits to the Fund exceeded withdrawals by Rs. 186 million; in 1962–3 and 1963–4 operations were expansionary by Rs. 54 and 66 million. The deposits are mainly derived from transfers of U.S. counterpart funds and sales-proceeds of 'free' foreign exchange contributed by participants to the Indus Basin Agreement of 1960.

expansion factors averages only Rs. 34 million per year during the six-year period, being negative in the last two years.[12]

It may perhaps be argued that if the State Bank was powerless to control the primary monetary effects of deficit-financing in the public sector, it could nevertheless have dampened inflationary pressures to some extent by curtailing the private sector's access to bank credit and by restraining the secondary credit creating potential of the banking system. There are two aspects of this question: the technical capacity of the State Bank to take such compensating action and the justification for it. The institutional limitations on open-market operations have been mentioned earlier. The use of the bank-rate instrument was largely pre-cluded by the Government's decision on the quantum of deficit finance and the rates of interest it would pay on its loans. In effect, the State Bank was left in the position of a residual holder of whatever part of the Government loan flotations the market was unwilling to absorb at the rates offered. [13] Nor could it bring pressure by curtailing its re-discount operations because whatever the fluctuations within each season, the level of its re-discounts outstanding varied little from year to year and remained in fact at such a low level that even its complete liquida-tion would have compensated hardly at all for the expansion in the public sector. Finally, with banks operating on excess reserves and with the Government's deficit bulking so large in relation to reserves, the power to vary reserve requirements would have had to be used with such severity as to unsettle the banking system as a whole and would have produced unequal effects on different classes of banks.[14] With the primary expansion largely outside

[12] There is some question whether the adjustment of time-deposits is quite justified. While not a component of money-supply as that term is defined in Pakistan, time-deposits are a very close money substitute and presumably add to the total liquidity of the economy in much the same way.

[13] The fact that the State Bank did not appear to actively support the market for Government bonds was perhaps due to its preparedness to meet seasonal requirements through an open discount window, thereby obviating the need for any large seasonal shifting of Government debt from the commercial banks to the State Bank. This was perhaps a slightly preferred course of action as it gave the State Bank some indirect supervision over the quality and purposes of bank credit to the private sector and prevented monetization of the public debt.

[14] The percentage by which average legal reserve requirements would have to be raised 'is equal to the ratio of the excessive Government deficit to the amount of bank reserves. . . . If banks have excess reserves, the increase in the ratio would have to be correspondingly greater'. (*See* Joachim Ahrensdorf, 'Central

State Bank control, there remained the possibility of sterilizing additions to bank reserves due to the Government's cash deficit. This could technically have been possible by requiring 100 per cent. marginal reserves against increases in deposits. However, the potential for secondary credit expansion was strictly limited by the small magnitude of the credit multipliers[15] in Pakistan, given the high ratio of currency to money-supply—roughly 0·66 throughout the 1950's—so that only one-third of the money created by Government came to be lodged with the banking system. Nor were these additional reserves used by the commercial banks to support credit expansion in the private sector to any extent except in the year 1956–7. The liquidity created by Government was substantially returned to it through investment in Government bonds. High marginal reserve requirements would have stopped this process of re-lending but, assuming the quantum of deficit to be fixed, the State Bank would presumably have been compelled to divert the bankers' deposits accumulating with it to precisely the same purpose.

It was the unwillingness of banks to use their growing deposit resources to expand credit to the private sector which provides the major justification for the State Bank's avoidance of general or aggregative restrictions on the *level* of bank credit. The banks apparently continued to apply the same rigid standards to loan applications and confined their operations to the traditional financing of the working capital needs of trade and industry, despite the massive additions to their liquidity.[16] With credit restricted to facilitating the movement of exports and imports and the short-term needs of large-scale industrial enterprises, any sharp curtailment of credit would have adversely affected trading channels and the growth of industrial output.[17] More-

Banking Policies and Inflation', *Staff Papers*, International Monetary Fund, Vol. VII, No. 2, p. 286.)

[15] The credit multiplier is the reciprocal of $c + r(1-c)$ where c is the ratio of currency in circulation to money and r is the legal or customary reserve ratio maintained by banks against deposits.

[16] There remains some doubt whether this may not have reflected lack of *scope* for expansion in a period when private activity was trammelled by a wide network of direct controls e.g., through severe import restrictions and allocation of essential domestic output. The sharp expansion in credit to the private sector after the return of a relatively 'freer' economy in the past few years may lend support to the doubters.

[17] This is the 'needs of trade' doctrine; it assumes that there can be no change in saving propensities at the margin, i.e., that no possibility exists for some

over, any sharp denial of credit facilities would probably have had 'bad' distributional effects by injuring small and marginal firms as well as new ventures whereas large well-established business houses would have managed to maintain unimpeded access to bank credit. Finally, the antagonism of the private sector which the State Bank's denial policy would have generated might easily have undermined whatever moral pressure it could bring to bear on Government to desist from its inflationary policy.[18]

While avoiding any curtailment of the *level* of credit, the State Bank did invoke selective controls to influence its *composition*. To prevent speculative activity on the stock exchange, especially in the new issues section, a directive was issued in June 1955 prohibiting the banks from making unsecured advances or making advances against the security of shares of a company in anticipation of their allotment, unless deposit of 50 per cent. or more of the application money was obtained. Next, confronted by the sharp expansion of credit to the private sector in the year ending June 1957, directives were issued to banks to limit their advances against imported manufactured goods, bullion, food-grains and oilseeds to a maximum of 60 per cent. of the value of such goods. To minimize the diversion of credit to non-restricted purposes, banks were simultaneously prohibited from making unsecured advances or advances secured by guarantees beyond a maximum of Rs. 50,000 to an individual party. These restrictions apparently had the desired effect of reducing the restricted category of advances. The total credit extended to the private sector changed little over 1957–8, suggesting that some diversion to other types of security could well have taken place. These restrictions were removed in November 1958 to relieve the strain on the banking system, following a precipitate fall in the prices

---

redirection of the borrowers' resources to the self-financing of output. The assumption may be true in the very short run, and not even then, if activities not financed by banks are simultaneously expanding (e.g. luxury housing in Pakistan) or if substantial idle balances are being accumulated. A gradual curtailment of credit would probably lead to greater savings rather than to lowered output or to a re-disposition of savings from less essential to more essential activities previously financed by banks.

[18] 'Central banks, especially when they are new and have little tradition and prestige to start out with, may feel, *perhaps not without justification*, that continued criticism along these lines will jeopardize their limited status in the community still further and may ultimately eliminate whatever admittedly little influence and effective power they have.' Ahrensdorf, op. cit., p. 299.

of consumer goods as inventories were run down in the wake of Martial Law regulations against the hoarding of goods. It was felt that with the severe penalties prescribed there remained little possibility of bank funds being employed for 'anti-social' activities.

A new phase in monetary policy was initiated in January 1959 with the raising of the bank-rate from 3 to 4 per cent. This resulted directly from abandoning the policy of deficit-financing and the willingness shown by the new Government to borrow from the market at more competitive rates of interest. The change in the bank-rate was rendered effective by a corresponding rise in the advance rates of commercial banks and some other credit institutions; the transition to a higher interest rates pattern was made without undue disturbance in the gilt-edged market.[19] The intent of the bank-rate change was not particularly restrictive and central bank accommodation remained freely available at the higher rate. Peak borrowings by commercial banks were about one-third of sanctioned limits in the 1958–9 busy season as the deposits in the banks were rising faster than bank loans, following the legalization of declared hidden wealth and the emergence of a balance of payments surplus in private sector accounts.

In the four years ending June 1964 the level of bank credit has nearly tripled to reach Rs. 4,791 million. The private sector claimed most of the increase, its borrowings expanding from Rs. 1,458 million to Rs. 4,186 million in this period. A marked expansion in economic activity as reflected in growth of national income at market prices (by Rs. 8,998 million in the first 4 years of the Plan), the removal of price and distribution controls over much of internal trade, a liberal import licensing policy which permitted a restocking of depleted inventories, the return of the food-grains trade to private hands and the sharp increase in private investment activity (net monetized capital formation in the private sector was Rs. 8,319 million in the four years ending 1963–4), are held responsible for this increase. Loans to provincial governments rose by Rs. 242 million over the same four years. Investments by the banking system in Government securities rose an additional Rs. 211 million.

[19] Ziauddin Ahmad, Ch. 9: *Central Banking in South and East Asia*, ed. G. Davies, Hong Kong University Press, 1962. The chapter provides an excellent review of State Bank policies through 1959.

Total deposits of the banks rose by Rs. 2,763 million to Rs. 5,706 million in these four years. The gap between deposits and bank credits was partly bridged by larger inter-bank borrowings[20] and later by borrowing from the State Bank. The outstanding figure for borrowing by scheduled banks has risen from Rs. 11 million in June 1960 to Rs. 386 million in June 1963. The borrowing shows an even larger expansion in 1963–4 when peak borrowing reached Rs. 958 million while outstanding at the end of June 1964 was a figure of Rs. 816 million.

Despite this remarkable increase in bank credit, financed so substantially by the central bank, there has been widespread criticism of monetary policy. The criticism appears to proceed at several levels of discourse.

At the most 'practical' level are the complaints of businessmen that there is a 'credit squeeze' in the country. Their outcry is partly directed against several selective credit controls which the State Bank imposed in 1960 and after for preventing the undue involvement of credit in certain sectors (for uses regarded as 'non-essential'). These include: (1) margin requirements of 50 per cent. against the issue price of shares of newly floated companies and 40 per cent. against the market value of shares of established concerns; (2) margin requirements of 40 per cent. on advances above Rs. 25,000 per borrower against cotton yarn (except for export) and imported manufactures (except industrial machinery, iron and steel); (3) prohibition of unsecured loans or loans secured by guarantee above Rs. 50,000 without State Bank permission; (4) restriction to a maximum of six months of the period for which advances can be made against stocks of wheat and rice. In January 1962 margin requirements of 25 per cent. were imposed in respect of letters of credit for import of twelve items and 30 per cent. for iron and steel. In May 1962 margin requirements of 40 per cent. were applied to advances against cotton textiles—whether imported or domestically produced. However, in April 1961 the margin on advances against restricted categories was reduced to 20 per cent. and advances up to Rs. 50,000 were exempted from margin requirements in East

---

[20] Over the past few years, U.S. owned counterpart funds have been transferred from the State Bank to certain foreign commercial banks. By October 1962 the transfers stabilized at Rs. 280 million. These banks have begun to function in the inter-bank market as alternative lenders of last resort.

Pakistan. In July 1963 the State Bank introduced some quantitative credit restraints. The statutory reserve requirements of the scheduled banks were raised to a uniform 5 per cent. of demand and time-deposit liabilities. Borrowings against Government securities were subjected to graduated penal rates. Each bank was assigned a quota equal to half of its reserve requirement. Borrowings up to the quota only would be at bank-rate. In excess of the quota higher rates were applied in a four-tiered structure reaching a maximum of 2 per cent. over the bank-rate for amounts exceeding six times the quota.

A major factor in the complaints of credit scarcity relates to the needs of small businessmen, especially in the less developed areas, who have emerged in the wake of the lifting of most direct or physical controls over the economy. This is especially true in the import trade where official policy has deliberately sought to introduce 'newcomers' by providing 'open general licence' or free licensing facilities of Rs. 25,000 per item. In the past, barriers to entry implicit in direct controls concealed the small operators' lack of access to bank credit. Now that these barriers have been lowered somewhat, their credit problems have come to the fore and a difficulty that is confined to only a segment of the trade has been generalized into a 'credit squeeze'.

A third, and perhaps the most important factor, has been the failure of the business community to adjust to the cessation of inflation and the re-emergence of a more competitive situation in the economy. There has been a tendency to hold inventories in the expectation that prices and profit-margins can be indefinitely maintained at high levels by keeping output off the market. An element of speculation is particularly noticeable in the holding of stocks of imported goods in the hope that the liberal import policy will have to be abandoned by Government. The use of bank finance for inventory building has apparently created pressure on the banking system which may bear little relationship to the normal requirements of trade and industry for working capital.

Moreover there is evidence that bank credit has been applied to longer-term purposes as a substitute for equity capital. There is a disposition in official circles (*vide* 1962 Annual Speech of the Governor of the State Bank) to explain the pressure for credit in terms of the accelerated commitments made by the private sector to the Industrial Investment Schedule. Against the target provisions for the entire Second Plan period of Rs. 3,660 million, an amount equal to Rs. 5,883 million was committed by the end of 1961. However, part of the investment has yet to materialize in actually installed and operating plant facilities. If credit demands are at all related to the Schedule, the inference must be that bank finance is being utilized for the purposes that are more appropriate to the capital market. The inference is supported by the sharp increase in bank advances against the security of machinery.

Finally and at perhaps the most fundamental level, the criticism is not that monetary policy has been restrictive in any absolute sense, but that it failed to be expansionary enough in relation to the available resources. Attention is drawn to the difficulties of disposal and the consequent accumulation of food-grains received under the P.L. 480 programme as well as the growing inventories of cotton textiles. According to this argument, the increase in stocks of these staple articles of consumption can be likened to an unintended rapid rise in external reserves. A high level of reserves is a luxury that a poor country can ill afford and the course of wisdom lies in utilizing them for imports of capital goods. In precisely the same way, accumulating stocks of food-grains and cloth can be regarded as providing the opportunity for capital formation based on the under-employed labour resources. This labour can be sent to work on capital building projects with a zero or very low foreign exchange content. Their wages can be financed by additional bank credit in the knowledge that the money created in this way will be spent on food and clothing, given the spending pattern of poor people in the country. In this view the failure to pursue an expansionary financial policy amounts to foregoing a unique opportunity for capital formation (through a works programme) that is presented by P.L. 480 grains and the surplus production of cotton textiles. The adoption of such a policy would have the incidental advantage, it is claimed, of escaping the dilemma on which the authorities are now impaled: many essential programmes, including the Indus Basin Settlement Works, can be financed only through the sales of P.L. 480 grains earmarked for the purpose. Good domestic crops with falling prices of wheat and rice have made for difficulties in disposal of imported wheat and forced the Government to cut the price at which the U.S. grains are sold, thereby further adversely affecting the price incentives of Pakistan's farmers.

Hence, either the P.L. 480 commodities remain unsold or local agriculture must suffer. A policy that increases purchasing power in the market for grains would simultaneously help to resolve both problems according to this analysis.

The preceding line of argument would be more convincing if there were greater assurances that the external sector would not be significantly weakened by the adoption of expansionist policies at home. Without much better information on consumer spending patterns than is presently available in Pakistan there is no guarantee that newly created purchasing power would in fact spend itself on surplus grains and cloth and exert little or no pressure on other goods which would otherwise have replaced imports or been exported. A deliberately inflated home demand could lead to a weakening of incentives to export or to adopt the improvements necessary for competing in world markets.

Without counteracting measures, the immediate prospects were for a continuance, and even an acceleration of the expansionary process that has been evidenced by monetary statistics since 1961–2. Provisional data for the calendar year 1964 indicate an increase in money supply of roughly 1·3 billion rupees. If time-deposits are included, the rise in liquidity is closer to two billion rupees. In January, 1965, the following credit measures were adopted: (a) imposition of 25 per cent. margin requirement against opening of letters of credit for all kinds of imports, (b) tightening of the Quota System and extension of its coverage and (c) raising of cash reserve requirements of banks from 5½ per cent. to 7 per cent. to be effective from 1 April 1965.

More significant is the renewed and growing dependence of Government agencies on the banking system. Apart from banking system investment in Government securities, both central and provincial, which have risen at an average annual rate of Rs. 290 million in the first four years of the Second Plan period, scheduled banks' loans to provincial governments have increased by another Rs. 75 million a year. The latter represents deficit-financing in the most direct sense, because under the counter-finance arrangements through which such loans are financed, the commercial banks are in fact merely channelling State Bank credit to the Government. The Second Plan had contemplated no *net* deficit-financing over the five year period. The increase in credit to the Government is rather surprising, since in recent

8

years many of the commercial functions performed by public agencies have been transferred to the private sector, most notably the food-grains trade.

A part of the monetary expansion would have been absorbed by the growth in *net* domestic product by an estimated 20 per cent. in the four years ending mid-1964. Another part would have been absorbed by the continuing monetization of the economy. The sharp rise in foreign assistance, as reflected in the striking increase in imports—from Rs. 2·5 billion in 1959–60 to Rs. 4·5 billion in 1963–4—would have engendered a need for higher cash balances to finance an enlarged volume of transactions flowing from the absorption of external resources of fairly massive proportions, relatively to the country's own resources. These and other factors may account for the fact that available price indices show a rise of no more than one and a half per cent. per annum. Notwithstanding all this, there is clearly room for caution in appraising an expansion of 31 per cent. in money-supply in two years ending June 1964 and of total liquidity with time-deposits of about 37 per cent. There are already indications that bank credit may have been perhaps too liberally available, especially for large borrowers, that it may have led to speculative inventory accumulation, that some of it has been diverted to long-term uses in the industrial sector and finally that it may be indirectly helping to maintain internal demand at a level which may imperil the momentum of import liberalization policy.

If the State Bank were disposed to move still further in the direction of restraining credit expansion, its chances of success are probably much improved by recent developments. The overwhelming dependence of the scheduled banks on central bank finance increases the leverage of the monetary authority. Excess reserves have disappeared and the emergence of the industrial sector as a year-round customer of bank credit has ironed out seasonal fluctuations in cash ratios. Money and capital markets are better organized to transmit the pressure of monetary policy from the point of initial impact to other parts of the credit system. The adoption of a responsible fiscal policy gives monetary policy room for manœuvre. At the same time, the shift in emphasis from physical to indirect or market controls places a greater responsibility on monetary policy for influencing the allocation of resources.

TABLE 15

Monetary Survey and Components[1]

(In millions of rupees)

	1956	1957	1958	1959	1960	1961	1962	1963
State Bank of Pakistan								
1.1 Foreign assets	2,004	1,787	1,505	1,753[9]	1,909	1,879	1,793	2,065
1.2 Claims on Government	1,444	2,301	2,841	2,772[9]	2,770	2,948	2,945	3,158
1.3 Claims on prov. governments	—	—	110	86	125	15	96	56
1.4 Claims on banks	30	94	42	19	43	347	445	440
$\Sigma_1 = 2$ Assets = Liabilities[2]	3,689	4,331	4,637	4,772	4,993	5,334	5,446	5,932
2.1 Note liabilities	2,835	3,206	3,373	3,411	3,566	3,609	3,645	3,953
2.2 Government deposits	90	16	175	160	115	62	211	160
2.3 Prov. government's deposits	82	51	—	17	9	7	49	8
2.4 Counterpart funds	160	606	642	669	827	919	662	809
2.5 Bankers' deposits	311	212	257	327	254	274	320	306
Scheduled Banks								
3.1 Cash/Deposits at S.B.P.	314	195	246	322	244	267	302	392
3.2 Claims on Government	694	704	872	960	1,024	1,086	1,073	1,065
3.3 Claims on prov. govts.	107	106	109	134	176	192	185	233
3.4 Claims on private sector	834	1,071	1,105	1,101	1,458	1,872	2,535	3,292
$\Sigma_3 = 4$ Assets = Liabilities[3]	2,050	2,154	2,481	2,749	3,172	3,782	4,484	5,457
4.1 Demand deposits	1,431	1,490	1,689	1,870	1,997	1,991	2,190	2,780
4.2 Time-deposits	564	569	700	753	946	1,228	1,507	1,935
4.3 Credit from S.B.P.	29	93	39	10	11	338	403	386
Related Data								
5–6 Treasury currency[4]	267	284	305	305	313	320	316	334
7–8 Savings Bank deposits[5]	402	443	490	486	493	492	494	520
9–10 Treasury IMF A/c[6]	22	22	22	22	84	84	84	84

TABLE 15 (cont.)

	1956	1957	1958	1959	1960	1961	1962	1963
Monetary Survey								
11.1 Foreign assets	2,021	1,804	1,522	1,770[9]	1,926	1,896	1,810	2,082
11.2 Claims on Government	2,785	3,711	4,487	4,501[9]	4,517	4,762	4,744	4,994
11.3 Claims on prov. govt.[7]	185	160	337	421	460	538	608	667
11.4 Claims on private sector[8]	857	1,095	1,137	1,132	1,490	1,906	2,597	3,387
Σ11 = 12 Assets = Liabilities	6,066	6,920	7,624	7,975	8,708	9,258	9,967	11,398
13.1 Money	4,557	5,011	5,362	5,560	5,856	5,882	6,105	6,987
12.1.1 Currency	3,053	3,432	3,627	3,646	3,815	3,846	3,865	4,157
12.2 Quasi-money	966	1,012	1,190	1,239	1,439	1,721	2,001	2,455
12.3 Government deposits	172	67	175	177	124	70	260	168
12.4 Counterpart funds	160	606	642	669	827	1,091[10]	687	809

Source: International Financial Statistics and Annual Supplements, with adjustments to compare with national sources.

[1] The Monetary Survey is a consolidation of the accounts of the State Bank of Pakistan, the Scheduled banks, the Post Office Savings Bank and the Treasury currency.

[2] State Bank balance-sheet totals for Issue and Banking Departments *less* held notes.

[3] Aggregate balance-sheet of scheduled banks *less* inter-bank balances.

[4] Treasury currency (one rupee notes and coins) is treated as part of money with contra-entry in claims on Government in line 11.2.

[5] Postal deposits are treated as part of quasi-money with contra-entry in line 11.2.

[6] Treasury IMF account is included in foreign assets to the extent of net IMF position and subtracted from line 11.2.

[7] Sum of lines 1.3 + 3.3 *plus* loans and advances by scheduled banks to provincial governments.

[8] Line 3.4 plus investment in private sector securities and shares by scheduled banks.

[9] Between August and October 1958, gold holdings of State Bank were revalued. Profits amounting to Rs. 114 million were applied to reducing claims on Government.

[10] Including U.S. Disbursing Officer's A/c with State Bank from 1961 onwards.

V

COMMERCIAL BANKING

THE territories now in Pakistan were reasonably well supplied with commercial banking facilities before Independence. Of the 3,496 offices of scheduled banks in undivided India on 31 March 1947, the Pakistan areas had 631, of which 487 offices were in West Pakistan. The smaller number of offices in East Pakistan was partly because some of the areas could easily be served from Calcutta, while the region east of the Brahmaputra lacked good communications and scheduled banks did not find it profitable to establish offices there. This gave scope for expansion of small (mostly non-scheduled) banks and of the 704 offices of such banks in the Pakistan areas (out of 3,498 in the whole of India) over 500 were situated in East Pakistan. Thirteen scheduled banks out of sixty-eight and 148 non-scheduled banks out of 603 in the subcontinent had their head offices in Pakistan territories.

Between the announcement of the Partition plan in June and Independence in August 1947 many of the banks transferred their headquarters, assets, and funds to areas likely to fall in the Indian Union. A sharp curtailment of credit resulted. The Hindus who had a virtual monopoly of banking business migrated *en masse* during the Partition disturbances so that most bank offices closed down. Prior to June 1947, there was only one scheduled Muslim-managed bank functioning in the Pakistan territories. Just before Partition, another transferred its head office to Karachi. A few banking offices continued to function after Partition, mostly branches of non-Indian foreign banks known as 'Exchange' banks. In West Pakistan, the numbers of offices of scheduled banks declined from 487 to sixty-nine immediately after Partition. In East Pakistan, the shock of Partition was not quite immediate and for some time the number of bank offices remained unchanged, but actual credit activity was greatly reduced as the bulk of non-Muslim deposits had been withdrawn. Many of the non-scheduled banks remained open only for repayment of deposits and collection of old loans; some restricted their business to the transaction of agency business.

Banking facilities were curtailed even for Government business. The Imperial Bank of India which was responsible for Government treasury work as agent of the Reserve Bank of India had only nineteen outlets functioning in the Pakistan areas after Partition against twenty-eight offices and fifty-three sub-offices in pre-Partition days.

The Government immediately undertook to alleviate the situation. With a view to restoring confidence, guarantees were issued to banks that premises previously occupied by them would not be requisitioned if they proposed to re-open later. A moratorium of three months was offered to any bank facing difficulty due to panicky withdrawal of deposits. Simultaneously, steps were taken to protect the interests of Pakistani depositors who had kept accounts in Indian banks by requiring every bank to designate one of its offices in each country to which depositors could apply for transfer of their accounts or to make arrangements for the encashment of Pakistani deposits through some other bank which continued to function. Government also assumed power to realize the assets of any bank to the extent of its outstanding liabilities in Pakistan if it failed to meet the genuine claims of depositors. A procedure was laid down for tracing depositors whose accounts had been inactive for long periods after January 1948. Many of these provisions were incorporated in an Indo-Pakistani Banking Agreement signed in early 1949. An Inter-dominion Implementation Committee was set up under the Agreement. The Agreement did not work successfully and became almost inoperative after the exchange deadlock with India.

Meanwhile, national banking enterprise, powerfully encouraged by Government and the State Bank began to fill the gaps created by Partition. The country's banks were encouraged to open new branch offices. Under the Banking Companies (Restriction of Branches) Act, 1948 (as amended), the opening of a new branch office by a bank requires the sanction of the State Bank. In June 1950, the State Bank decided to reserve banking outside the large cities for Pakistan banks. Foreign banks were restricted to the port towns or the large cities from which substantial trade was carried on with other countries. The resultant increase in the number of Pakistani bank offices more than offset the withdrawal of numerous Indian banks. Between 1 July 1948 and 30 June 1954, 129 offices, all belonging to Indian banks, had Pakistani banks. In the last few years, the growth of banking services has been spectacular.

TABLE 16

DISTRIBUTION OF BANKING OFFICES

Banks	As on 1 July 1948				As on 30 June 1964			
	No. of Scheduled Banks	No. of Bank Offices			No. of Scheduled Banks	No. of Bank Offices		
		West Pak.	East Pak.	Total		West Pak.	East Pak.	Total
Pakistani[1]	2	23	2	25	13	744	362	1,106
Indian	29	45	106	151	10	10	24	34
Exchange	7	16	3	19	11	27	11	38
Total	38	84	111	195	34	781	397	1,178

[1] Excluding Agricultural and Industrial Development Banks which are not commercial banks.

The Pakistani banks have an additional 12 offices abroad reflecting their success in the foreign exchange business which was a preserve of the oversea banks in the past.[1]

There has been a marked rise in their deposits and in credit extended by them. From 29 per cent. of total deposits at the end of 1948 their share rose to 75 per cent. at the end of June 1963, with the share in current deposits being three percentage points higher. There has been a pronounced fall in the share of the Indian banks from over 40 to under 7 per cent. The Exchange banks held their own until the middle of 1959, maintaining their share of deposits at 31 per cent. Thereafter, the share declined to under one-quarter of total deposits, even as the absolute level more than doubled over 1948. There is a similar pattern on the side of bank assets, although in the earliest years, the share of Pakistani banks in bank credit lagged behind deposits. At the end of 1949, it was only 19 per cent. and, in fact, until almost the end of 1952 the Pakistani banks appeared to be more successful at attracting deposits than at lending money and a substantial proportion of their funds were locked up in investments in Government securities. This was largely the outcome of their initial

[1] United States aid regulations appointing 'designated' banks for handling documents on commodity aid may have helped the foreign business of some of the Pakistani banks.

unfamiliarity with business conditions in the new state, the inexperience of management and staff and the ability of the foreign banks to retain old clients, whether refugee or settled businessmen with whom their connexions went back many years. The banking crisis precipitated by India's decision not to recognize the Pakistan exchange rate provided the first real opening for the country's banks. With large-scale central bank finance, the Pakistani banks, especially the newly formed National Bank, were able to double their share of bank credit by 1951. By the middle of 1953, the share in bank credit was almost equal to that of deposits and in subsequent years tended to exceed it, mainly because the National Bank continued to obtain 'counter-finance' facilities from the State Bank.[2]

Among the foreign banks, it is the Indian banks which have lost business most heavily. They were specialists in financing the subcontinent's internal trade, and particularly the land-borne trade of the eastern region. Their importance diminished as the volume of Indo-Pakistan trade declined. The Foreign Exchange banks, with headquarters outside the subcontinent, have provided more competition. They built up a profitable business during the long period when they had no serious competition in their primary field of activity, viz., the financing of foreign trade. Although now virtually confined to the port towns, they have become more diversified in their clientele and are particularly active in financing many types of foreign managed enterprises like the tea estates, the petroleum companies and oversea trading firms.

They have been criticized on the grounds that their operations tend to retard the development of local banks, which may have done well in an absolute sense but not so well as national banking in neighbouring India. Their highly selective business clientele also helps to aggravate the concentration of bank credit, e.g., the average size of loan made by foreign banks was Rs. 71,305 at the end of June 1964 as compared with Rs. 21,909 for local commercial banks (i.e., excluding ADB and IDB). In their favour it can be said that they provide valuable traditions, facilitate inter-connexions with metropolitan money-markets and have

---

[2] Counter-finance designates the arrangement under which Pakistani banks are able to draw from the State Bank amounts equivalent to loans granted to central and provincial governments for food and jute purchases.

helped in the country's search for foreign capital by contributing —through their head offices—to the share-capital of PICIC and by purchasing earlier maturities of IBRD loans to Pakistan. However, the recent diversion by the U.S. Treasury of substantial amounts of U.S.-owned counterpart funds (Rs. 277 million by June 1964) to American banks has generated criticism of 'unfair' discrimination. On their part, foreign banks have reacted sharply to provisions of the Banking Companies Ordinance of 1962 which requires all banks to maintain a reserve fund in Pakistan to the extent of 5 per cent. of their deposits and to constitute it forthwith by transfer of moneys from their head offices.

Among Pakistani banks, two need special mention: the National Bank of Pakistan and the Habib Bank. The former was established in 1949 by special legislation. Government contributed 25 per cent. of its share-capital and has the right to appoint its chief executive. This official interest derives from the bank's function as the agent of the State Bank for handling Treasury business and providing remittance facilities[3] at places where the State Bank did not have offices of its own. The Bank was launched to meet the emergency caused by the trade deadlock with India and initially, its operations were confined to the financing of the trade in jute, cotton and other agricultural commodities. It was permitted in March 1950 to undertake normal commercial banking functions. In 1952, the National Bank took over the State Bank's agency work from the Imperial Bank of India. The Bank's aggressive loan policies have made a powerful contribution to the growth of credit facilities in the country, especially for the marketing of jute and cotton. It has undertaken special financing connected with Government price-support schemes for the two commodities and also the food procurement and stock-piling programmes of the provinces. On December 31, 1964, the bank had a network of 443 offices in the country and seven abroad. Its deposits stood at Rs. 1,996·8 million, or approximately 30 per cent. of total deposits. Its share in bank credit was slightly higher and it was giving special attention to the

[3] 'In principle, the advisability of handing over Treasury business to a private institution in the management of which the Government did not have a reasonable share was open to question.' Cf., Moin Baqai, *The National Bank of Pakistan*, Selected Papers on Pakistan Economy, Vol. 2 (State Bank of Pakistan, 1955), p. 87.

financing of small business. The Bank had a paid-up capital of Rs. 30 million and reserve funds of Rs. 37 million in 1964.

The Habib Bank Ltd. is the only scheduled bank in the sub-continent which transferred its head office to Pakistan territory. It was established in 1941 and at the time of Partition, the bank had a paid-up capital of Rs. 5 million and reserve funds of Rs. 2·5 million; at the end of 1964 the figures had risen to Rs. 35 million and Rs. 28 million respectively. Starting with two offices in the Pakistan areas, the bank now has 325 offices throughout the country and two abroad. It has undertaken a programme of expanding overseas through an allied concern which had six offices at the end of 1964. The deposits of the Bank at that date were Rs. 1,624 million or a little under one-quarter of total deposits. The Habib Bank has made a substantial contribution to the supply of trained banking personnel. The National Bank and the Habib Bank together conduct more than half the country's inland banking business and are responsible for about one-half of all bank offices. Since 1962 there has been remarkable growth in banking. Conditions have become highly competitive with the establishment of three new banks, viz. United Bank Ltd., Standard Bank Ltd. and Commerce Bank Ltd. At the end of 1964 these banks had 214, 40 and 32 offices respectively.

The following discussion of commercial bank deposits is in over-all terms, although Table 17 shows the distribution of deposits by (i) nationality of bank, (ii) ownership of depositor, (iii) interest paid, (iv) size of account and (v) turnover. An analysis of this classification is not attempted because the data is available in this detailed form for a few years only. The earliest over-all data is for 22 August 1947 when total deposit liabilities were Rs. 1,040 million, of which Rs. 650 million were demand and Rs. 390 million were time liabilities.[4] Within less than a year (2 July 1948) total deposits had fallen to Rs. 881 million, wholly caused by a reduction of Rs. 256 million in time deposits. The decline reflected the large-scale transfer of funds to India by the departing minority population while incoming refugees preferred to hold surplus funds in demand deposits. As bank-ing services were restored, deposits began to rise and the trend was accelerated by the boom in export incomes launched

[4] Figures for 1947 include inter-bank borrowings while later figures exclude them. The discrepancy is not significant and the data are roughly comparable.

by the Korean War. Deposits reached a peak of Rs. 1,527 million in November 1951. By the middle of 1952, there was a sharp decline to Rs. 1,288 million as commodity markets weakened and a heavy import surplus on private account drained away liquidity from the banks. The emergence of cash deficits on Government account helped to restore bank reserves and to rebuild bank deposits after 1953. Demand deposits rose continuously until 1959–60 to reach about two billion rupees. There was a decline in 1960–61 but it was slight and the rising trend was resumed as they rose to Rs. 3·3 billion in mid-1964. The rise in demand deposits has been much faster than that of currency so that the deposit-component in the money supply has risen significantly. This indicates spectacular success on the part of the banking system in securing a larger portion of the liquidity that has been generated during the last decade. It also suggests the possibility of some contraction of the non-cash sector of the economy.

Time-deposits have risen much faster than demand deposits in the last few years. The average rate of increase has been roughly 35 per cent. in each of the three years ending 1962–3. In the same period, their ratio to total deposits has risen from 32·2 per cent. to 41·0 per cent. The shift in favour of time-deposits reflects several factors, including the conversion of hoarded money into interest-bearing deposits announced by a new government in 1958, the improvement subsequently in the political climate and economic prospects,[5] the opening of bank offices in small urban areas where bank accounts are used for the custody of savings while current transactions are conducted mostly for cash and a temporary diversion to time-deposits of funds appropriated for public agencies (like WAPDA) or newly subscribed capital of companies pending completion of their spending plans. A substantial part of the counterpart funds transferred from the State Bank to foreign commercial banks are also held as time-deposits (roughly Rs. 203 million in June 1964).

The main earning assets are call money, loans and advances, bills purchased or discounted, and investments. The non-earning

[5] 'From a time when money balances were mistrusted and even eschewed, there was undoubtedly a long period of rising desires for real balances. . . . This period has now ended and it is very possible that a shift away from money balances has begun—a shift not to the near-moneys of flight—gold and jewelry—but to the near-moneys of safety, time-deposits, co-operative shares, savings certificates, etc.' Cf. Porter, op. cit.

TABLE 17

CLASSIFICATION OF DEPOSITS (30 JUNE)

(Percentage of Total Deposits in categories ii, iii, iv)

Description of Deposits	1962			1964		
	Total	Current Deposits	Savings and Fixed Deposits	Total	Current Deposits	Savings and Fixed Deposits
Total accounts (nos.)	822,837	323,145	465,917	1,632,960	522,779	1,046,084
Total amount (in 000 Rs.)	3,679,036	1,643,334	1,518,035	5,760,814	2,279,058	2,432,346
Average size (in Rs.)	4,471	5,086	3,258	3,528	4,360	2,325
(i) By nationality of reporting bank						
Pakistani:						
Accounts (nos.)	636,935	256,917	353,010	1,425,610	462,899	907,964
Amounts (in 000 Rs.)	2,523,769	1,183,199	929,856	4,528,522	1,794,794	1,781,460
Average size (in Rs.)	3,962	4,605	1,635	3,177	3,877	1,962
Foreign:						
Accounts (nos.)	207,350	59,880	138,116	185,902	256,917	353,010
Amounts (in million Rs.)	1,232,292	484,264	651,586	1,155,268	1,183,199	929,856
Average size (in Rs.)	5,943	3,930	4,718	6,214	4,605	1,635
(ii) By ownership						
Official foreign	8·26	4·65	14·98	5·90	4·92	9·35
Other foreign	4·85	6·53	3·23	3·24	4·53	2·23
Central Government and agencies	6·67	7·78	—	4·47	3·74	2·76
Provincial government and agencies	5·69	5·32	4·60	11·02	10·78	6·64
Local bodies	4·08	3·44	3·68	6·29	2·54	7·58

Manufacturing, mining and quarrying	8·02	10·19	5·23	6·28	8·81	5·95
Construction and utilities	2·16	2·72	1·93	2·41	2·76	1·06
Commerce	7·93	13·33	2·58	7·33	13·96	2·40
Transport	1·45	1·20	0·96	1·39	1·46	0·68
Agriculture, forestry, fishing, etc.	1·43	1·48	1·74	1·79	1·83	2·35
Other business	10·38	12·99	2·99	10·27	14·25	30·2
Trust funds, non-profit organizations	6·70	5·71	8·70	4·93	4·69	4·89
Personal	32·28	24·66	48·74	34·69	22·72	51·56

(iii) By rates of interest

0·00 %	50·6	99·3	29·5	48·6	96·3	30·5
0·25%–1·25%	0·9	—	1·0	0·8	2·0	1·0
Over 1·25%–2%	8·1	0·1	1·1	10·2	0·2	1·5
Over 2%–2·50%	22·8	0·2	58·4	23·8	—	58·4
Over 2·50%–3%	13·0	—	5·0	12·9	—	4·0
Over 3%–4%	3·8	0·2¹	5·0	5·8	0·2	6·0
Over 4%	0·4	0·2	—	0·5	1·3	—

(iv) By size

Less than Rs. 5,000	30·7	—	—	31·98	—	—
Rs. 5,000–10,000	8·3	—	—	5·98	—	—
Rs. 10,000–20,000	8·0	—	—	7·04	—	—
Rs. 20,000–50,000	6·8	—	—	7·70	—	—
Rs. 50,000–100,000	5·9	—	—	5·86	—	—
Rs. 100,000–500,000	15·6	—	—	13·13	—	—
Rs. 500,000–1,000,000	5·0	—	—	5·89	—	—
Rs. 1,000,000–4,000,000	10·2	—	—	8·77	—	—
Rs. 4,000,000 and above	9·3	—	—	10·14	—	—

Source: State Bank of Pakistan

assets include cash in vaults, balances with the State Bank of Pakistan and balances with other banks. Separate data on all items are available from 1953 although series on reserves, advances and bills reach back to 1948. As against the statutory minimum of 5 per cent. of demand and 2 per cent. of time-deposits, the banks maintained substantial excess reserves during the earlier years. In 1948, balances with the State Bank were 29·3 per cent. of deposits, indicating extreme caution induced by the prevailing economic dislocation. This persisted through 1949 after which excess reserves declined and by the middle of 1950 the deposits/cash ratio was down to 14·7 per cent. It fell sharply in 1952 as deposits were drained away by the import surplus while earning assets could not be reduced as quickly. After 1953 the banks began to rebuild excess reserves and this trend persisted until 1956. The next two years witnessed a sharp rise in bank credit and excess reserves were correspondingly reduced. Excess liquidity reappeared in the latter part of 1959 as the increase in deposit reserves was unaccompanied by a corresponding rise in bank credit. The situation changed after 1960 and by 1962 excess reserves were reduced and later eliminated.

The second assets item which comes closest to being a liquid asset is 'call money', which consists almost entirely of inter-bank loans. However, advances to banks appear to be larger than call money, the difference representing advances for longer periods.

The proportion of assets constituted by call money, or even the larger category of inter-bank advances, was not sizeable until quite recently because the money-market was not fully developed. Transactions are even now confined almost exclusively to Karachi where something approaching continuous activity exists. The Karachi market itself is largely, if not wholly, an 'inter-bank affair' in which certain banks, inclined to follow more conservative lending policies than their deposit resources permit, act as lenders while the more active banks are borrowers. Activity is at its height during certain months of the year and the volume of outstanding inter-bank credit at such times may be quite high. Beyond a point, however, the absorption of funds leaves little or no surplus funds with any individual bank and then the interest rate quotation (which reached as high as 5½ per cent. in 1961) becomes quite nominal as the banks turn to the State Bank for finance at fixed rates. On the other hand, at the bottom of the slack season, funds might go begging at as low as ¼ per cent. per annum. This picture has changed significantly with the transfer to American banks of counterpart funds in amounts large enough to establish them as alternative lenders of last resort. In 1960–61 inter-bank borrowing reached a peak of Rs. 301·4 million (as compared to Rs. 73·4 million in 1958–9). In 1961–2, the peak level was slightly over Rs. 284 million. In June 1963, advances to banks were Rs. 286·1 million and constituted 3·1 per cent. of the total assets of the scheduled banks.

A large portfolio of advances and bills discounted in pre-Partition years was reflected in a credit/deposits ratio of 45 per cent. In July 1948, the ratio was down to 22 per cent. After a rise in 1951 and a decline in 1952 the ratio rose continuously until 1957 as in addition to larger credit extended to the private sector, the provincial governments borrowed heavily in connexion with food procurement and other state trading programmes. The rise in the rupee value of trade following devaluation in July 1955 was responsible for further expansion. A series of selective credit restrictions were imposed by the State Bank in June 1957 and this seemed to slow down the rate of growth of credit and in 1958 credit to the private sector actually declined. In June 1959, the ratio was 49·6 per cent. In each succeeding year the ratio has risen—to 55 per cent. in 1960, 68·4 per cent. in 1961 and 78·1 per cent. in mid-1963. For individual banks, the ratio may have even exceeded one hundred per cent. during the busy season. The reasons for this credit expansion and its bearing on monetary policy have been discussed in the preceding chapter. Here some of the implications of the massive credit expansion for the commercial banks are considered.

The rise in credit/deposit ratios has meant considerable strain on the liquidity position of the banks. There has been massive and continuous resort to State Bank credit for the financing of normal operations. Excess reserves have been almost eliminated and free reserves (required reserves less borrowing from the State Bank) have become wholly negative. The ratio of capital and reserves to deposits has weakened significantly. These developments are hardly conducive to the long-range growth of the banking system despite the fact that the working results of individual banks show great improvement in the short run. With deposit rates averaging slightly above 1 per cent. and advance rates averaging well above 5 per cent. and with residual funds hitherto available from the State Bank at 4 per cent., the expansion in credit has brought large profits to the banking industry. A portion of these profits have been appropriated to reserves under the Banking Companies Ordinance of 1962 which requires transfer of 20 per cent. of profits (before tax) to a reserve fund until the amount of the fund equals the paid-up capital. The fixation of a minimum percentage of paid-up capital and reserves to total deposits has been suggested as a means of more adequately protecting the interests of the depositors.

If the banks are to finance the growing credit needs of the economy without impairing further their liquidity, greater efforts are needed for mobilizing deposits. In past years, the banks were largely the beneficiaries of the expansionary process induced by deficit-financing operations, whether in the public or the private sectors. They have not considered it necessary to offer attractive deposit rates as an instrument for mobilizing deposits. This attitude may need revision, especially on a selective basis for new and small depositors. Greater convenience in bank procedures and improvements in the range of services offered may help enlarge clientele. The safety factor may be enhanced by the introduction of a Deposit Insurance Scheme with the cost absorbed by the banking industry. Fiscal incentives and greater secrecy of bank accounts by exempting banks from reporting information to income-tax or police authorities also need attention.

The major residual category of bank assets is 'Investments'. Data on the types and maturity distribution of bank investments are available from March 1953 when the banks held Rs. 486 million.[6] There was a continuous rise in investments, in line with deposits up to 1960–61. In 1961–2, there was hardly any change in the total figure which concealed, in fact, a net decline in investments in Government securities. The rapidly growing credit demands of the private sector made the banks reluctant to invest in low interest bearing Government paper. From 44·9 per cent. in 1958–9, the share of investments in total earning assets declined to 24·2 per cent. in mid-64. This was achieved by investing at a diminishing rate in Government securities as deficit-

---

[6] Figures for earlier years can be inferred from commercial bank holdings of Central Government bonds which were Rs. 408 million in March 1950. These investments have held consistently about 80 per cent. of the total.

financing operations were curtailed. In 1961–2, there was a net retirement of Government credit as shown in the following table, only to be followed by renewed lending:

TABLE 18

CHANGES IN BANK CREDIT AND INVESTMENTS IN GOVERNMENT BONDS
(In millions of rupees)

Year	Change over preceding year in		
	Total Bank Credit	Credit to Government	Investment in Government bonds
1957–58	+ 92·8	+ 63·8	+170·7
1958–59	+ 76·5	+ 82·8	+112·7
1959–60	+315·4	− 41·9	+106·1
1960–61	+585·4	+171·5	+ 78·3
1961–62	+658·7	− 4·0	− 19·7
1962–63	+808·5	+ 51·5	+ 39·9
1963–64	+1,121·3	+227·2	+112·9

Source: State Bank of Pakistan.

There is apparent an inverse relationship between investments in Government paper and credit to the private sector. Central Government treasury bills and securities constituted 76·3 per cent. of total bank investments in the middle of 1963, with provincial bonds accounting for another 16·7 per cent.

The maturity distribution of bank investments is shown below, as percentages of the total:

TABLE 19

MATURITY DISTRIBUTION OF BANK INVESTMENTS

Year (end June)	Total (In millions of rupees)	Treasury Bills	Securities Maturing In			
			Under 5 years	5 to 10 years	10 to 15 years	Over 15 years
1954	651	8·5	63·8	24·6	2·0	1·1
1955	703	6·1	72·5	16·9	1·6	1·0
1956	781	8·0	77·8	11·7	2·5	—
1957	813	6·4	81·2	8·7	3·7	—
1958	949	6·8	86·8	4·3	2·2	—
1959	1,104	4·0	74·7	7·3	14·0	—
1960	1,198	—	74·8	7·1	18·1	—
1961	1,278	—	66·0	14·9	19·1	—
1962	1,258	—	75·2	18·0	6·8	—
1963	1,298	—	76·9	17·8	5·1	0·3
1964	1,438	—	72·5	25·9	0·1	1·5

Source: State Bank of Pakistan.

There is a clear tendency for a lengthening out of the debt, especially after 1957. Treasury bills (90 days) constituted as much as 8·5 per cent. of the total in 1954 but have gradually declined and disappeared altogether from bank portfolios in 1960

9

TABLE 20

CLASSIFICATION OF BANK CREDIT[1] (1955–64)

(As percentage of total)
(30 June year)

(i) By major economic groups

Classification	1955	1956	1957	1958	1959	1960	1961	1962	1963	1964
Agriculture, forestry and fishing	1·4	1·4	1·0	2·8	3·7	2·0	2·2	3·4	2·0	2·7
Mining and quarrying	0·3	1·4	0·5	0·1	0·6	1·0	0·7	0·4	0·3	0·5
Manufacturing	20·5	29·7	28·6	34·3	31·0	35·5	31·7	31·7	34·5	33·0
Construction	3·1	1·9	0·8	1·6	1·6	1·0	0·6	2·9	2·7	2·0
Electricity, gas and water services	1·8	0·5	0·4	0·9	0·5	0·4	2·3	0·8	0·2	0·3
Commerce	59·5	59·9	62·0	47·9	43·3	48·0	45·3	39·3	47·5	45·6
Transport and storage	1·9	0·9	0·8	1·5	1·1	1·0	1·4	1·7	2·0	2·4
Services	8·7	1·7	2·7	2·0	12·0	4·9	7·7	10·5	7·9	7·9
Others	2·8	2·6	3·3	9·0	8·2	6·5	7·9	9·3	2·7	5·6
All economic groups (in millions of rupees)	866	914	1,098	1,176	1,265	1,578	2,019	2,589	3,275	4,302

(ii) By securities pledged[2]

Classification	1955	1956	1957	1958	1959	1960	1961	1962	1963	1964
Precious metals	1·7	1·5	1·3	1·5	1·7	1·6	2·1	2·1	2·1	1·7
Stock exchange securities	5·6	6·3	5·4	10·7	6·5	9·6	6·2	8·3	9·1	8·8

	30.6.58	31.12.58	30.6.59	31.12.59	30.6.60	31.12.60	30.6.61	30.6.62	30.6.63	30.6.64
Merchandise	50·8	63·0	65·2	68·4	62·3	65·8	67·3	66·6	64·0	61·8
Machinery and fixed assets	9·8	8·7	7·0	4·7	3·5	2·4	1·9	2·9	3·1	3·1
Real estate	2·6	1·4	2·0	1·4	1·7	2·6	4·8	1·3	1·8	2·4
Financial obligations	3·4	3·7	4·6	2·8	2·1	3·8	5·0	3·9	4·4	4·4
Others	26·2	15·3	14·5	10·5	22·2	14·2	12·7	14·9	15·4	17·8
All securities in millions of rupees)	723	781	975	1,059	1,097	1,427	1,831	2,351	2,980	3,924

(iii) By interest rates[3]

	30.6.58	31.12.58	30.6.59	31.12.59	30.6.60	31.12.60	30.6.61	30.6.62	30.6.63	30.6.64
Up to 2%	5·1	2·5	2·6	2·5	2·7	2·2	2·2	2·2	1·6	2·1
Over 2%–3%	13·0	14·6	0·5	0·5	0·7	1·0	2·4	0·2	0·3	0·2
Over 3%–3½%	10·8	11·5	18·7	10·7	13·0	9·2	17·9	14·4	13·9	15·6
Over 3½%–4%	19·2	20·3	1·6	2·1	1·9	1·7	1·7	1·7	2·3	2·9
Over 4%–4½%	17·3	19·0	10·0	11·9	10·7	9·9	5·5	8·3	6·6	6·4
Over 4½%–5%	20·5	17·7	21·1	21·0	15·9	16·9	17·0	21·5	21·2	17·3
Over 5%–5½%	2·1	2·1	16·5	17·6	19·5	18·0	13·3	11·8	9·4	7·8
Over 5½%–6%	8·1	9·2	20·6	25·3	26·0	31·1	25·7	23·8	23·3	22·8
Over 6%–7%	2·1	2·2	6·8	6·4	6·8	7·4	11·7	13·2	16·9	21·7
Over 7%	1·8	0·9	1·6	2·1	2·7	2·6	2·7	2·9	4·4	3·2
Total (in millions of rupees)	1,059	1,224	1,097	1,403	1,427	1,797	1,831	2,351	2,980	3,924

Source: Banking Statistics of Pakistan (State Bank of Pakistan), Vols. 1–5.

[1] Bank credit is defined in State Bank statistics as 'Advances' plus 'Bills Purchased and Discounted'. Advances made by the Agricultural Bank of Pakistan and the Industrial Development Bank are excluded from this table.

[2] Classification by securities pledged and by interest rates covers 'Advances' only.

[3] Exclusion of Agricultural and Industrial Developments Banks by estimate only.

as the Government dispensed with borrowing short term from the banks. In mid-1957, Treasury bills and securities maturing in less than five years constituted as much as 92·5 per cent. of total investments. By 1960, only three-quarters of investments were in this category. Maturities between ten and fifteen years have risen in the same period from 3·7 to 18·1 per cent. Similarly, the category of 5–10 year bonds declined continuously from 54·8 per cent. in 1953 to 4·3 per cent. in 1958 but has since risen somewhat thereafter.

Having reviewed the main constituents of commercial bank liabilities and assets, we turn to an analysis of (i) the purposes for which bank credit is extended[7], (ii) the security or collateral for advances, and (iii) the rates of interest charged on advances.

(i) The earliest classification of bank advances dates from 31 March 1953 and shows that 54·2 per cent. were committed for 'commerce' and another 16 per cent. for 'manufacturing'. A sector-wise analysis of 'bills purchased and discounted' is available from the middle of 1954 and raises the share of 'commerce' in total bank credit (i.e. advances and bills taken together). With the rapid growth of large-scale industry, the banks have directed increasing amounts for meeting working capital needs[8] and the 'manufacturing' sector now accounts for one-third of the total. The share of commerce has correspondingly declined to 45·6 per cent. in the middle of 1964.

After these two sectors, 'services' come next, covering community, recreation and other personal service enterprises. Their share has fluctuated widely. After reaching 8·7 per cent. in 1955, this sector declined in importance during the next three years and then rose sharply to 12 per cent. in 1959. A substantial portion is extended to the hotel industry which has been greatly stimulated by Government efforts in recent years, especially its inclusion in the Export Bonus Scheme. Entitlements against

---

[7] The statistics can indicate only the proximate purpose; credit obtained for a stated purpose may be diverted to other uses and the end-use may be indeterminate because it is the other expenditures which would have been curtailed if bank credit had not been forthcoming which are logically financed by it.

[8] Total working capital invested in registered factories was Rs. 1,227 million in 1959–60, according to the *Census of Manufacturing*. Bank credit to industry at the end of June 1960 was Rs. 566 million so that a little under half of working capital requirements appear to have been financed by the banks. According to the First Plan document, the corresponding share in 1954–5 was 10 per cent. only.

foreign exchange earned by the hotels are available for importing hotel needs. Advances are usually made against the mortgage of immovable property and third-party guarantees. Other types of businesses included in this category are cinemas, film studios, restaurants, dry-cleaners, etc.

The remaining sectors are only marginal. The banks have not lent to the agricultural sector to any significant extent, the amounts ranging between Rs. 35–50 million in recent years. Almost two-thirds of loans for 'agriculture, forestry and fishing' are made by the banks to the European tea-estates and a few to foreign-owned orchards and other agricultural estates in West Pakistan. As noted in Chapter VI, various legal and administrative complications involved in mortgaging agricultural land or hypothecating standing crops as security, together with the absence of licensed warehouse receipts or other acceptable collateral, have prevented the commercial banks from operating more actively in agricultural finance. The banks normally enter the picture when agricultural produce reaches marketing agencies for processing and transporting to consuming centres and perhaps more than one-half of all credit to 'commerce' may be for the marketing of agricultural products.

Construction advances amounting to Rs. 15–25 million are made primarily to building contractors with little or no funds extended for residential housing. The amounts are minute in relation to the massive construction programmes under way in the country. Delays in receiving payment of bills, especially from the Government departments, create a difficult credit problem as funds must be laid down in advance for purchases of materials, payment of wages, etc. In pre-Independence days, the commercial banks were prepared to discount 'on-account' Government bills but the facility has been greatly restricted in Pakistan and is available only to very large firms, especially those with foreign connexions, leading to allegations that insufficiency of credit was impeding local enterprise in this sector.

Loans to public utility undertakings (electric, gas and water services) have ranged between Rs. 5–15 million and rose sharply in 1961 to Rs. 23·5 million. Some of the power-stations in East Pakistan used to be privately owned in the past and were financed by the foreign banks. The recent increase may be due to financing of P.I.D.C. electricity undertakings.

The mining and quarrying sector accounts for another Rs. 10–15 million, although until recently almost the whole of this was advanced to foreign petroleum companies for the extraction of natural gas. The transportation sector also receives about Rs. 10–15 million. While established road and inland transport operators have no particular working capital needs because of the short time lag between the carriage of goods and the receipt of freight, there has been a scarcity of slightly longer-term credit for purchases of cars, trucks, motor boats and other vehicles. Before Independence, it was possible to finance such purchases by executing *hundis* in favour of the car-dealer who in turn was able to get them discounted with commercial banks. Some of the indigenous bankers also undertook the discounting of hire-purchase bills.[9]

Finally, there is a miscellaneous category of advances which fluctuated within a range of 2·5 to 3·5 per cent. of total advances until 1957 and thereafter have risen to 8–9 per cent. in the middle of 1958. It is perhaps not without significance that this trend should emerge after extensive selective credit restrictions were applied by the State Bank. However, this category includes activities not adequately described by banks in submitting their returns and it may not be safe to read too much into the statistics. It is known that the category includes market loans to share-brokers, personal loans to bank employees, Government servants and other stable income groups. Some light on the subject may be shed by advances classified according to securities pledged.

(ii) This classification (part (ii) of Table 20) shows that advances[10] against stock-exchange securities have ranged between 5–10 per cent. of the total, being as high as 9·6 per cent. in 1960. While the character of the security is not an infallible guide to the purpose, it does suggest that a substantial part of the miscellaneous purpose advances may have been made for the purchase of shares by individuals or for holding inventories by professionals. Loans against precious metals and financial obligations (e.g., life insurance policies, savings-bonds, time-deposits) ac-

[9] There has been a certain amount of financing for such purposes by the co-operative banks and this is evidenced by the large number of transport co-operatives formed in the country which tend to be co-operative in name only, being organized for the sole purpose of obtaining access to co-operative banking funds.

[10] For obvious reasons, this classification can only cover advances as credit in the form of 'bills discounted and purchased' would have as security the instrument of the bill itself.

count for another 1·5–2 per cent. and 2–5 per cent. of advances respectively and would certainly include many personal loans.

The largest proportion of advances, about two-thirds, are made against the security of merchandise and this is in line with the predominant share of 'commerce' in bank credit. The greater part of advances to 'manufacturing' would also be made against stocks of goods-in-process or unsold finished products, which would come under 'merchandise'. Some industrial loans would probably be made against the security of machinery. Most agricultural loans would be expected to be made against the security of real estate (i.e. title-deeds of immoveable property) although the recent rise may be related to increased loans to the hotel industry. For the rest, it is not possible to relate security to purpose of credit, especially in view of the substantial residual category which accounts for anywhere between 10–26 per cent. of total advances by security pledged.

(iii) The third classification, restricted as in the case of securities to advances, is by interest rates.[11] It is available on a semi-annual basis from the middle of 1958. The breakdown by selected ranges rates is shown in part (iii) of Table 20. It clearly records an upward leverage executed on the entire interest rate structure by the raising of the bank-rate in January 1959. Prior to that, advances up to 3 per cent. constituted 17 to 18 per cent. of the total; in the middle of 1959, this category declined to 3·1 per cent. and did not move far from this level until after the end of 1960. However, the substantial increase in the 2–3 per cent. range in the middle of 1961 apparently reflects the much higher level of advances made to provincial governments in 1960–61 which are made on the best possible terms, and even below the bank-rate. For advances to the private sector, interest rates are in most cases quoted in terms of percentage points over bank-rate and this is evidenced by the movements after the bank-rate increase. The class interval of 3½ to 4 per cent. accounted for one-fifth of all loans up to the end of 1958, suggesting that the best business firms were accommodated at ½ to 1 per cent. above the bank-rate. Starting from 1959 there is a sharp reduction, so that less than 2 per cent. of all advances now appear below the bank-rate. About one-fifth of all advances were made

[11] It is interesting to note that advances ranging between Rs. 25–35 million have been made at zero rate of interest.

at 1 per cent. above the new bank-rate after 1958. There is a tendency however, for the proportions to change. The same applies to the next two steps, with a distinct tendency after 1959 for advances in the 5½ to 6 per cent. class to gain at the expense of the preceding two class intervals. The highest rates, over 6 per cent., have applied after the end of 1960 to almost 15 per cent. of the total advances, as against 8–9 per cent. earlier, reflecting the pressure for funds induced by the spectacular rise in bank credit in this period. Even so, the rate-structure appears to be almost too low when viewed in the perspective of the great capital scarcity that prevails in a poor country like Pakistan. It is evidence of the hiatus that separates the 'organized' sections of the money and financial markets and the vast unorganized hinterland of the economy, with its millions of small farmers, artisans and traders who either lack for credit or secure it on terms that bear no relationship to the rates at which the commercial banks lend to the minority that is privileged to have access to them.

Even within the privileged group credit has gravitated to the more substantial elements of the community. This tendency was recognized as one of the three outstanding problems in the banking field, the other two being the insufficiency of credit for sectors other than commerce and large-scale industry and the uneven spread of banking facilities.[12] Statistics prepared by the State Bank indicate a striking concentration of bank advances:

TABLE 21

DISTRIBUTION OF COMMERCIAL BANK ADVANCES BY SIZE
(In thousands of rupees)

Size of Advances*	31. 12. 1957		31. 3. 1962		30. 6. 1964	
	Accounts (No.)	Amount	Accounts (No.)	Amount	Accounts (No.)	Amount
Less than Rs. 25,000	26,104	57,166	71,802	204,104	141,837	455,798
Rs. 25,000–100,000	1,803	89,557	5,174	243,416	10,097	477,596
Rs. 100,000–500,000	903	203,892	2,017	409,468	2,743	575,464
Rs. 500,000–1 million	179	127,961	289	203,092	487	331,131
Rs. 1 million–5 million	184	385,886	291	589,409	398	806,540
Rs. 5 million and above	33	338,301	42	795,369	87	1,277,053
	29,206	1,202,763	79,615	2,444,858	155,649	3,923,582

* The upper limit of the range is exclusive of the limit amount.
Source: Reports, Credit Enquiry Commission (1959), Credit Committee (1962) and State Bank of Pakistan.

[12] The discussion of these problems follows closely chapters 11 and 12 of the *Report*, Credit Enquiry Commission, op. cit.

At the end of 1957, over 70 per cent. of bank credit was employed in advances above half a million rupees and about 60 per cent. was locked up in 22 accounts above one million rupees. If, as is likely, a number of loan accounts may have been controlled by the same family group, the actual concentration would be greater. At the other end of the scale, small advances under Rs. 25,000 did not exceed 5 per cent. of total credit and the amount was spread over 26,104 accounts. Some of the largest advances, however, were extended to provincial governments. Some decline in concentration has taken place after 1959. At the end of June 1964, the share of advances above half a million rupees declined to under 61·5 per cent., although this was out of a larger total value of advances. On the other hand, small advances (i.e., less than Rs. 25,000) had risen to 11·6 per cent. of total advances and the number of accounts to 141,837.[13]

It has been contended that apart from the provincial governments, some of the largest loans were made to enterprises managed by the P.I.D.C., a semi-government agency. As for the big private borrowers, bank credit was presumed to adjust passively to the consequences of a public policy which permitted the establishment of large private undertakings in the first place. Moreover, large loans were naturally more attractive to banks because of their lesser risk, the sound collateral which big businesses could offer as security and the expectation of additional bank earnings from handling the foreign exchange and other ancillary business emanating from them.

On the other hand, small loans are less profitable and the risks of lending far greater. Many small borrowers are not well educated, lack in managerial ability, and are sometimes unable even to prepare and maintain proper accounts. There is a general tendency to operate on a very minor equity and a reluctance to disclose the true financial picture to a banker, partly for fear of acknowledging the over-trading implicit in a high debt/equity ratio. Again, most small businessmen are organized as proprietary concerns, often over-dependent on the talents of a single individual and affording the bank no guarantee of continuity or fair dealing. In the event of default, the banks have a legal

[13] By way of contrast, although not strictly relevant to the issue, the distribution of deposits indicates that 58 per cent. of deposits were in accounts having less than Rs. 25,000.

recourse but the proceedings may be time-consuming and involve the banks in expenditures quite out of proportion to the income expected from small loans or the amounts involved in default. Indeed the much higher cost of investigating, supervising and accounting for small loans made them unprofitable quite apart from the greater risks involved.[14]

Implicit in the above analysis is an assumption that rates of interest charged cannot be raised to compensate the banks for the higher costs per rupee lent and to cover the risk-premium. While there is no question but that these rates would be higher than the conventional pattern presently established, there is no reason to believe that the rates would necessarily be prohibitive. This is indicated by the terms on which credit was provided by the indigenous bankers, like the *Multani shrolfs*, to small businessmen in pre-Independence days. It is possible that with higher interest rates and given certain urgent legal reforms relating to the recovery of bank dues, it may be possible for the commercial banks to expand their direct lending commitments to small borrowers. Through the establishment of some credit intermediaries like 'guarantee brokers' or discount houses specializing in investigating, accepting and discounting *hundis* emanating from small borrowers or through the agency of a public institution which would 'guarantee' small loans on certain conditions, the banks could also enlarge their indirect contribution to this sector.[15]

The second problem in the banking field is sectoral concentration of credit. As noted earlier, banks have tended to confine their operations to two major sectors and to prefer the security of 'merchandise'. This is partly attributable to the fact that in several sectors, such as transport, mining or public utilities, the need is largely for medium- and long-term credit. The banks in Pakistan have felt that with the predominant share of demand liabilities their deposit resources prevent undertaking anything more than short-term commitments. In other sectors, like construction or community services, the security which potential borrowers can offer is real estate or other fixed assets which did not constitute self-liquidating paper and were often illiquid in

---

[14] Cf. para. 260 of the *Report*. For additional legal impediments to small loans see in particular paras. 252–255 and 260.

[15] The Commission suggested that a proposed Small Business Corporation be empowered to guarantee loans made by banks on easier terms to small business (para. 269).

the sense that sales of assets for recovering defaulted loans were difficult to effectuate quickly or without lessening of value. These objections have validity, although their force may have diminished in recent years with the sharp increase in the ratio of time-deposits which now constitute almost 40 per cent. of total deposits. The theory of the 'self-liquidating' paper has been weakened by banking practice in many countries where it has been found both safe and proper to earmark a certain proportion of loans for longer-term purposes. Finally, the access to central bank credit which commercial banks enjoy should dispel exaggerated fear of illiquidity in a time of emergency. By co-ordinating efforts with the specialized finance corporations the commercial banks may be able greatly to increase their usefulness to the economy in future years.

The last problem is that of the geographical inadequacy of banking facilities. This is most strikingly evident in the distribution of deposits and advances by major cities as on 30 June 1964:

TABLE 22

DEPOSITS AND ADVANCES DISTRIBUTED BY MAJOR CITIES[1]

As on 30 June 1964

(Figures for each city expressed as percentage of Total)

Cities	Deposits			Advances		
	Accounts (No.)	Amount (Million Rs.)	Average Size (Rs.)	Accounts (No.)	Amount (Million Rs.)	Average Size (Rs.)
All-Pakistan	1,632,960	5,761	3,528	529,955	4,342	8,193
W. Pakistan:						
Karachi	23·06	35·00	5,352	5·18	40·38	63,811
Lahore	11·08	14·72	4,687	4·17	9·70	19,056
Rawalpindi	4·38	3·80	3,072	1·19	1·17	8,065
Lyallpur	2·57	2·32	3,181	1·01	2·69	21,879
Hyderabad	2·31	1·67	2,554	1·41	1·80	10,454
Multan	1·77	1·20	2,404	1·35	1·20	7,256
Peshawar	1·80	1·27	2,501	0·66	0·93	11,529
20 other	11·83	8·38	2,494	9·31	5·64	4,933
E. Pakistan						
Dacca	8·77	9·88	3,976	3·62	19·80	44,824
Chittagong	5·86	6·67	4,015	4·54	6·03	10,880
Narayanganj	1·55	1·50	3,440	0·31	2·19	57,143
Khulna	1·67	1·10	2,335	2·27	0·86	3,089
7 other	4·21	2·60	2,168	17·92	1·47	671
All Others:	19·14	9·89	1,822	45·33	5·27	950

Source: State Bank of Pakistan.

[1] Including deposits and advances by Agricultural and Industrial Development Banks.

In cumulative terms, six cities account for three-quarters of all deposits while in the case of advances, only four cities—Karachi, Dacca, Lahore and Chittagong—take up the same proportion of the total.[16] Geographical differences are pronounced, not only between the two provinces but within each province. While a provincial distribution cannot be precisely determined a rough approximation is possible. West Pakistan appears to hold 77 per cent. of deposits and 71 per cent. of advances; the progressive curtailment of the operations of non-scheduled banks has been especially unfortunate for East Pakistan. The terrain, difficult communications and the general lack of *pucca* structures needed for installing bank vaults or storing goods pledged with the banks have discouraged them from opening offices in the latter province. The total number of banking outlets, taking scheduled and non-scheduled banks together, is far less in proportion to the population of East Pakistan, although this is due in greater part to the less developed commerce and industry of the region. However, proposals for subsidizing the opening of new offices by Pakistani banks in the less developed parts of the country merit serious consideration because there might be a vicious circle joining the inadequacy of banking with the lack of development. A solution to the problem of geographical coverage would also help alleviate the problem of credit for small businesses that predominate in the mofussil areas of the country.

Some progress in alleviating the problems of small borrowers is under way. In January 1964, the National Bank of Pakistan established a Peoples' Credit Department, specializing in small loans (up to Rs. 50,000) granted on easier terms. Other banks are also attending to these needs, stimulated perhaps by the pronounced increase in competition within the banking industry recently and the willingness of the State Bank to allow banks to borrow at the bank-rate (i.e., even in excess of 'quota' amounts) to the extent of their loans of Rs. 25,000 or below.

---

[16] Data on advances must be interpreted with caution as in a branch banking system the point at which credit is extended may have no relation to the area where it is utilized. Moreover, the inclusion of the Agricultural Bank in Table 22 inflates the share, in strictly commercial banking credits, of small towns from where its loans are made. Similarly the inclusion of the Industrial Bank inflates the share of East Pakistan, especially of Dacca.

APPENDIX NOTE

NON-SCHEDULED BANKS

Before Independence, there were 190 non-scheduled banks in the Pakistan territories. With the *en masse* departure of minority populations, their number was reduced in West Pakistan from 84 to 15. In East Pakistan, as many as 80 continued to operate. Many were gradually liquidated because of failure to comply with banking laws. In 1962, the number of reporting banks was down to 42 (of which 27 were in East Pakistan) and the number of their offices was 49. Eleven banks were incorporated outside the country, mostly in India. The over-extended condition of many banks is reflected in the much larger figures for advances and bills discounted, indicating that while deposits had been withdrawn bank credit had not been liquidated to the same extent. The figure was as high as 243 per cent. of deposits in 1949 but had declined to 96 per cent. in 1962. Paradoxically, many of relatively solvent banks were holding substantial cash balances, including deposits with the State Bank and other banks, the figure for 1962 being as high as 64·7 per cent. of deposits. Investments have accounted for another 7·2 per cent. of deposits so that the total of earning assets exceeds deposits by a substantial, if diminishing, margin.

TABLE 23

STATISTICS OF NON-SCHEDULED BANKS
(In millions of rupees)

Year	No. of Banks Reporting	Deposit Liabilities	Cash Balances and Money at Call	Advances and Bills Discounted
1950	95	27·5	4·9	49·7
1951	91	28·9	6·8	41·3
1952	81	27·9	9·6	36·2
1953	69	26·0	9·2	32·4
1954	65	23·6	9·0	27·7
1955	61	17·0	6·9	26·7
1956	57	18·9	4·1	23·6
1957	60	15·1	5·8	27·0
1958	54	12·4	8·4	18·9
1959	51	15·2	11·2	15·0
1960	44	19·6	11·8	16·1
1961	43	26·6	13·8	20·3
1962	42	15·7	10·1	15·0
1963	40	18·3	12·8	14·4

Source: State Bank of Pakistan

It is evident that in relation to the scheduled banks, the non-scheduled banks have ceased to be of any significance and hence do not merit detailed consideration. However, in a recent report, the State Bank has cautioned that any failures would undermine confidence in the entire banking system. It has called for liquidation of all remaining weak units and efforts to make the more viable financially stronger by reform and merger.[17]

[17] *An Appraisal of the Credit and Monetary Situation* (Economic Adviser, State Bank of Pakistan) Karachi, 1962.

VI

AGRICULTURAL CREDIT

RURAL credit needs in Pakistan are classified according to the period of time for which credit is required. Seasonal finance for periods generally not exceeding nine to fifteen months is needed for buying seed and fertilizer, paying wages and maintaining the cultivator's family and cattle until the harvest. Medium-term credit repayable over two to five years is required for buying livestock or simple implements and sometimes for minor improvements like levelling of land or repair of wells. Long-term credit is needed for purchase of land or heavy agricultural machinery and for major improvements on the land, such as sinking tube-wells, constructing embankments, laying field-drains and irrigation channels or planting orchards. The period of repayment varies but usually extends over ten years.

In addition to these 'functional' needs, there is an insistent demand for 'personal' credit to meet social obligations and to pay for litigation, weddings, illness or house repairs. Being intrinsically 'unproductive', institutional arrangements do not provide for it. While the discussion in this chapter is confined to problems of 'functional' credit, it is useful to recognize the magnitude of unproductive indebtedness. The Dacca University Socio-Economic Research Board survey in four districts in 1956 revealed that nearly two-thirds of the debt incurred by the surveyed families was for 'family expenditures'. In West Pakistan, inquiries have been conducted since Partition in the Punjab in 1951 and 1957.[1] According to the 1951 study, about 36 per cent. of the families surveyed were in debt, the average debt being Rs. 414. Of the amount, 28·2 per cent. was incurred for 'domestic purposes'. In 1957, 54·8 per cent. of surveyed families were found to be in debt. Of the average debt of Rs. 452, 34 per cent. was for the same purpose. The 1951 Survey showed 'social

---

[1] Since the various studies were made by different groups and using different definitions, the figures for unproductive indebtedness are comparable only in a very general way.

ceremonies' as accounting for another 15·6 per cent. of debt; in the later study, the cost of weddings alone was responsible for nearly 8 per cent.

Several factors contribute to the acute problem of agricultural indebtedness in Pakistan. Firstly, the size of the typical agricultural enterprise is very small—millions of cultivators operate on tiny farms and the loan agency must deal with great numbers of applicants for small loans. Institutional factors are important, for it is only the coming of a money economy to the rural areas and of laws which permit the lender to have access to courts for collection that make the credit problem what it is today. These vast legal and economic changes have come about without a corresponding change in the outlook on life of the average farmer. Hence he is not credit conscious in the modern sense and the cost of administering a loan is out of proportion to its size. Moreover, the level of near-hunger at which the majority subsists makes for an almost irresistible temptation to divert credit obtained for productive purposes to unproductive ends. Even when the funds are properly used, there is a tendency to divert the fruits of increased productivity to raising consumption rather than to repaying debts.

Secondly, the ordinary agriculturist does not have good collateral to offer. Apart from personal surety, acceptable to friends, relatives and sometimes to co-operatives, there are only three types of collateral available to farm people: land, crops and ornaments. In the absence of licensed warehousing facilities or assurance that the crop will be marketed through the credit agency, the security of crops is often meaningless. As for land, its availability depends primarily on the land-tenure situation. Even a land-owning cultivator may be unable to borrow because of various restrictions on the transfer of land. Land-alienation legislation was designed to prevent the transfer of land to money-lending classes and to prevent the loss of essential farm assets in foreclosure proceedings. An unintended effect of the land reforms in West Pakistan in 1959 and the restrictions placed on the alienability and partibility of holdings is to further impair the value of land as security. Finding an alternative security to land is a major problem of rural credit.

Thirdly, a majority of cultivators do not work economic holdings. If the holding is uneconomic (and subsidiary sources of income are unreliable), the cultivator has not the means to maintain his family from the produce of the land itself and must remain in perpetual need of funds. Credit for such an individual is difficult to provide since he does not possess dependable means of repayment.

These three conditions resulted in the evolution of a set of non-institutional credit agencies in the subcontinent: money-lenders, traders, and *zamindars*. The money-lender was in the past the most common source of credit. He lent money on personal surety and did not press for repayment of capital so long as interest was paid. There was no publicity attached to his loans, which was eminently necessary for protecting the *izzat* of the borrower. In return, he charged an exorbitant rate of interest, rarely less than 18 per cent. and often more than 50 per cent. per annum. The money-lender's influence was demoralizing since loans were so easily available that they were readily spent, and because the money-lender did not care how they were spent.[2]

The oppression of the money-lender was felt acutely in the depression years after 1929. Several laws were passed for controlling his activity[3] but were not entirely effective as no alternative source of credit was made available to the indigent peasant. The superior bargaining power of the money-lender, the illiteracy of the ordinary debtor, the absence of satisfactory inspecting machinery, and the lack of sufficiently deterrent penalties contributed to infringement of these laws. To the extent that the laws were effective, they produced two results. In some areas they created a new set of money-lenders who belonged to the agricultural class, such as landlords, and they led to a contraction of credit facilities where alternative agencies did not emerge.

Partition led to an almost total exodus from West Pakistan of the money-lenders as most were Hindus or Sikhs. In East Pakistan also, money-lending by professional *banias* gradually declined. Table 24 shows sources of credit in the country. While the eclipse of the money-lender appears complete, there may be some semantic disguises here and some of those described as

[2] For an excellent description of the money-lender and his system, cf. Darling, *Punjab Peasant in Prosperity and Debt*, Chapters X and XI.

[3] *Vide* Punjab Regulation of Accounts Act (1930), Bengal Money-Lenders Act (1939), Punjab Registration of Money-Lenders Act (1938).

'friends and relatives' or 'well-to-do rural people' may more accurately be described as 'money-lenders'. In any case, these groups have shown a strong preference for conditional sale of land or other legal subterfuges to evade restrictions on transfers of land from peasants. In East Pakistan, 'well-to-do' lenders may insist that the borrower execute a mortgage of a portion of his holding in complete usufructuary mortgage. This involves the transfer to the creditor of the possession of a portion of land with an annual production equal in value to the payment necessary to amortize the loan. After a specified number of years (not exceeding fifteen), the land is returned to the owner free of all encumbrances. In most cases, the debtor is retained as a *bargadar* and becomes entitled to half of the produce. Even so, less than one-tenth of land transfers in the province are reported under such mortgages, the rest being sold outright.

The village shopkeeper and others interested in the purchase of agricultural produce have been a major source of credit. Sometimes the shopkeeper feeds and clothes the agriculturist and meets his requirements until the harvest. The supplies are often made at higher than prevailing market rates, thus including a hidden interest charge. If the shopkeeper also markets the farmer's produce, he either obtains repayment in kind or specifies that the grower should not sell his crop through another party. Alternatively, credit is provided by traders interested in the purchase of the growers' produce, especially crops like cotton, jute, tobacco and sugar-cane. The grower enters into a contract with the dealer, stipulating supply of produce at predetermined prices or with price unfixed until delivery or later. The former alternative is more general and the grower receives a percentage of the price in advance. Sometimes the loan is provided by processors, e.g. cotton-ginners. No interest may be charged but the price fixed is probably unfavourable to the producer. Alternatively, the price is reduced when the final payment is made. A discount known as *ghati* is charged against loans made by cotton-ginners to *zamindars* in the Sind region.

Since Partition, the new trader classes in West Pakistan have been drawn mainly from enterprising *zamindars* or even small agriculturists who have discovered in trading a more lucrative source of income. They have either operated with personal funds or obtained credit from processors of crops who in turn draw on

TABLE 24

SOURCES OF CREDIT AND CAUSES OF INDEBTEDNESS

(percentages of total)

	Board of Economic Inquiry (Punjab)	Socio-Economic Board, Dacca University				Socio-Economic Research Project Punjab University
		Narayanganj	Rangpur	Rajbari	Feni	
A. SOURCES OF CREDIT						
1. Relatives and friends	63·2	59·5	58·6	53·9	41·3	62·8
2. Well-to-do rural people/landlords	16·9	17·9	23·3	13·7	31·6	0·2
3. Co-operatives	13·2	0·4	—	1·4	0·4	14·3
4. Government	2·9	0·3	6·0	5·3	5·7	13·4
5. Shopkeepers	2·5	12·8	4·5	17·3	10·3	0·4
6. Marketing intermediaries	—	2·2	5·2	2·1	1·0	4·7
7. Money-lenders	1·3	3·9	1·4	2·8	8·9	1·1
8 Other sources	—	3·0	1·0	3·5	0·8	3·1
B. CAUSES OF INDEBTEDNESS						
1. Family expenditure[1]	51·4	67·4	74·7	63·5	69·6	62·0
2. Capital expenditure in farming[2]	29·9	8·1	12·5	8·3	8·4	19·6
3. Non-farm business expenses	13·5	11·9	3·0	10·1	6·4	1·2
4. Current expenses of farming[3]	3·7	9·8	8·5	13·4	12·3	12·0
5. Repayment of debt	1·3	1·8	1·3	4·3	2·8	3·2
6. Other miscellaneous purposes	0·2	1·0	—	0·4	0·5	2·0

Sources: Tables I and II, *Report*, Credit Enquiry Commission, 1959.

[1] Includes expenditure on (i) family consumption, (ii) residential construction or repairs (iii) social ceremonies, (iv) litigation (v) medical expenses, etc.

[2] Includes expenditure on (i) purchase of land, (ii) purchase of farm equipment, (iii) livestock purchases, (iv) construction of fencing for farms, etc.

[3] Includes expenditure on (i) purchase of seeds and fertilizer, (ii) hire of labour and equipment, (iii) payment of rents, etc.

Note: According to the Agricultural Census of 1960, 9·2 per cent. of the rural debt of Rs. 930 million in East Pakistan was from official sources; the percentage was 9·7 out of Rs. 1,296 million in West Pakistan.

institutional sources of credit. Sometimes the grower obtains credit directly from commission men or dealers.

The landed proprietor was a traditional source of credit, particularly if he was residing on his lands and he became more important after Partition in many areas. The recent land reforms may deter landlords from providing credit to tenants not wholly under their control.[4] No contract for the loan is generally made and no interest ordinarily charged though it is common practice for the *zamindar* to collect the loan from sale of the tenant's marketable surplus which the latter is often compelled to sell through him. Sometimes the price paid by the *zamindar* may bear no close relationship to the proper value of the produce and thereby involve an element of interest.

INSTITUTIONAL CREDIT

Some institutional sources of credit have also developed in the rural areas, including co-operatives, Government agencies and specialized banks.

The *co-operative movement* in the subcontinent is predominantly a credit movement. It was officially inaugurated under the Co-operative Credit Societies Act, 1904, which regulated the licensing of credit societies on an unlimited liability basis. Eight years later, the Co-operative Societies Act, 1912, made it possible to organize societies on a limited liability basis. Above the primary credit societies there developed 'central' co-operative banks which collected deposits from townspeople and from primary societies which had surplus funds and channelled them to other affiliated societies in need of funds. Later the central banks in most provinces were affiliated to form provincial co-operative banks which mobilized funds in a similar manner from the cities, channelling them back to the co-operative movement at the lower levels. A federal credit structure was thus built up. Co-operative land mortgage banks for meeting medium- or long-term credit needs were also established, but they stood somewhat apart, both in regard to the nature of credit and the security against which it was provided.

The movement expanded quickly under the impetus of rising

[4] For a discussion of the effects of the land reforms of 1959 in West Pakistan, cf. Chapter IX and Appendix I of the *Report*, Credit Enquiry Commission (1959).

agricultural prices and land values during and after World War I. This introduced an element of weakness which was revealed with the onset of the depression in the thirties. Thousands of credit societies failed as falling agricultural prices made it impossible for borrowers to repay loans which had been advanced against personal surety or the security of inflated land values. Since most credit societies had been organized on an unlimited liability basis, solvent members were held responsible for the debts of defaulters. In East Pakistan, the co-operatives never did recover from the Great Depression. The application of the Bengal Agricultural Debtors Act to debts owed to co-operatives was a serious blow since it compulsorily reduced their loan recoveries.

The outbreak of the Second World War in 1939 found the movement struggling to find a new equilibrium and a basis for further advance. Earlier expectations of prompt liquidation of overdues were not fulfilled owing to the somewhat erratic course of prices of agricultural produce. The War did impart a stimulus to supply societies or consumer stores and to marketing societies.

Partition affected the co-operative movement at all its levels. There was a large-scale withdrawal of members and deposits. Non-Muslim technicians (managers, accountants, auditors, inspectors) who had largely staffed both co-operative institutions and departments migrated to India. The social upheaval caused by the massive exchange of population in West Pakistan created a serious vacuum of leadership. Both incoming refugees and the local population were preoccupied by the imperatives of personal adjustment to the new environment. Many who were previously active in the movement were drawn to the profit-making opportunities in trade and transport vacated by the departing population. Many ex-co-operators sought to exploit their old connexions with the co-operative banks by obtaining finance for their own profit.

In this effort, they were assisted by the prevailing chaos. Provincial governments virtually compelled the co-operatives to undertake the financing of commercial activities by relaxing by-laws which restricted lending to members only. The co-operative banks provided minimum banking facilities, acted as treasuries in some of the provinces and operated as agencies for the procurement of food-grains, paddy, cotton and other field crops on behalf of the Government. They undertook the distribution of controlled items such as sugar, kerosene and cloth in the rural areas. Many small evacuee concerns—wheat-flour mills, rice mills and cotton ginning and pressing factories—were allotted to them for management. As private enterprise revived, the co-operative banks did withdraw from their purely trading and industrial activities. They showed no disposition to withdraw from commercial lending even after commercial banks were re-established. The effect of the Partition was thus 'to turn the upper tier of the co-operative movement into ordinary banking, financing the very merchants against whom it was designed to protect the small man and neglecting the primary societies'.[5]

In East Pakistan, Partition merely worsened the problems inherited from the depression years. The movement had been built on the basis of Bengal as a single province. The new boundary-line cut across the area of operation of many societies. Since recoveries from individuals and societies across the border were not possible, a number of central banks lost whatever solvency they had managed to recoup from the Depression experience. They were disaffiliated from the apex bank which had its head office at Calcutta and which failed to credit the deposits of the co-operative institutions left in Pakistan territory. (It also failed to collect loans due it from such institutions.) In 1949, fifty-seven of the eighty-two central banks in East Pakistan were running at a loss and nearly 24,700 primary credit societies were under liquidation.

Not all the effects of Partition were adverse. The movement was forced to shift from purely credit to multi-purpose activities. Many commission shops and purchase-sale societies were organized in the *mandi*-towns to save the marketing organization from complete collapse. But this welcome change proved to be short-lived. After 1951–2 there was a continuous decline in the value of purchases made by multi-purpose societies in West Pakistan. As private traders re-entered the field, growers seemed to prefer to deal with them because of the poor management of the co-operative societies. In several cases where the management was initially efficient, the office-bearers often deserted the co-operative societies and established themselves in business,[6] illus-

---

[5] *Report*, Food and Agriculture Commission, p. 179.
[6] *Report*, Credit Enquiry Commission, para. 217.

trating the basic poverty of leadership in the movement after Partition. In East Pakistan, the primary credit societies were replaced wholesale by multi-purpose societies at the union level, with 3,949 societies being registered by 1953. However, of the 9,197 societies extant in 1957, most were active only in the credit field.

The marginal contribution of co-operative credit in the surveyed areas has been indicated in Table 24. The statistics appear consistent with other findings for the country as a whole.[7] The first part of Table 25 relates to the primary agricultural credit societies. For West Pakistan, the data are given separately for the limited and unlimited liability societies because of their somewhat contrasting experience. The former type are found in the Sind region where the village societies have been amalgamated into larger societies covering a whole *taluka* (or *tehsil*).[8] There are several *zamindara* banks in the same region, which are also primary societies, but situated in large district towns and with a membership restricted to substantial landowners. Assuming that each member represents a family of five, the population presently covered is perhaps 7 per cent. In East Pakistan, only statistics of the multi-purpose union societies are used as the village credit societies have been virtually liquidated. The population covered is almost the same as in West Pakistan. The rise in membership in the country has not kept pace with the rise in the rural population over the decade.

While the share-capital of the societies in West Pakistan has tripled, this improvement must be treated with caution as in many societies, share-money is deducted from loans granted to new members. The capital does not constitute genuine contributions unless the credit is repaid in full, which is not generally the the case. The 'working capital' of the societies, which is an all-inclusive category, embracing deposits, borrowings from higher financing institutions or Government, share-capital and reserves, has more than quadrupled. A part of this is in deposits attracted by the *taluka* and *zamindara* 'banks' from the general public in the towns. Most of the increase of the unlimited liability societies

[7] The discussion in the next few pages draws heavily on Chapters V and VI, *Report*, Credit Enquiry Commission. Individual references are therefore not given. AFM was Secretary of the Commission.

[8] *Taluka* societies with a paid-up share-capital of Rs. 10,000 are designated as 'banks'.

TABLE 25

CO-OPERATIVE CREDIT MOVEMENT

1947–48 and 1960–61

(In thousands of rupees)

| | WEST PAKISTAN | | | | EAST PAKISTAN | | | |
| | Unlimited Liability | | Limited Liability | | Union Multi-purpose Societies | | Rural Credit | |
	1947–48	1960–61	1947–48	1960–61	1947–48[1]	1960–61	1947–48	1960–61
A. PRIMARY SOCIETIES								
1. No. of societies	9,021	11,873	50	109	2,570	3,705	26,664	289
2. No. of members	231,811	435,378	14,183	38,411	285,960	773,218	658,125	9,834
3. Working capital[2]	24,331	86,416	5,447	39,564	2,624	35,684	38,101	816
4. Share capital	3,884	10,975	863	3,970	1,349	6,156	4,142	129
5. Reserve/other funds	11,144	18,606	1,250	5,586	413	1,107	15,379	363
6. Deposits	2,852	14,763	2,010	11,542	257	551	1,688	74
7. Borrowings	6,451	42,071	1,324	18,466	605	27,870	16,892	250
8. Loans outstanding	15,806	67,841	3,883	27,192	488	33,266	18,815	[a]
8.1 of which overdue	4,394	15,344	2,148	4,541	160	4,187	15,210	[a]
9. Loans during year	2,652	53,054	442	28,111	731	27,723	1,973	[a]
10. Profit/Loss (−)	−144	+1,641	+115	+481	+157		−1,699	[a]
	APEX BANKS[4]		**CENTRAL BANKS[4]**		**APEX BANKS**		**CENTRAL BANKS[4]**	
B. CENTRAL AND APEX BANKS								
1. No. of banks	3	3	29	30	1	138	83	56
2. No. of members	15,107	7,012	11,884	n.a.	83		29,598	6,484

	A	B	C	D	E	F	G	H
2.1 Individuals	2,104	4,675	2,914	n.a.	—	—	4,069	2,967
2.2 Societies	13,003	23,357	8,970	n.a.	83	138	25,402	3,517
3. Working capital	94,947	132,522	103,125	205,109	2,428	44,823	40,783	34,566
4. Share-capital	2,212	6,371	1,821	3,904	259	5,973	4,638	3,028
5. Reserve/other funds	5,242	10,024	7,909	16,809	—	82	12,414	1,901
6. Deposits	87,471	68,522	90,890	136,876	569	1,191	11,602	4,680
6.1 Individuals	27,077	n.a.	82,726	n.a.	57	n.a.	10,083	n.a.
6.2 Societies	5,122	n.a.	8,164	n.a.	118	n.a.	1,519	n.a.
6.3 Banks	55,272	n.a.	—	—	394	n.a.	—	n.a.
7. Borrowings	22	47,605	2,505	47,520	1,600	35,553	12,068	24,957
7.1 Government	22	n.a.	—	n.a.	1,600	1,400	39	n.a.
7.2 State Bank	—	n.a.	—	n.a.	—	34,153	12,029	n.a.
7.3 Co-op banks	—	n.a.	—	—	—	—	—	n.a.
8. Loans outstanding	93,026	93,123	42,427	128,616	2,169	41,897	25,762	28,803
8.1 Individuals	28,384	12,058	10,229	75,206	136	1,907	6,828	362
8.2 Societies	64,642	81,065	31,198	53,410	2,043	39,837	17,934	28,441
9. Overdue loans	n.a.	12,838	n.a.	52,312	n.a.	2,908	n.a.	5,459
9.1 Individuals	n.a.	9,353	n.a.	44,711	n.a.	1,865	—	113
9.2 Societies	n.a.	3,485	n.a.	7,541	n.a.	1,043	n.a.	5,345
10. Profit/Loss	+882		2,303	1,347	n.a.	n.a.	-207	+135

1 Figures for Union Multi-purpose Societies refer to 1949–50.
2 Working capital includes paid-up share-capital, reserve and other funds, deposits and borrowings.
3 Figures are included with Union Multi-purpose societies.
4 Figures are for 1959–60.

Source: Report, Credit Enquiry Commission (1959) and State Bank of Pakistan: *Agricultural Credit in Pakistan* (Agricultural Credit Department, 1962).

in West Pakistan and of the multi-purpose societies in East Pakistan is due to outside borrowings, suggesting that in both wings the rural societies are functioning mainly as purveyors of credit rather than as mobilizers of savings.

Turning to lending operations, the expansion in loans has been in line with the rise in working capital. In West Pakistan, the village societies had outstandings in excess of Rs. 600 million but almost one-quarter of this amount was overdue. In East Pakistan, about one-sixth of loans outstanding in 1960 was overdue but this ratio may be deceptive as there has been a sharp increase in loan commitments after 1958-9 and not enough time has elapsed since for unrealized loans to be declared overdue. A large number of societies in both wings (excepting only the limited liability societies in West Pakistan) must be in a weak financial position owing to large-scale defaults by their members.[9]

At the secondary level of the movement, the financial position is not much more encouraging. In East Pakistan, the number of central banks has been reduced from 82 at the time of Partition to 56 in 1960 of which 24 were classified by the Registrar of Co-operative Societies as good, i.e., viable but not liquid, another 13 were 'tolerable', i.e., not viable but could be revived with financial assistance, and the remainder were practically insolvent. In West Pakistan, thirty central banks operate only in the Punjab and Bahawalpur regions. Their financial position is stronger but rather uneven so that the over-all statistics, though not impressive, tend to conceal the rather weak financial position of some banks.

There are three apex co-operative banks in the province, of which two have branch networks in the areas corresponding to the former provinces of the Frontier and Sind, while the third— the Punjab Provincial—is exclusively an affiliating institution and is in process of conversion into a 'super-apex' bank for the

---

[9] This is confirmed by the reports of Government auditors quoted by the Credit Enquiry Commission. Of the 10,985 societies in 1956-7 in West Pakistan, 2,421 were placed in the 'D' class, i.e., they were defunct and on the verge of liquidation, while another 2,194 societies were in the 'C(ii)' category, i.e., they were nearly defunct. In East Pakistan of the 4,713 societies listed as 'living' agricultural societies, 1,231 were classified as 'D' and 3,002 as 'C' class, defined in official reports as societies 'working not very satisfactorily'. Later figures are not available but may not be much better. (*Report*, op. cit., para. 51.)

province. In East Pakistan, a new apex bank was established in 1948. Its paid-up capital of Rs. 5·97 million represents in large part earlier advances made by the provincial government which became frozen in commercial lending and were then converted into share capital. In fact commercial lending has been the be-setting weakness of central and apex co-operative banks through-out the country. Although designed to operate as higher financing agencies for the co-operative societies affiliated to them, many of the banks have come to be dominated by individuals, who were admitted to direct membership and have succeeded in attracting a major share of the funds lodged with the banks. Although com-mercial lending was ostensibly profitable, excessive overdues and bad debts had actually undermined the solvency of the co-operative banks.[10]

Many factors have contributed to the impasse in the co-operative movement, especially at the primary level. The histori-cal factors associated with the Depression and the Partition have been discussed already. Of the remainder, some can be termed internal to the structure of the co-operative credit organization as it has developed in the country while others are external to it. Among the former, the odium that came to be attached to the principle of unlimited liability has been mentioned. The prin-ciple of 'one village one society' laid down by the MacLagan Committee in 1919 had many features to commend it such as mutual knowledge and close supervision of such a society by its members. In practice, these advantages either did not materialize or were more than counterbalanced by the disadvantages of a low turnover which forced the society to depend on untrained and honorary office-bearers who either did not exert themselves at all or only for their own benefit. In most cases the society became a mirror of the factional strife of the village.

The major 'internal' impediment, however, was the fixation of credit limits for loans made on personal surety. A land-owning member in the former Punjab and Frontier provinces was allowed a maximum credit of 20 times the land revenue paid by him, while for a landless tenant the ceiling was fixed at 15 times of *half* the land revenue payable on his rented holding. In the former Sind, the maximum was four times land revenue includ-ing *abiana* (water-rate) which was charged separately elsewhere

[10] *Report*, paras. 93–99, 112–117.

in West Pakistan. While these limits may have had some relevance in the thirties when most of the land revenue rates (still in effect) were assessed, the ceilings become totally inadequate as prices of items for which the cultivator required credit rose. The individual credit limits could be doubled if the cultivator was willing to offer the security of land. Thus the extension of credit by the co-operatives came to depend increasingly on the mortgage of land, and the effective coverage of the movement was gradually restricted to landed individuals, while other sections of the population were effectively discouraged by the low limits applying to them.[11]

The foremost among the 'external' factors is the character of the uneducated and faction-ridden leadership. In this environment of apathy and ignorance it was inevitable that the primary impulse for co-operative organization should have arisen, not spontaneously from below, but from the act of a government anxious to improve the conditions of farm people by emancipating them from the clutches of middlemen and moneylenders. While the officials who helped establish the movement in its early days were often acting in an individual capacity, a large bureaucracy has grown up with the passage of time. Presently, the Co-operative Department in each province was headed by a Registrar,[12] who was invested with wide powers of supervision, control and arbitration over all co-operative societies in his jurisdiction. The departmental structure depended heavily on the qualities of men at the top. Lack of care in selection, a failure to train the men selected properly and lack of continuity of tenure combined in the past to weaken the capacity for effective leadership. While senior officials become desk officers, the field staff remained poorly qualified for the tasks of educating the membership in co-operative ideals and practices. In effect, the officials responsible for the movements have been unable to provide just the right degree of guidance. 'Where too much guidance has been given, there has been no sense of participation on the part of the membership; where too little has been given the people may have merely participated in failure.'[13]

---

[11] The ceilings have been doubled in 1961 while 'service' co-operatives now being organized at union level can give credit in kind without specific limits.
[12] Replaced by a Commissioner of Co-operatives in 1961 in West Pakistan.
[13] *Report*, Food and Agriculture Commission, p. 181.

The weakness of the official machinery has been most pronounced in relation to the co-operative banking structure. The apex and central banks in West Pakistan deploy resources exceeding Rs. 400 million. There are 125 banking offices which accept deposits from the general public and lend them more or less like the commercial banks. While the State Bank of Pakistan has wide powers of control of the commercial banks and exercises them in the interests of depositors, it had until July 1962 no jurisdiction over the co-operative banks.[14] The Co-operative Department which had the responsibility for control and inspection has discharged it ineffectively, or not at all, because of a lack of trained staff. In fact, the powers of the Registrar may well have been exercised in the past in a manner detrimental to the co-operative banks. The Registrar is empowered to fix limits on the funds which any co-operative enterprise can borrow from financial institutions. The limits are technically binding only on the borrowing society. The Credit Enquiry Commission found that in recent years, the 'limits' served, in fact, as official 'recommendations' to the co-operative banks who regard them as 'orders' to grant unsecured advances to the full extent of the limits. The recommendatory powers of the Registrar thus became powerful instruments of patronage in the hands of the Department, attracted unhealthy political influence, and prevented them from discharging their duties either efficiently or impartially.

A substantive impediment in the growth of the movement has been its inability either to generate an authentic rural leadership which could replace the official elements or withstand the powerful economic pressures brought to bear by private business interests. The farmer's need for credit is matched in intensity by his need for an access to the urban market. In the absence of appropriate marketing arrangements for their members' produce, the co-operative credit societies have been helpless against the competition of middlemen who have catered for both of the grower's needs. Multi-purpose societies organized at the primary level had, in turn, little chance of success so long as the higher stages of the marketing or processing chain were controlled by elements hostile to the co-operatives. In this generally hostile environment, the co-operatives' main chance of success lay in the

[14] For later development, *see* section on State Bank below.

'countervailing' power of Government. Here despite much lip-service to co-operative ideals, there has been no consistent or well articulated official policy in support of the co-operative movement.

Before discussing measures recently introduced or planned for strengthening agricultural credit facilities through the co-operatives, it is useful to discuss the other institutional agencies now operating in the same field.

State Credit. Governments in the subcontinent have provided agricultural credit, mainly in times of flood, famine or other natural calamities. Special enactments for this purpose were placed on a permanent basis by the Land Improvement Loans Act of 1883 and the Agricultural Loans Act of 1884 (replaced in West Pakistan by a new act in 1958). Under the former Act, long-term loans can be made for land improvements. Under the latter, short-term loans can be made for relief of agricultural distress, purchase of seed and cattle and for other agricultural purposes. Sales of improved agricultural implements on a hire-purchase basis and credits to settlers in newly colonized areas were included in the new West Pakistan law.

Loans by the provincial governments are known as *taccavi* in West Pakistan and 'agricultural loans' in East Pakistan, where they are almost exclusively extended under the Act of 1884. The grant and collection of loans is a responsibility of officials of the provincial Revenue Departments. The security of land is re-quired for loans under the 1883 Act while distress loans are usually given on a personal bond, although in East Pakistan, an attempt is made to lend to borrowers in groups, so that the liability can be both joint and several. The question of security is, in any event, not too important since recovery can be effected as arrears of land revenue. In the event of default, recovery pro-cedures involve not a civil suit, but the summary arrest of the defaulter and his lodgement in jail for periods not exceeding one month in a year.

While fluctuations in the earlier years reflect the impact of emergencies such as floods or crop failure, there has been a rising trend in disbursements (Table 26) in recent years as the pro-vincial governments have tried to satisfy the increasing clamour of farmers for loans to purchase cattle and fertilizer (in East Pakistan) or to install tube-wells and equipment to develop new lands in West Pakistan. Provision of credit to farmers who become provisional owners under the Land Reforms of 1959 in the latter province is also included in these figures.

Government credits to agriculturists have been criticized on several grounds. To start with, the recovery experience has not been satisfactory. In East Pakistan the recovery percentage was only seven in 1957–8 and recoveries are reported to have been delayed or dues substantially remitted in several years for political reasons. (In 1958–9, following the exclusion of political influence, the rate of recoveries rose to 26 per cent.) In West Pakistan, the percentage of unrecovered balance to the annual demand in respect of arrears was as high as 47·7 per cent. but if the loans given to refugees soon after Partition are excluded because the circumstances prevailing at that time made recovery

TABLE 26

STATE CREDIT

(In thousands of rupees)

| | Act of 1883 and Act of 1884–1958 | | Act of 1884 and Cattle Loans | |
| | West Pakistan | | East Pakistan | |
	Advances	Recoveries	Advances	Recoveries
1950–51	5,721	2,474	1,281	3,899
1951–52	1,379	4,076	5,168	4,206
1952–53	2,015	3,711	8,536	3,515
1953–54	5,529	3,803	3,508	3,353
1954–55	3,002	4,970	6,257	5,039
1955–56	3,594	2,626	1,124	2,934
1956–57	6,903	2,704	27,991	493
1957–58	12,500	2,386	1,218	1,523
1958–59	13,000	2,591	20,888	8,143
1959–60	20,992	5,523	13,006	3,182
1960–61	11,040	9,324	13,500	9,773
1961–62	12,162	10,176	21,546	5,000
1962–63	9,465	6,939	29,008	33,970
1963–64 (B.E.)	12,700	n.a.	40,000	n.a.
1964–65 (B.E.)	13,000	n.a.	40,000	n.a.

Note: Recoveries of any year are not comparable with payments for same year. The recovery relates to the *demand* for that year.
Source: State Bank of Pakistan.

almost impossible, the ratio is believed to be less unsatisfactory. However, recovery percentages cannot take account of remissions which are entirely in the nature of losses incurred by the provincial government in their agricultural credit operations.

Secondly, Government loans have not always been popular with borrowers. While the usual rate of interest is $5\frac{1}{2}$ per cent. in West Pakistan and $6\frac{1}{2}$ to 7 per cent. in East Pakistan, the cost of loans may be greatly increased by the exaction of petty officials. Revenue officials are overburdened with other responsibilities so that long delays ensue in the issue of loans and in their recovery. In any case, their concern is mainly with the mechanics of lending and does not extend to the manner in which loans are utilized. There has been a tendency to squander the funds received partly because of their inadequacy for most productive purposes (e.g. in East Pakistan the law fixes a maximum of Rs. 25 for any individual loan) and partly because of a widespread impression among farm people that such loans represent either the State's generous refund of a part of their land taxes or political largesse which need not be repaid.

Finally, while the contribution of *taccavi* to agricultural credit is minor in terms of need, it has not been small in relation to the flow of credit from alternative institutional sources. There has been some apprehension that the continuance of lending on the scale attained in the last few years may well impede the progress of the specialized credit agencies discussed next.

Specialized Banks. The major institutional innovation in the country has been the establishment of a specialized statutory agency functioning on strictly banking lines. The Agricultural Development Finance Corporation (ADFC) was set up by the Central Government in 1952 to operate in a field previously reserved for provincial administration. Its capital was subscribed exclusively by the Centre. The almost total absence of medium or long-term credit facilities for agriculture (apart from small amounts disbursed under the Land Improvement Act of 1883) provided the *raison d'être* for the ADFC. The only alternative source—co-operative land mortgage banks—had shared in the débâcle of the co-operative movement after the Depression as loans granted against the mortgage of land became virtually uncollectible when land values collapsed.[15] It became evident as

---

[15] In the Punjab, which had inaugurated the first land mortgage bank in 1920 in the subcontinent, there were only seven banks at the time of Partition with a total 'working capital' of Rs. 235,000—all of it sunk in overdue loans; most were under voluntary liquidation. In East Pakistan, there were 15 banks with a total working capital of Rs. 2·23 million of which Rs. 1·5 million had been borrowed from other co-operative banks. They were also moribund.

the years passed that the co-operatives were failing even to meet the short-term credit needs of their members and that the existing constitutional division of responsibilities made it impossible for the Central Government to resolve problems which the provinces seemed unable to meet. The Agricultural Bank of Pakistan (ABP) was therefore established in 1956 with a wider scope and special responsibilities for financing the seasonal credit needs of small farmers. It was envisaged as functioning in the role of a super-apex institution for the co-operative banking system. As an earnest of this special role, the provincial governments subscribed Rs. 5 million each to its paid-up capital while the Central Government provided Rs. 20 million. Meanwhile, the ADFC had also moved into seasonal finance, as there was little demand for longer-term credit in East Pakistan. With no apparent difference in their functions, a territorial division of jurisdiction was made between the two institutions. The resulting duplication of staff and services led to their merger in February 1961 into the Agricultural Development Bank of Pakistan (referred to hereafter in this section as the Bank). The Bank has an authorized capital of Rs. 200 million of which Rs. 82·5 million was paid-up at the time of establishment (Rs. 50 million from ADFC and Rs. 32·5 million from ABP). The Bank inherited 47 branches, 5 subbranches, and 22 pay-offices. The network has since been reorganized and expanded. In the middle of 1964, there were 110 offices of which 61 were located in West Pakistan and the rest in East Pakistan, i.e., there was an office at every district headquarters and in nearly half of *tehsil* or sub-divisional headquarters. The loan operations of the Bank and its two predecessors are shown in Table 27. It is evident that through the middle of 1958 when only the ADFC was operating, lending was on a relatively modest scale. With the addition of the Agricultural Bank, lending rates rose perceptibly in the next two years. At the time of merger, the ADFC had outstanding credits of Rs. 53·5 million (of which Rs. 30·2 million were in West Pakistan) while the ABP had lent Rs. 24·7 million (of which Rs. 16·1 million were in East Pakistan). The merger led to uniformity in lending policies and procedures and to greater efficiency in the servicing of loans. This was reflected in a sharp rise in activities, as can be seen from the statistics for 1961–2 and 1962–3.

TABLE 27

SPECIALIZED CREDIT AGENCIES[1]

(In thousands of rupees)

Year	West Pakistan			East Pakistan			All-Pakistan
	No. of Approved Applications	Amount of Loans Sanctioned	Amount of Loans Disbursed	No. of Approved Applications	Amount of Loans Sanctioned	Amount of Loans Disbursed	Amount Outstanding
1952–53	3	126	80	1	21	—	80
1953–54	74	2,107	616	167	673	191	887
1954–55	87	1,558	1,086	134	688	415	2,309
1955–56	122	1,133	988	479	817	684	3,074
1956–57	245	2,905	1,749	1,726	2,388	1,652	6,256
1957–58	641	6,491	3,627	2,643	7,985	3,718	12,645
1958–59	2,329	11,846	5,658	15,312	11,276	8,601	24,732
1959–60	12,411	33,341	24,772	52,039	21,742	19,078	60,492
1960–61	22,999	36,500	30,899	115,003	41,078	37,575	97,436
1961–62	25,018	50,467	46,912	116,404	44,488	40,544	148,126
1962–63	15,277	42,392	40,671	90,578	38,284	37,669	197,901
1963–64	12,411	55,203	46,651	92,109	40,324	38,344	—
Cumulative	89,668	242,400	203,706	478,775	211,428	189,087	—

Source: Reports, ADFC, ABP and ADBP.
[1] Covers Agricultural Development Finance Corporation up to 1956–7. Agricultural Bank of Pakistan included from 1957–8. Both were replaced by Agricultural Development Bank in February 1961.

The slow start and halting growth of the earlier years is not surprising. The statutory agencies were pioneering in a completely new type of lending in the subcontinent. There was no staff trained in the problems of administering agricultural credit on strictly banking lines—an enterprise far more complex than either co-operative or commercial banking. In a vast country of small farmers, the agency could not make an impact without a branch network and this required large numbers of field staff and experienced supervisors which were just not available. The constitutional dichotomy made vain the hope that the Bank would work through the co-operatives. Long delays occurred in obtaining exemptions from provincial laws which had placed restrictions on the sale, mortgage and transfer of agricultural property in an effort to prevent the passing of land into the hands of money-lenders.

Other impediments derived from the uncertain status of owners whose lands were affected by the East Bengal State Acquisition and Tenancy Act or the Land Reforms of 1959 in West Pakistan. Large numbers of cultivators in the latter province were allottees of evacuee lands and not able to transfer it by mortgage.[16] Where there were co-owners to the land the statutory agencies were required to insist that every owner adhere to the mortgage. Where co-ownership rights were not clearly defined in the Record of Rights or where no Record was available, the mortgage of land was ruled out altogether. Still other restrictions made it impossible to accept hypothecation of crops excepting tea, cotton and sugar-cane. Again, while the agencies were authorized to extend loans up to Rs. 500 on the basis of personal surety, the amount was too small for most purposes in West Pakistan, while in East Pakistan sureties were often not forthcoming. Difficulties connected with judging the solvency of the surety led the ABP to withhold any loans against personal surety. In effect, this meant that only persons owning land and prepared to mortgage it were enabled to apply for loans. Long delays ensued between application and sanction of loans and between sanction of loans and their disbursement because the verification of particulars of applicants, e.g., titles to land, encumbrances, if any, on the land, and the registration of mortgage-deeds were time-consuming procedures. These and other problems were

[16] This restriction was removed in June 1962.

highlighted by the Credit Enquiry Commission and corrective actions followed in respect of many of them.

The last few years have therefore seen a perceptible, almost spectacular, rise in the activities of the Bank. Much progress has been made towards cultivation loans to ordinary agriculturists against the hypothecation of crops through arrangements with marketing agencies to whom the grower sells his crop, e.g., ginneries in the case of cotton, rice mills for paddy, sugar-refining mills for sugar-cane growers residing in the vicinity of mills, and brokers in the case of tea. By the end of 1963 Rs. 31·8 million had been advanced against the hypothecation of tea (Rs. 8·29 million), paddy (Rs. 5·33 million), sugar-cane (Rs. 14·09 million) and cotton (Rs. 3·70 million). Loans against personal surety have also increased after the doubling of the ceiling to Rs. 1,000 in each case. Marketing loans are being given for tobacco and jute.[17] Special purpose loans are being extended for development of fisheries, tea-estates and cottage industries. More significant perhaps than these quantitative results is the matter of distribution of loans. In the middle of 1962, 89 per cent. of all borrowers owned no more than 12·5 acres (93 per cent. in East Pakistan) and accounted for 68 per cent. of all credit granted. The average size of loans was Rs. 350 in the latter province, suggesting that loans were mostly for seasonal purposes, or purchase of cattle. In West Pakistan, 68 per cent. of loanees were small owners; only 23 per cent. of total loans had been granted to them. The average loan was Rs. 1,700 indicating greater use for longer-term purposes by larger landowners.

While progress registered to date is impressive, it is likely to create problems of its own. Firstly, there is the increasing risk of defaults. From inception through end-1963, the ratio of recoveries is estimated to be 77 per cent. in East Pakistan and 78 per cent. of the amounts outstanding in West Pakistan.[18] As commitments move up, there is a distinct danger of overdues accumulating and eventually turning into bad debts. While the dues of the Bank can be recovered as 'arrears of land revenue', it is known that the Revenue Authorities have large annual de-

---

[17] Marketing loans were Rs. 0·3 million for jute and Rs. ·02 million for tobacco at end-1963.

[18] *Financial Institutions* (Office of Economic Adviser, Government of Pakistan, Rawalpindi), 1964, p. 69.

mands of their own to collect and are not likely to give priority to the dues of the Bank. Foreclosure proceedings are an ultimate recourse but may not always be effective if past experience is any guide. There is quite a widespread unwillingness on the part of cultivators, especially in East Pakistan, to bid for land which is put to auction for realizing dues. Where co-ownership interests are involved, it is particularly difficult for outsiders to try for a share in what is after all, a family undertaking. Interest rates on Bank loans have been raised from a uniform 5 per cent. prevailing before 1959 to 7 per cent. for loans up to five years and 6 per cent. for longer-term loans. There is an additional penal charge of ½ per cent. in case of default. There remains a question whether this rate structure provides sufficient margin both to meet the high initial expenses of a rapidly expanding branch network and to generate the reserves needed to write off overdues when they finally become bad debts.

Secondly, there is a danger that the mere provision of credits in cash without parallel arrangements for supply of the means for increasing agricultural productivity—improved seed, fertilizer and improvements—will only generate inflationary pressures in the countryside. The problem can be seen most clearly in the case of cattle loans which are being extended to a large number of cultivators in East Pakistan. Short of imports, there is no way of increasing the supply of cattle in the province quickly; the only result of extending cattle loans would thus be to raise prices.

Thirdly, lending commitments have risen in 1961–3 at a rate which may not be maintainable unless new capital resources are made available to the Bank. Its paid-up capital is now Rs. 100 million while loans sanctioned in 1962 alone were almost of that order. A certain proportion are seasonal loans, which are revolved each year, so that repayments offset new lendings. Moreover, some of the special purpose lending has been financed by appropriations from various funds. For example, a sum of Rs. 5 million has been placed at its disposal by the Tea Development Committee for financing loans to the tea-estates. A sum of Rs. 20 million was provided out of the allocations for the 'Crash Programmes' for making loans in the areas where these programmes were under way. Similarly sums have been allocated for the development of fisheries or for repair of cyclone damage. However, commitments must be expected to increase from year to year for the Bank's normal operations. So far as seasonal finance is concerned funds may be secured from the State Bank of Pakistan which has rapidly raised its lending facilities. However, central bank credit is not likely to be available for medium- or long-term lending (except for allocations from the Rural Credit Fund described in the next section). The continued availability of State Bank finance is likely to depend partly on the repayment experience of the Agricultural Bank, partly on the over-all monetary and credit situation in the economy, and partly on decisions as to the appropriate distribution of agricultural credit as between the ADB and the co-operatives.[19] Meanwhile, the Agricultural Bank's efforts to raise deposits have thus far been less than successful. This is perhaps inevitable, given the deficit economy of the agricultural sector in Pakistan. Unless substantive arrangements can be made for regular Government allocations to the Bank's capital, finance may become perhaps the most important limitation on the expansion of the activities of the Bank.

State Bank of Pakistan. The State Bank does not directly finance the agriculturist. It can and does provide finance for the purpose through the institutional agencies, viz., Agricultural Development Bank (ADB) and the apex co-operative banks. Under the State Bank Act of 1956, it can purchase or discount bills of exchange and promissory notes maturing within fifteen months and bearing two good signatures, of which one must be that of a scheduled bank. It can make loans or advances for periods not exceeding 90 days against several types of security, including promissory notes of the institutional agencies supported by documents of title to goods. However, the documents of title to goods must be negotiable and this is not possible in Pakistan so far because of the absence of licensed warehouses. The Act also empowers the State Bank to advance medium-term loans under Section 17(2)(d) to co-operative banks for a maximum period of five years for financing development of agriculture or animal produce. Finally, the Bank can make funds available to any institution or bank established for the purpose of promoting agricultural development in the country, on such terms and conditions as it may determine.

---

[19] The proper co-ordination of functions between these two institutional agencies remains one of the unresolved issues of policy in the country today. (*See* discussion in concluding section.)

It has been providing loans and advances to the institutional agencies mainly against Government securities or against the guarantee of the provincial government. Its commitments have risen sharply after 1958–9 as shown by the following data on limits sanctioned and utilized in recent years:[20]

TABLE 28

STATE BANK SEASONAL CREDITS FOR AGRICULTURE

(In millions of rupees)

	Sanctioned Limits			Maximum Utilization		
	Total	Co-operative Banks	ADB	Total	Co-operative Banks	ADB
1950–1—1958–9[1] (average)	31·9	31·9	—	22·6	22·6	—
1959–60	88·8	63·8	25·0	75·0	50·0	25·0
1960–1	127·5	72·5	55·0	115·5	60·5	55·0
1961–2	202·4	127·4	75·0	183·4	109·3	75·0
1962–3	266·5	173·9	92·6	n.a.	n.a.	92·6

Source: State Bank of Pakistan.

[1] For yearly distribution, see Table 23, Report Credit Enquiry Commission.

An amendment to the State Bank Act in March 1961 established a Rural Credit Fund from which medium-term credits repayable in three years can be advanced to the co-operative banks and medium- and long-term credits to the specialized agricultural credit agency. The Bank is also authorized to charge to the Fund any short-term loans made to co-operative banks which have to be converted into medium-term credits if satisfied that the debtor bank is unable to repay the initial credits in time. The Fund is fed from the profits of the State Bank and total appropriations to it amounted to Rs. 30 million at the end of June 1963. A medium-term credit was sanctioned for the first time to co-operative banks in 1961–2 and extended in 1962–3. In that year, a special medium-term was given to East Pakistan by way of converting short-term loans granted in the previous year in areas which were later ravaged by floods.

State Bank credit has been made available at concessional rates. In earlier years rates as low as 1½ per cent. were offered to the

[20] The increase in commitments to the co-operatives has been more pronounced in East Pakistan. Starting cautiously with Rs. 3·5 million to the Provincial Co-operative Bank in 1957–8, its credit limit rose to Rs. 43·2 million in 1961–2. For a description of the arrangements made in the province for using State Bank credit, *see Report,* Credit Enquiry Commission, paras. 389–90.

provincial co-operative banks in order to ensure that rates to ultimate borrowers were kept at reasonable levels in the face of the several links in the co-operative credit chain. At each level of the movement it was necessary to keep a margin between borrowing and lending rates to meet establishment expenses and to build up reserves. A part of the subsidy implicit in the concessional rates was applied in certain years to paying the costs of education and training of co-operative personnel. The concessional rates were suspended in 1958–9 for two reasons. Since the co-operative banks were continuing to lend for both commercial and agricultural purposes, there was no way of really knowing that the State Bank funds were not diverted to commercial purposes. Secondly, the banks were passing on the benefits of the concessional rate to borrowers *only* to the extent of their borrowings from the State Bank and, to this end, selected customers were arbitrarily designated as beneficiaries of State Bank credit by being granted loans at lower rates. The Credit Enquiry Commission suggested that if the commercial lending of the co-operative banks were terminated and the State Bank had powers of inspection and control, it would be appropriate to restore the concessional rate arrangements.

Following the recommendations of the Commission, the co-operative banks have been required to withdraw from commercial lending and are reported to be doing so according to a phased programme. The Banking Companies Ordinance of 1962 gave the State Bank powers to inspect and issue directions to co-operative banks.[21] The concessional rate policy was restored in 1960–61 and loans are now granted to the co-operative banks at a rate of one per cent. below bank-rate and to the Agricultural Bank at $\frac{1}{2}$ per cent. below bank-rate.

The State Bank has expanded its Agricultural Credit Department in order to inspect co-operative banks on a regular basis

---

[21] *See* Section 3, of the Banking Companies Ordinance. Under Section 40, the State Bank may inspect a co-operative bank at any time and report to the Central Government which may prohibit the bank from receiving fresh deposits or direct the State Bank to wind it up if its affairs are conducted to the detriment of the interests of its depositors. Under Section 41, the State Bank is empowered to issue such directions as it deems fit to any bank if satisfied that the directions are (a) in the public interest or (b) required to prevent the affairs of the bank being conducted in a manner detrimental to the interests of the depositors or prejudicial to the interest of the bank itself or (c) required to secure the proper management of the bank.

and has appointed Agricultural Credit Advisers in both provinces to develop plans for a more rapid expansion of agricultural credit. In August 1961 the Bank appointed a 'Rural and Co-operative Advisory Committee' to provide permanent machinery for consultation and co-ordination on rural credit matters. This is an issue of far reaching importance and the State Bank is perhaps in a good position to provide leadership in this field.

Assessment and Prospects

In concluding this chapter, we may review the lines on which the agricultural credit structure is now being developed and touch on some outstanding problems. There is a general consensus that the co-operative represents the ideal machinery not only for dispensing credit but also for meeting the marketing, supply, and other service needs of the millions of small agriculturists in the country. It is also recognized that enduring success can be achieved mainly by reorganizing and strengthening the movement at the primary level.[22] The Credit Commission envisaged the primary credit society operating as a single-purpose limited liability, large-sized unit covering an area of a Union Council, managed by paid staff and affiliated to a marketing society situated at a higher level; all credit-worthy residents within its area of jurisdiction would be members, co-operative dues would be realizable as arrears of land revenue and in specified circumstances, the co-operative department could supersede the management of a primary society. Loans would be granted for short- and medium-term needs for periods up to three years and individual credit limits would be based primarily on repaying capacity and recovery experience. The development now proceeding within the framework of the Second Five Year Plan has been influenced to a varying degree by the Commission's recommendations.

In West Pakistan, a scheme costing Rs. 16·6 million is being implemented. It provides for the establishment of 700 large-sized co-operatives of the type suggested by the Commission. However, instead of staff being paid for in part by the apex banks, it is

[22] At the secondary and apex levels the gradual elimination of commercial lending and the transfer of control in matters of credit from the Co-operative Departments to the State Bank, give some assurance that the co-operative banks will in time become efficient instruments for financing the primary societies affiliated to them.

proposed that each society have Rs. 10,000 as participation in capital, the funds being channelled by the provincial government through the co-operative banks. This technique, in effect, creates endowment funds, the income from which allows for the payment of qualified personnel. In addition, the larger capital base helps in increasing the limits up to which the society can borrow from higher institutions. Each society is also to be given Rs. 5,000 for building storage for farm supplies and for members' produce on its way to the marketing society. Eighty-two of the latter are being organized with Government participation of Rs. 25,000 in each as share-capital and with a like amount provided as loan for construction of godowns. Up to June 1962, 228 of the larger size societies had been organized and nine of the marketing societies. Another 1,250 smaller societies were to be provided grants-in-aid for paying salary of trained secretaries.[23]

In East Pakistan, the provincial government proceeded in a different direction. It has decided to stick with the multi-purpose societies already existing at the Union level. One hundred multi-purpose societies are to be developed a year from 1963–4 to provide credit, marketing and supply facilities to their members, there being an average of 750 members per society. Each selected society is to be provided Rs. 75,000 for short-term loans for cultivation and marketing. Godowns are to be constructed by the Government for the societies. Thirty central multi-purpose societies are to be organized to function as marketing associations for the primary societies. They will purchase the produce of members as well as non-members and supply them with fertilizer, seeds, and farm equipment. A long-term interest-free loan of Rs. 75,000 is provided to each central society to be paid back in fifteen years. Each society is also provided with a godown.[24]

The remaining union multi-purpose societies will continue to be financed through the central banks, the number of which is

---

[23] This project is in doubt. However, service co-operatives are being organized for the distribution of fertilizers, seeds and implements. The Agricultural Development Corporation in West Pakistan proposes to channel the distribution of fertilizers through these co-operatives. By June 1962, 2,591 service co-operatives had been organized. This compares with 3,000 union councils in the province.

[24] For details of plans accepted by the provincial government, see *Action Plan* for East Pakistan, State Bank of Pakistan, 1962.

to be reduced from 54 to 17, i.e., one in each district. The existing offices of the sub-divisional banks may continue to operate as branches of the district banks. It is proposed to build up their 'owned funds' through infusions of Government capital and by contributions from the primary societies. Deposits of non-members are to be paid off with a 20-year loan from the Government. Similarly, the capital base of the apex bank is to be raised to Rs. 5 million by contributions from the central banks and the Government, which would continue to subsidize its operations but on a gradually declining scale.

Several methods of reorganizing the movement at the primary level are under simultaneous experiment at the present time. This has the distinct merit of providing evidence as to alternative types of arrangements from which the most suitable can be selected for more general adoption at a later date. The decision to concentrate on developing only that number of primary societies for which trained staff and financial resources can be found is a welcome change from the past emphasis on ambitious quantitative targets and the corresponding neglect of quality.[25] The systematic linking of credit with marketing and service co-operatives is most welcome. Whether these arrangements can withstand the hostility of private trading interests remains to be seen.

Meanwhile, several important things remain to be done. Co-operative dues are not yet realizable as arrears of land revenue in the former Frontier and the Punjab, where most of the loans for short-term purposes are given against personal sureties. Even where dues are realizable as revenue arrears, the procedures especially in East Pakistan tend to be cumbersome. With repayment a discipline still weak in the countryside, the dependence on tangible security (such as an automatic charge on land or crops) and final recourse to compulsory proceedings for collecting debts seem unavoidable if the co-operatives are to attract the savings of the community and not to remain as passive channels for funds borrowed from the banking system.

Secondly, while the need to train large numbers of managers, accountants, inspectors and other technicians is appreciated, there is less awareness of the perhaps greater need for developing

[25] This unfortunately does not appear to be true of the service co-operatives which have been organized *en masse* in West Pakistan.

real leadership and devotion to the ideals—and demands—of the co-operative movement at the grass roots. The 'Comilla Project'[26], which seeks to develop local interest and leadership for an internally motivated effort to meet problems through the co-operative organization, may well set a model for the intensive education that is needed in the villages if the movement is really to strike root instead of remaining an imposition from above, officially inspired and managed, regarded by most country folk as no more than a convenient tap for easy credit. The task is truly a tremendous one and should not be underrated.

Finally, there is a problem of co-ordinating co-operative credit with the facilities provided by the ADB and by the provincial Revenue Departments (*taccavi*). While there is agreement on the advantages of the co-operative agency, there is at the same time no disposition to wait upon its growth. Herein resides a dilemma: if alternative facilities are available, a cultivator has less motivation to work through a co-operative enterprise; if exclusive reliance is placed on co-operatives, many individuals would have no facilities at all. The obvious solution would be to work through co-operatives wherever they exist but this may require that co-operatives cater to the needs of non-members in their respective areas, which is not necessarily desirable.

A special committee appointed by the Government to review the proposals of the Credit Enquiry Commission[27] laid down that the statutory agency—now the Agricultural Development Bank—should stop making short-term loans in any area where a credit co-operative is organized and confine itself to long-term agricultural loans. This policy has remained in abeyance partly because of the patent inadequacy of the co-operative credit network and the inability of co-operatives to meet the needs of all creditworthy residents in their area of operation because not all residents care to or are permitted to join because of village

---

[26] *See* First Annual Report Rural Co-operative Pilot Experiment for Comilla Thana (1961). The site of the experiment is an 80 square mile administrative area attached to the East Pakistan Academy for Village Development as a working laboratory for rural development.

[27] For a description and analysis of the Special Committee's conclusions as applying to the Agricultural Bank of Pakistan, one of the predecessors to the ADB, *see* G. M. George, Report to the Government of Pakistan on the Agricultural Bank of Pakistan, *FAO Report* No. 1321 (Rome, 1961).

faction. In part, the enforcement of the policy would completely stultify the operations of the ADB. Almost two-thirds of the loans entertained by the Bank are for short-term purposes and the proportion is much higher in East Pakistan and among small farmers throughout the country who just do not have the capacity—on an individual basis—to utilize loans productively for long-term development purposes.[28] After many years of halting effort, credit has at last begun to flow into the countryside at a rate that promises to make some impact. The needs of the farmer are so great that one is tempted to argue that no restrictions should be placed on any agency and that competition among them should be welcome. On this line of argument, even the ministrations of the Revenue machinery could as well be allowed to continue and expand. However, the dangers of this course of action are also great. For the problem is to provide credit without generating excessive indebtedness and the danger is that the farmer may be tempted to borrow where he can, using one agency's funds to pay off another, with the aid of willing accomplices.[29] Of these three agencies, only the co-operative can make some pretence to actual supervision of the use of credit. The others are just not in a position to ensure that loans will be effectively used for increasing agricultural production and that the income generated by productive use will be applied to repayment. A *modus vivendi* must be worked out. In the present impasse the Agricultural Bank is prevented from lending through the co-operatives altogether. The task of the Bank would be rendered much simpler and less expensive if it could deal through the co-operatives at least in respect of their members while continuing to deal directly with non-members. As for *taccavi*, the solution indicated in the Second Plan is that it be confined to areas where no co-operative society or branch of the Agricultural

[28] During 1959–60, for example, development loans for amounts up to Rs. 1,000 (which presumably were to small agriculturists) accounted for only Rs. 816,000 out of Rs. 7,906,000 lent out by the Agricultural Bank to small farmers. *Ibid.*

[29] *See* Report of the Food and Agriculture Commission, 1960, pp. 183–6. The Commission suggests that the Agricultural Bank withdraw from the front line altogether and that the Agricultural Development Corporations recommended by them should take up the granting of loans in kind. The *taccavi* system is characterized as the 'somewhat indiscriminate hand-out of small amounts by officials to meet disasters or to assist in some cases men of influence' and with 'an even worse reputation for repayment than the co-operatives'.

Bank exists, where colonization is in progress and in special cases in areas where land reforms are being implemented.

Even after institutional agencies have developed to their full potential, two major problems in the agricultural credit field will be unresolved. There will remain literally millions of farmers who will not be credit-worthy, on an individual basis. The Credit Enquiry Commission estimated that almost one-half of owner-cultivators in West Pakistan and 60 per cent. in East Pakistan are 'non-subsistence' land holders, i.e., cultivators who do not have repaying capacity at the existing level of productivity of their tiny and fragmented holdings. Significant increments in productivity cannot be achieved without substantial changes in agricultural practices, methods, and technology, which in turn require co-operative effort on a broad front. The mere grouping of such cultivators into co-operative credit societies may not be sufficient because the problem is not one just of finance but of over-all rehabilitation. In other words, the institutional agencies must wait upon the engendering of co-operative effort ranging from common cropping patterns to joint cultivation, before they can begin to finance the non-subsistence holders of land on a sound basis.

Nor can these agencies be expected to lend to cultivators for non-productive purposes. Yet there is a genuine need here which must somehow be satisfied. When confronted by personal disaster such as death or illness in the family, the cultivator often must either sell some part or all of his land immediately or in most cases eventually, as in cases of conditional sale. Slightly less unfortunate is the farmer who can obtain *khaikhalashi* terms in East Pakistan, i.e., credit granted against the usufructuary mortgage of land. In effect, the borrower achieves repaying capacity through a temporary process of disinvestment, i.e., through a loss of the part of income from land which he would have otherwise derived from ownership of the land. Since institutional credit is unavailable, a landless rural proletariat has emerged and its ranks are continuously swelled by the growth of population which creates more non-subsistence land-holders who command no credit and have nowhere to turn when misfortune strikes. The serious social consequences of the growth of this class in Pakistan's rural areas poses perhaps the most baffling problem in the field of agricultural credit today.

VII

CAPITAL MARKET

WHILE a capital market is yet far from being fully developed, several constituent parts of the market, such as insurance companies and stock exchanges, are in process of growth. A special place is occupied by postal institutions consisting of savings banks, a life insurance fund, and a scheme of savings certificates. Several specialized institutions have been set up, with Government participation, for meeting the capital needs of industry, housing and agriculture. A National Investment (Unit) Trust has started functioning from 1 January 1963.

1. INSURANCE

About 250 insurance companies were operating in the areas that constituted Pakistan before Independence but the majority closed down soon afterwards. At the end of 1948 only seventy-six companies were operating, of which eight were Pakistani. During a transitional period through March 1948, the Superintendent of Insurance in India administered the Insurance Act (1938) and Rules (1939) in both countries. To encourage registration of companies in Pakistan, the Insurance Act was amended, reducing the deposits required under Section 7(1) of the Act by 50 per cent.[1] As a result, many non-Indian companies applied for registration. Most Indian companies wanted further concessions and an interim solution was reached in April 1948 (replaced by an Agreement in December 1948). The agreement permitted the Indian companies to hold 25 per cent. of their adjusted liabilities[2] in Government of Pakistan securities, 15 per cent. in Indian

---

[1] Restored to 100 per cent. by the Insurance (Amendment) Act, 1951.

[2] 'Adjusted liabilities' as defined under Section (27) of the Act, are the sum of the amount of the liabilities of an insurance company to the holders of life insurance policies in Pakistan on account of matured claims and the amount required to meet the liability on policies maturing for payment in Pakistan, less (i) the amount of any statutory deposit made under Section (7) in respect of its life insurance business, (ii) any amount due to the insurance company for loans against surrender value of policies.

and another 15 per cent. in Pakistan-approved securities, i.e., the investment of only 55 per cent. of the adjusted liabilities of Indian companies was prescribed. This agreement did not work satisfactorily after enactment of evacuee property legislation and the exchange rate deadlock in September 1949.

In 1953 Section 27 of the Insurance Act, governing investments, was amended with a view to treating all insurance companies uniformly, regardless of the country of origin. From 1 July 1953 all insurance companies were required to invest at all times assets equivalent to not less than the full sum[3] of their 'adjusted liabilities' in Pakistan in the following manner: (a) 30 per cent. in Pakistan Government securities, (b) another 30 per cent. in Pakistan Government or Pakistan-approved securities, and (c) the balance of 40 per cent. in Pakistan-approved securities or in approved investments. Insurance companies were given until 30 June 1957 to readjust their investments. At the end of 1960, insurance companies were required to invest a sum of Rs. 161·0 million (local insurers Rs. 74·8 million and foreign insurers Rs. 86·2 million) in Government and other approved securities. Their actual investments were in excess and totalled Rs. 171·3 million. As against required investments of Rs. 48·2 in Government securities, the actual figure was Rs. 127·3 million, suggesting a narrowness of investment portfolios which in part reflects the underdeveloped character of the capital market and in part contributes to it. The latter was in turn attributable to various legal restrictions on what constitute 'approved' investments under the Insurance Act. By an amending ordinance in August 1961, Government took powers to notify any investments to be 'approved' and the proportions required to be invested were modified, viz. (a) 30 per cent. in Government securities, (b) 10 per cent. in Government or other approved securities and (c) the balance of 60 per cent. in 'approved' investments.

In 1963, the number of insurance companies doing business in Pakistan was 75 of which 33 were Pakistani concerns. Of the 42 foreign companies, 22 were incorporated in the U.K., another 8 were Indian, and 5 were American. Of the total number, only 28 companies (24 Pakistani and 4 foreign) were doing life

---

[3] The Insurance (Amendment) Ordinance 1960 requires *general* (i.e., non-life) insurance companies to invest in excess of their liabilities by an amount of Rs. 0·5 million or 10 per cent. of the net premium income, whichever is higher.

business, either alone or in addition to other classes of business, while the remaining 47 were exclusively conducting non-life or general business (viz. fire, marine, and miscellaneous insurance).

Considerable expansion has been recorded in the volume of insurance business since Partition. Table 29 indicates the growth in the volume of life insurance business from 1948 to 1963 with the respective shares of Pakistani and foreign companies. A substantial rise both in *new* business written each year and in the business *in force* has taken place over the years. There were 15,000 to 17,000 new policies written annually (line 1) up to 1952, with a perceptible increase from 1953 onwards, as foreign insurers became more active. After 1957, there was another spurt, due in part to greater efforts by local insurers. The amounts of new business written (line 2) show similar trends, in slightly accentuated form. The local companies had a preponderant share in new business written up to 1951, after which it declined continuously through 1954, as foreign insurers increased their activities (e.g., from 2,944 new policies in 1951 to 12,622 policies in 1954). With the exit of the established Indian companies following the nationalization of life insurance in their country and the transfer by an African company of its business to a Pakistani concern, the relative share of local insurers improved in and after 1955. Several new local concerns were established after 1957 and with the foreign insurers reduced to four, the latter's business appeared to stabilize in recent years at roughly one-third of total new policies written. It is significant however, that the *amount* of new insurance written by the local insurers is consistently lower than their share in the number of new policies written by them. This is reflected in the lower average sum assured per policy by the local insurers. In 1963, for example, it was Rs. 7,233 as against Rs. 8,907 per policy written by the foreign insurers. Even more significant is the fact that the share of local insurers in the amount of total business *in force* or outstanding at the end of each year (line 4) has been consistently lower than the amount of new business written by them. While the local insurers have been more aggressive in securing new business, they have been less successful than the foreign insurers in sustaining what they did secure, i.e., the percentage of lapses of policies of local insurers has been substantially higher. The percentage of lapses in respect of the business secured from 1957

12

TABLE 29

LIFE INSURANCE TRENDS[1]
1948–1963
(Totals in thousands of rupees)
(The second row of items 1 through 5 show percentage of total relating to Pakistani insurers)

	1948	1951	1952	1953	1954	1955	1956	1957	1958	1959	1960	1961	1962	1963
A: New Business														
1. No. of policies	15,067	15,187	17,228	20,729	24,378	29,452	27,992	36,498	34,961	41,991	43,798	59,562	68,371	79,716
	79.3	80.6	62.0	51.9	48.2	49.1	62.7	67.8	64.6	67.6	65.3	71.2	74.3	75.8
2. Sums assured (Rs.)	45,624	73,694	88,734	114,865	133,054	160,858	167,900	219,933	199,605	257,990	274,847	372,524	467,490	608,960
	76.0	64.9	52.7	45.7	46.1	48.2	56.3	63.7	56.3	60.1	58.8	64.9	72.3	71.7
B: Business in Force[2]														
3. No. of policies	53,945	48,268	63,191	74,730	87,872	105,380	106,007	118,791	157,277	153,109	154,544	224,418	262,067	275,264
	77.3	70.3	58.2	55.7	54.0	52.3	61.8	66.1	54.4	64.3	59.7	62.5	62.0	67.8
4. Sums assured and bonuses (Rs.)	153,777	193,857	255,805	332,235	413,252	524,160	594,219	688,483	848,978	941,250	1,008,580	1,355,430	1,630,636	2,058,208
	73.5	59.3	51.4	48.1	46.7	45.3	49.7	51.2	47.3	51.8	48.3	51.7	58.1	58.1
5. Gross premium income (Rs.)	7,143	9,789	13,721	17,845	22,712	28,451	30,872	40,906	47,405	52,174	59,172	n.a.	86,794	107,574
	68.5	57.4	50.9	76.9	45.0	42.5	45.9	43.0	44.2	48.4	45.7	n.a.	55.0	56.9
C: Total Life Funds (Rs.)[3]	30,658	39,687	51,439	61,500	76,433	103,892	90,321	122,084	131,607	159,937	187,124	256,249	319,366	371,531
	65.2	63.5	57.8	56.5	55.8	56.9	47.9	43.1	48.7	49.3	47.5	45.3	47.5	51.1
D: Payments to Policy Owners	2,356	2,217	3,123	3,019	3,835	4,649	3,232	5,409	5,317	7,663	7,181	10,884	12,590	16,624
of which % death	37.6	40.0	39.1	31.9	35.2	32.2	39.8	36.8	35.7	26.8	33.6	n.a.	33.2	29.3
,, % endowment	50.7	39.0	41.5	46.7	40.7	49.4	29.5	30.0	22.4	36.5	39.0	n.a.	36.5	40.5
,, % surrender value	10.6	20.7	18.7	21.1	22.7	17.4	30.4	32.2	41.6	36.2	26.7	n.a.	29.5	29.5
,, % annuities	1.1	0.3	0.7	0.3	1.4	1.0	0.3	1.0	0.3	0.5	0.7	n.a.	0.8	0.7

Source: Pakistan Insurance Yearbooks
[1] Excludes Postal Life Insurance Fund and Pension Funds which are exempted from the provisions of Insurance Act, 1938.
[2] Excludes pre-Partition policies of non-registered companies and business of Postal Life Insurance Fund.
[3] Represents total assets of life reserves and is calculated by taking the terminal funds of the preceding year and adding the net balance of income over outgo of each succeeding year.

through 1963 for the three biggest Pakistani life insurers[4] and the
same number of foreign companies[5] now operating in the country
is shown in the following Table:

TABLE 30

LAPSES IN SUMS INSURED ACCORDING TO MEAN DURATION*

(Expressed as percentage of New Business of specified years)

(1957–1963)

	1958 (0–2 years)	1959 (0–1 year)	1960 (0 year)	1963 (0 year)
Local Insurers				
Eastern Federal	49	37	9	14
Habib Insurance	39	30	8	7
Ideal Life	40	33	11	8
Average	43	33	9	10
Foreign Insurers				
Prudential	23	21	4	6
Norwich Union Life	8	8	3	2
American Life	33	26	9	9
Average	21	18	5	6

* Mean Duration is the calendar year of lapse *less* calendar year of entry; thus
0 year shows percentage of lapses in the same year in which the sums insured
were written.

Source: Pakistan Insurance Year Book, 1961.

[4] The local insurers are selected on the basis of (1) number of policies outstanding at the end of 1963, (2) amount of business in force and (3) the amount
in Life Insurance Reserves. Together they constitute over 90 per cent. of total
business commanded by local insurers. Their statistics for end-1963 are as
under:

	(1) No. of Policies	(2) Sums assured (In thousands of rupees)	(3) Life Insurance Funds (In thousands of rupees)
Eastern Federal	64,369	455,140	74,339
Habib	30,847	220,052	43,773
Ideal Life	22,942	122,863	24,870

(*Source: See* next footnote.)

[5] Some comparable statistics for the foreign insurers at the end of 1963 were
as follows:

	(1) No. of Policies	(2) Sums assured (In thousands of rupees)	(3) Life Insurance Funds (In thousands of rupees)
Prudential	201,271	6,333,341	59,490
Norwich	87,528	2,510,005	54,497
American	25,034	434,045	59,517

Source: Pakistan Insurance Year Book, 1964.

The rate of lapses for local insurers has averaged about twice as high as that for the foreign. There is a tendency for lapses to be greatest in the year immediately following that in which the policy is written because the policy would not have had time to acquire a surrender-value. Equally disturbing is the high proportion of benefits paid out by way of surrenders of policies (Section D of Table 29), in relation to terminal benefits—i.e., on death or at the end of the endowment period. Since 1956, surrender-value benefits have ranged between 25 to 40 per cent. which is unusually high, when compared both to earlier years and to experience in other countries. Lapses and surrenders represent losses not only for the withdrawing policy holder but also for the insurance industry. The 'renewal expense ratio' of six out of eleven local insurers was found in 1960 to be in excess of 20 per cent. with three having a ratio exceeding 50 per cent.[6] (The four foreign insurers had a ratio under 18 per cent.) The main reason for this disparity is that local insurers, particularly the new ones, pay a much larger percentage of first-year premium income to their agents in order to make it worth their while to sell for them rather than for established insurers. The sales effort of the industry needs to be stepped up considerably if the potential market for life insurance in the country is to be fully exploited. *Per capita* life insurance in Pakistan was a little over Rs. 14 in 1961, as compared with approximately Rs. 62 in India where economic conditions and income levels are broadly similar.

Turning to non-life insurance, there were 65 insurers operating either exclusively in this sector of the industry, or in addition to life insurance, of which, at the end of 1963, 26 were Pakistani companies. The growth of business is indicated by figures of gross premiums. (Table 31.) While the total premiums have risen from about Rs. 20 million in 1949 to Rs. 122 million in 1963, there have been marked divergences in the experience of the three major components of the business, viz., fire, marine and motor-vehicles. The bulk of the fire coverage pertains to machinery installed and inventories of large-scale industrial units and export commodities awaiting shipment at ports and interior dispatching

[6] The balance of 'management expenses' after deducting first-year management expenses, when expressed as percentage of renewal premium income is designated the 'renewal expense ratio'. Under Rule 60 of the Insurance Rules, 1958, 90 per cent, of the first-year premium income is generally taken as 'first-year management expenses'.

TABLE 31

GROSS PREMIUMS ON NON-LIFE INSURANCE[1]
(1953–63)
(In thousands of rupees)
(Figures in brackets show percentage of business shared by local insurers)

Year	Fire	Marine	Miscellaneous	Total
1953	21,621 (29·6)	10,446 (32·4)	7,173 (37·0)	39,240 (31·7)
1954	20,882 (30·4)	13,834 (31·0)	7,209 (39·0)	41,925 (32·1)
1955	21,629 (28·2)	16,453 (37·3)	7,806 (34·9)	45,888 (32·6)
1956	26,643 (32·0)	21,007 (38·4)	8,712 (37·2)	56,362 (35·2)
1957	26,195 (34·1)	20,967 (39·8)	10,937 (40·4)	58,101 (37·3)
1958	25,188 (38·6)	21,924 (45·2)	11,400 (38·8)	58,512 (41·1)
1959	25,737 (41·5)	22,456 (47·7)	12,881 (43·1)	61,074 (44·1)
1960	30,872 (37·6)	26,386 (46·5)	15,034 (47·5)	72,292 (42·9)
1961	32,471 (49·2)	34,114 (56·9)	17,458 (55·1)	84,043 (53·6)
1962	43,307 (54·8)	38,169 (62·2)	23,292 (62·2)	104,768 (59·1)
1963	48,202 (58·9)	46,787 (66·1)	27,131 (63·9)	122,120 (62·8)

[1] Figures are for gross premiums written direct in Pakistan, and exclude premiums written by local insurers outside Pakistan. In 1960, Pakistani companies received Rs. 2·80 million from fire, Rs. 0·02 million from marine and Rs. 0·27 million from miscellaneous premiums written outside the country.
Source: Pakistan Insurance Year Book, 1951–63.

centres. The business has risen rather slowly in relation to the industrial growth of the economy and it is suggested that fire risks are more often than not covered only on the insistence of lending institutions. Moreover, the present level of fire premiums appears rather low when it is realized that in respect of a number of industrial units, the risk carried on any single undertaking is well in excess of the total fire premium collected in the country in a single year. It is perhaps fortuitous that formerly claims in any particular year have not exceeded more than one-third of *net* premium income (*net*, i.e., of reinsurances ceded and accepted) per annum.

Next in importance is marine business where no distinct trend is visible until 1954 because of the considerable fluctuations with the country's trade, which reached its lowest point in 1953. A decision taken by Government in 1954 to issue import licences on a C. and F. basis instead of a C.I.F. basis did provide a stimulus to the writing of marine premiums directly in Pakistan. The growth of foreign as well as coastal trade has meant that marine business has more than doubled in 1963 as compared with 1959, and the share of local insurers has also risen from 47·7 per cent. to 66·1 per cent. in the same period. The premium base remains low in relation to risks covered. Assuming an average premium rate of one-half per cent., annual collections of Rs. 26 million mean that the approximate sum insured under marine covers must be in excess of Rs. 5,000 million in cargo alone in 1960. In addition, the marine insurance market insures the hulls of all Pakistani shipping companies for an amount in excess of Rs. 250 million. There have been rather substantial claims in recent years. In 1963, 40 per cent. of all net premium income of local insurers was absorbed in claims alone.

Miscellaneous business is almost entirely restricted to third-party liability in respect of motor-vehicles which is obligatory under the law. The local companies appear to have forged ahead after 1958 and now write roughly more than 60 per cent. of the total business. The expansion of other categories of miscellaneous business requires much greater initiative than has so far been in evidence in the coverage of such risks as personal disability and sickness, theft and burglary, occupational accidents, travel and public liability insurance.

Non-life business does not yield much of a surplus for use in the country's capital market. This is partly because the maximum amount or 'limit' that each insurance company can retain on any single risk is strictly related to the maximum loss it can afford to sustain out of its own resources. This means that a substantial part of the gross premium income must be ceded (i.e., paid to other companies) for obtaining reinsurance facilities either within the country or outside.[7] The ratio of net premiums to gross premiums indicates that as much as one-half of fire, 40 to 50 per cent. of marine and 25–40 per cent. of all miscellaneous

---

[7] Under present law 30 per cent. of all fire, marine and motor-vehicles business must be compulsorily ceded to the Pakistan Insurance Corporation (*see* the section below) and this applies to every single risk covered, even if the *whole* risk could conceivably have been absorbed by the company itself.

business is ceded, with local insurers surrendering a somewhat larger percentage of their gross premiums because their capital and reserves enforce much lower retention limits on them. Nor are they able to attract as much reinsurance business from other sources as the foreign insurance companies which have world wide connexions and reserves accumulated over long periods of time. The local companies also incur higher commissions costs, especially in respect of their fire business, suggesting that it is more often secured through chief agencies instead of being written directly by the company itself. On the other hand, expenses of management of local insurers, as a percentage of net premiums, are consistently lower than for foreign insurers. Taking claims, commissions, and expenses together, the non-life departments leave little over 10 to 15 per cent. of gross premium collected for adding to surpluses.

The surpluses are of course much higher in the case of life insurance business, being about 60–65 per cent. of gross renewal premium and other income. Section C of Table 29 shows that the accumulation of Life Insurance funds has averaged about Rs. 31 million a year during the last decade.[8]

The combined reserves and *other assets* of life and non-life companies amounted to Rs. 578 million at the end of 1963 of which Rs. 317 million belonged to Pakistan insurers. The distribution of these assets is indicative of the insurance industry's contribution to the financing of the capital requirements of the economy. Over one-third were invested in Government securities, including foreign governments (0·8 per cent.) and municipal, port and improvement trust securities (1·8 per cent.). Another 11·8 per cent. were held in the form of bank deposits and cash—a preference for liquidity which is not easy to explain. Investments in the shares of Pakistani companies constituted another 22·8 per cent. of total assets, with local insurers responsible for over 15 per cent. of such holdings. Loans to policy holders were another 6·5 per cent. and may well have been for personal or short-term capital needs of borrowers. Mortgages on property, which account for a fairly substantial share of the insurance industry's assets in more advanced countries were only 4·1 per cent. of the total, a reflection of the legal and administrative impediments to

---

[8] The rate of accumulation rose, however, to almost twice this rate in the last two years ending 1963.

mortgage lending which have discouraged banks and other credit institutions as well. The remaining assets were agents' balances, outstanding premiums and interest (7·8 per cent.), land and house property, (6·2 per cent.), accrued interest and other miscellaneous assets (2·6 per cent.). The restrictive provisions of the Insurance Act have been held mainly responsible for the present pattern of investments. (Additional restrictions on the foreign companies are imposed by the State Bank of Pakistan, particularly in respect of investment in shares of Pakistani Companies.) Local insurers have invested 28·1 per cent. of their assets in the shares of Pakistani companies against 16·3 per cent. for the foreign insurers. Recent amendments in the Insurance Act, various taxation incentives provided to life insurance companies[9] and the increasing share of local insurers in a growing insurance business provide grounds for expecting a larger and more diversified contribution to the financing of the needs of the capital market by the insurance industry.

Until 1952, insurance companies were remitting large sums of foreign exchange to obtain reinsurance facilities on non-life business in foreign countries. To reduce this liability Government by special legislation established the *Pakistan Insurance Corporation* in 1953 with an authorized capital of Rs. 10 million, of which 51 per cent. was reserved for the Central Government. Initially, Rs. 2 million was issued and subscribed; in 1962, the issued capital was raised to Rs. 5 million. The legislation empowers the Corporation to transact all forms of reinsurance; to assist in promotion of new insurance companies, to help organize training schemes and to underwrite the issue of stocks, shares, bonds or debentures of insurance companies. To start with, all insurance companies were required to reinsure at least 10 per cent. of all their fire, marine, and miscellaneous business with the Corporation. In 1958, the proportion of business compulsorily reinsurable with the Corporation was raised to 30 per cent. with the understanding that a substantial part of the additional business ceded would be redistributed among the companies under a pooling scheme. The business so retroceded provides a

[9] The 1962–3 central budget raised from 50 to 75 per cent. the income-tax deduction allowed to insurance companies in respect of amounts paid to or reserved for or expended on behalf of policy holders; this should leave a large surplus *after tax* with the companies and enable them to reduce premium rates or increase their bonuses to policy holders.

well-balanced portfolio of the national business and since the reciprocity given by the Corporation is higher than that available to national companies under their conventional treaty arrangements, there has been both an improvement in reinsurance portfolios and in the profitability of the same. With a view to effecting further savings in foreign exchange, the Corporation extended its activities in 1956 to treaty and facultative reinsurances and by 1960, savings were estimated to be in excess of Rs. 5 million. It has been able gradually to attract inward reinsurances of reciprocal business from abroad, with resultant receipts of premiums paid by foreign concerns for the protection afforded to them by the Corporation. By 1958 the inward remittances were approximately half of the outward remittances. Moreover, the Corporation has ceded about 35 per cent. of this foreign business to national companies to strengthen their net accounts and also to attract more voluntary reinsurance business from abroad. The Corporation operates a National Co-insurance Scheme, on lines similar to those in Western countries, for handling Government and semi-Government business. It is based on the joint efforts of the Pakistani companies, which share in providing insurance cover on companies' combined policy forms at reasonable rates for Government risks. This scheme is serviced and administered by the Corporation.

Another field of activity has been the promotion of local insurance companies. In addition to rendering advice on technical matters of organization, the Corporation has actively assisted in establishing one insurance company in West Pakistan and two in East Pakistan by participating in capital, granting reinsurance treaties on favourable terms and after managing them initially, it has handed them over to private interests. The Corporation has pioneered in training insurance personnel, especially life agents and inspectors, and is thus helping to alleviate a major bottleneck in the growth of insurance facilities in the country. There remains a dearth of experienced underwriters and claim adjusters; a reliance on standard tariffs for various classes of marine risks has tided over the shortage of the former but may well be self-defeating unless such tariffs are regarded as strictly temporary expedients while a cadre of trained and qualified workers is being built up in the school of experience. In 1962, the Corporation was entrusted with the management of the Export Credit Guarantee Scheme (*see* Ch. II).

2. POSTAL INSTITUTIONS

The postal institutions in Pakistan offer facilities for mobilization of savings in the form of (a) savings deposits, (b) savings certificates, and (c) life insurance. These savings are used exclusively for the capital needs of the public sector.

(a) *Postal Savings Deposits*

Savings bank work is conducted at over 8,300 post offices and some branch offices. The offices serve only as deposit-institutions and are prohibited from entering into the financing of business. As there is a wide network of branches in the interior, many at places which do not possess any commercial banking facilities, these constitute a medium for the mobilization of rural savings. An account can be opened with a minimum initial deposit of only Rs. 2; the rate of interest varies from 2·5 per cent. to 4 per cent. depending on the outstanding balance and the nature of the account. Interest on such accounts is exempt from income tax. The average annual growth of deposits was Rs. 23 million in the decade ending 1963. This conceals a slowing down in the growth after 1958; at the end of 1963, deposits were Rs. 537 million. This is attributed to increasing commercial activity in the country, purchases of newly developed land by farmers and the extension of commercial bank offices to the smaller towns.

(b) *Savings Certificates*

A small savings scheme is operated through the post offices. Before November 1954 this was in the form of twelve years' savings certificates and six years' defence savings certificates, redemption yield on which amounted to 4⅛ per cent. and 3·5 per cent. simple interest respectively. With effect from 15 November 1954, these were replaced by ten years' and five years' certificates. Although the period of maturity was reduced the rate of interest was maintained at 3·5 per cent. in the case of five years' certificates and raised to 4·5 per cent. for ten years' certificates. In 1959, the yield to maturity on newly issued 10-year National Development certificates was raised to 6 per cent. simple interest.

In October 1960, National Prize Bonds were introduced which carried no interest but offered substantial prizes to lucky bond holders. The new issue attracted considerable public interest and by the middle of March, 1965, investment in prize bonds totalled Rs. 159·1 million. There is evidence that this has been partially at the expense of postal savings certificates, sales of which have tended to slow down as apart from their lottery feature the bonds are freely transferable and carry no limit on individual holding. Postal certificates can be encashed after twelve months from the date of issue. The maximum permissible limit of holding is Rs. 25,000 in the case of individual investors, Rs. 50,000 in the case of joint-investors and Rs. 200,000 for charitable institutions and funds. At the end of 1964, the aggregate investment in savings certificates amounted to Rs. 707·5 million. Both Savings Bank deposits and postal saving certificates are a part of the 'Unfunded Debt' of the Government; together they have contributed about Rs. 95 million to central capital receipts in recent years.

(c) *Postal Life Insurance*

The Post Office has operated a life insurance scheme for over seventy-five years. Originally meant exclusively for the benefit of postal employees, the coverage of the scheme has been progressively enlarged and its facilities are now available to anybody with an assured means of regular income. The Fund offers both whole life and endowment policies for any amounts, with a minimum as low as Rs. 100 so that the scheme can cater to lower income groups. A non-medical life policy was introduced in 1960, with a view to encompassing the rural population which is unable to submit to medical examination because of the virtual absence of qualified medical personnel in the countryside. Premiums are collected as deductions from salaries and can be deposited at post offices, and the ultimate responsibility for payment of claims lies with the Pakistan Government. The scheme works on a non-proprietary basis and all policies are eligible for profit sharing. Postal life funds are wholly invested in Government securities.

After Partition the Government of Pakistan assumed responsibility for 10,000 policies valued at Rs. 9 million in respect of policy holders who were either residents of Pakistan or had opted for service in Pakistan. Despite the attractive terms offered, the volume of new business during the years 1948–53 was meagre. In November 1953 the scheme was completely reorganized. A central office was established at Karachi under an independent director who was made responsible both for the administration of the Insurance Fund and maintenance of accounts. He was also entrusted with the task of popularizing the scheme and running it on business lines. Since then, various measures have been adopted which have resulted in a substantial increase in the volume of business. The number of policies at the end of 1963 was 84,569 and total sums assured amounted to Rs. 264·2 million. In effect, the Postal Fund is by far the largest single life insurance organization in the country.

3. STOCK EXCHANGES

There are two registered stock exchanges in the country, at Karachi and Dacca, with some unorganized dealings in Lahore. The Karachi Exchange is the only really active market, the volume of business at other centres being small. Registered in 1949, Karachi provides a market-place, both for gilt-edged securities and for the equity issues of public limited companies. At the time of registration, the Exchange had only nine members on its rolls; the number has since risen to 180.

In 1948, a securities market was virtually non-existent and gilt-edged stocks were treated by banks and other institutional investors as unmarketable. The State Bank, as manager of the public debt, undertook to foster this market by laying down procedures for transaction in central and provincial government securities through approved brokers. As a result the market broadened gradually. Through judicious open-market operations, the State Bank has sought to keep the gilt-edged market on an even keel with a view to minimizing undue fluctuations in security values. (The monetary policy implications of this effort have been discussed in Chapter IV.)

Until 1952, activity in the equity section of the Karachi Exchange was on a limited scale, due mainly to the paucity of investment capital and hesitancy on the part of the business community to participate in stock exchange dealings. Following the severe restriction of imports in 1952–3 and the decline in the export trade, a large volume of funds became available for diversion to the share market. Flotations of several industrial scrips were heavily oversubscribed and sizeable capital gains were obtained. This set off a speculative boom which was curbed in 1954 and share values tended to stabilize thereafter, at more realistic levels. The devaluation of 1955 and the temporary spurt in exports which followed it stimulated the market, which was further strengthened by the artificially high profits resulting from the inflation then prevailing. This trend was abruptly halted on the advent of the Martial Law and the steps taken by the authorities to bring down prices. Confidence gradually returned, however, as the beneficial effects of the economic policies launched by the new régime became evident.

Official series on stock exchange prices and valuations are available with 1959-60 as base. There is a general index covering all 130 shares listed at the end of 1963 and a sensitive index of 52 shares. There is also an index of Government securities and a valuation series based on market prices of the scrips in the general index as shown below:

TABLE 32

INDICES OF SCRIPS ON KARACHI STOCK EXCHANGE
(1959/60=100)

End of	General Index	Sensitive Index	Securities Index	Valuation Series (In millions of rupees)
July 1960	92·62	91·85	99·87	1,766·4
June 1961	95·32	94·85	99·80	2,024·6
June 1962	108·43	106·69	99·94	2,294·1
June 1963	123·23	118·85	100·07	2,476·6
June 1964	115·14	117·27	100·13	2,691·5
Mar. 1965	115·18	118·50	100·19	2,732·3

Source: State Bank of Pakistan: *Index Numbers of Stock Exchange Securities,* Dept. of Statistics (1963) and later issues.

The decline in the market after June 1963 was attributed to the introduction of taxes on wealth, capital gains and gifts, the cancelling of 5 per cent. rebate on corporate taxes for industrial companies and the taxing of closely held companies and family corporations at a tax 5 per cent. higher than on public companies. The wealth tax on private companies was abolished in the Budget for 1964–5.

Even when public floatations were made, there was a tendency to offer only a small proportion of the capital to the general public in order to secure control firmly within the sponsoring group. Heavy oversubscriptions of new issues, especially those sponsored by a select few groups, have been general, indicating the potential demand and the apparently growing preference for investment in shares. A recent study of non-corporate private savings in the form of financial asset accumulation shows corporate share-holdings to be the most important form of savings after currency holdings and bank deposits.

TABLE 33

NON-CORPORATE PRIVATE SAVING IN FINANCIAL ASSETS

(In millions of rupees)

Form of Saving	Average				
	1949–1958	1959	1960	1961	1962
Currency holdings	319·7	102·2	338·1	−128·1	52·1
Bank deposits	50·5	147·6	61·3	164·0	298·2
Postal saving schemes	49·5	59·2	58·6	69·9	82·4
Provident funds	25·3	52·2	53·9	70·6	68·9
Life insurance	14·9	30·4	38·8	52·1	66·4
Corporate shares	61·0	163·7	162·7	98·2	131·1
Co-operatives	−1·9	n.a.	n.a.	n.a.	n.a.
Gross savings	519·0	555·4	713·4	326·7	699·1
Less borrowings*	−13·9	−57·1	−57·4	−67·1	−70·0
Net savings	507·0	498·3	655·9	259·6	629·1

*Loans taken by individuals from Government agencies, Agricultural Bank, House Building Finance Corporation and Refugee Rehabilitation Finance Corporation.

Source: Pakistan Development Review, Vol. IV, No. 1. For derivation and limitations of data, see pp. 3–4 and 25–50.

With the rapid growth of industrial activity and of incomes in the urban sector, the role of stock exchanges is bound to expand, especially in view of the measures being taken to diversify ownership of shares. Under the powerful goad of the 5 per cent. tax differential mentioned earlier both existing and new companies are becoming 'public', i.e., offering at least 50 per cent. of their voting shares to the lay public, the National Investment Trust and the Government. The Trust was established in 1962 as an 'open-ended' mutual fund to encourage share-holding by small investors by providing them the advantages of a diversified portfolio and skilled management. To the end of 1964 the Trust sold 8,435,000 'Units' and repurchased 1,780,000. The value of outstanding Units was Rs. 77·1 million at the end of 1964. The Trust has been afforded the right to allotment of 20 per cent. of any new share floatations. Its operations are expected to have a stabilizing influence on the stock exchange in coming years. Other measures to widen the base of the stock market include the authority granted recently to the National Bank and the Industrial Bank to underwrite share floatations. PICIC has pioneered in this field by underwriting the shares of medium-sized companies, by encouraging the issue of convertible debentures and, in some cases, by requiring the conversion of family enterprises into public limited companies as a condition of providing finance. (*See* Table 34.) Finally, foreign insurers have been permitted to invest in Pakistani share companies on a selective but restricted basis in recent years.

4. SPECIALIZED FINANCIAL INSTITUTIONS

In earlier chapters, the functions and activities of some specialized financial institutions have been discussed. This section reviews aspects of the operations of all the specialized agencies as are common to them, with special reference to the sources of their funds. Table 34 provides selected data from latest balance sheets on the scale of their commitments.

The specialized agencies finance *private* sector activities which private financing institutions such as the commercial banks or the insurance companies or the stock exchanges have been unable to finance. While the working capital requirements of large-scale enterprises generally and of many medium-scale enterprises have been adequately met by the banking system, there has been a persistent shortage of long-term capital for almost all purposes and of working capital for small-scale enterprises in all sectors, particularly in agriculture. The former has reflected the pervading shortage of savings in the economy, the inadequacy of institutional mechanisms which would provide liquidity to the saver and venture capital to the entrepreneur and the larger returns available in commerce and personal money-lending. The

TABLE 34

SELECTED DATA ON SPECIALIZED FINANCE INSTITUTIONS (1962–64)[1]
(In millions of rupees)

	A.D.B.P.[5]	I.D.B.P.[6]	H.B.F.C.[7]	P.I.C.I.C.[8] (As at 30 December 1964)
	(As at 30 June 1964)			
Paid-up capital	100·00	30·00	50·00	40·00
Reserves	0·24	6·59	4·54	11·55
Borrowings	142·87	425·37	115·54	306·94
Deposits	8·77	44·61	35·00	2·88
Total assets or liabilities (excluding contra items)[2]	257·08	510·36	212·19	374·29
Cash	1·69	34·00	—	26·09
Loans and advances	245·78	464·40	163·56	297·51
Investments	3·60	4·78	46·22	49·55
Cumulative commitments[3]	453·83	692·37	245·48	775·1
Total commitments—end of 1st Plan	55·1	72·3	68·0	91·0
Projected commitments in 2nd Plan	n.a.	600·0	200·00	750·0
Cumulative guarantees/ Underwriting agreements[4]	nil	336·1	nil	13·0

Sources: Annual Reports and Economic Survey for 1963–64 (Office of the Economic Adviser, Govt. of Pakistan, Rawalpindi), 1964.

[1] Figures are 30 June 1964 in respect of ADB, MBFC and IDB and 31 December 1964 for PICIC.

[2] Excluding 'per contra' items from both assets and liabilities. Difference between the items and totals covers miscellaneous liabilities such as reserves provision for taxes and accounts payable and miscellaneous assets such as income from interest and commissions, accrued income on investments and accounts receivable.

[3] Refers to amounts of loans sanctioned and is a gross figure, i.e., it takes no account of repayments. Loans sanctioned but later cancelled or withdrawn have been excluded. Data cover loans through March 1964 for ADB, June 1963 for IDB and HFC and March 1964 for PICIC.

[4] Refers to underwriting guarantees issued by PICIC in respect of share-flotations and exchange guarantees in respect of foreign exchange loans to private borrowers granted by Government but channelled through IDB.

[5] The Agricultural Development Bank (ADB) was established in February by merger of the Agricultural Development Finance Corporation established in 1952 and the Agricultural Bank of Pakistan established in 1957. Related data items are based on consolidated statistics of the two institutions prior to merger.

[6] The Industrial Development Bank (IDB) replaced the Pakistan Industrial Finance Corporation (est. 1949) in July 1961.

[7] The House Building Finance Corporation (HBFC).

[8] The Pakistan Industrial Credit and Investment Corporation (PICIC) is a public limited concern established under the Companies Act.

latter reflects the great risks attendant upon lending to the unorganized small-scale enterprise sector in the country.

The specialized agencies represent an attempt, largely under official auspices,[10] to meet some of these needs. The earliest, and perhaps least successful, effort was made with the establishment of the Pakistan Refugee Rehabilitation Finance Corporation in 1948, now largely dormant. The Industrial Finance Corporation came next in 1949 and the Agricultural Development Finance Corporation and HBFC in 1952. By the time of the First Plan it was becoming evident that at least in the sphere of large-scale industry, the shortage of saving was less of a limitation on industrial expansion than the capacity to convert the same into foreign exchange needed to buy capital goods. PICIC was organized on the pattern of the development banks sponsored by the World Bank in several countries with the primary objective of attracting foreign capital, both private and official. PIFCO lending operations declined after 1956–7 as it could not provide loans in foreign currency. There was a diversion of demand to PICIC but from 1961, it was decided to channel foreign credits negotiated by Government for the private sector through PIFCO. (As noted above, the Industrial Development Bank replaced PIFCO in 1961.) In the agricultural sector, it became evident that long-term finance hitherto extended by the ADFC was not enough. There was an acute need, especially in the eastern wing, for working capital which the co-operatives were not satisfying. Hence the Agricultural Bank of Pakistan was established in 1957. The two agencies were merged in 1961 into the Agricultural Development Bank.

The Credit Enquiry Commission, 1959, focused attention on the inequitable distribution of credit in the economy and the tendency even of the specialized agencies to concentrate on large-sized loans. On the Commission's recommendations the Industrial Finance Corporation was converted into an Industrial Development Bank in 1961 and its maximum lending limits were fixed so that its funds would be made available for medium-sized and smaller industrial units. It is required to administer

---

[10] The slight exception to exclusive official auspices is found in the case of PICIC which is registered as an ordinary public limited concern under the Indian Companies Act. However, it was largely sponsored by official initiative headed by the governor of the central bank. It has received interest-free loans of Rs. 60 million from the Central Government which are unsecured and it has 3 Government Directors on its Board. Its foreign borrowings are guaranteed by the Government.

13

a sum of Rs. 2·5 million previously allocated for small industries. IDB was also entrusted with the financing of residual sectors, including mining, inland water transport and the hotel industry.

While the existing institutional coverage appears to be reasonably comprehensive, the specialized institutions operate within certain limitations. They are predominantly loan-making agencies and their commitments to any individual enterprise must bear some relationship to the equity invested by the borrower. It is this equity in the form of physical or other productive assets which provides the security or the collateral required against loans. Over the years there has been a trend towards softening these requirements and PICIC has adopted more flexible instruments of financing which include some admixture of loan and equity financing, e.g. debentures convertible into shares, income notes carrying no fixed rate of interest, etc. Even so, these institutions must operate within the constraint set by the equity/loan ratio appropriate to the project financed.[11]

Indeed, this constraint applies equally to the resources which the specialized agencies can command for their own operations. A portion of these resources must be derived from equity and the portion that can be borrowed is directly related to the paid-up capital or other funds which are analogous to the equity of a private undertaking. In the case of PICIC, the limit of its borrowing capacity is six times the sum of paid-up capital, reserves and special Government advances which rank for payment *after* the debts, liabilities and capital of the Corporation. The borrowing powers of IDB by way of accepting deposits or by the issue and sale of bonds and debentures, together with contingent liabilities by way of guarantees and underwriting agreements, cannot exceed five times its paid-up capital and reserves. Similar restrictions apply in the case of HBFC and ADB, both of which have secured their capital base from budgetary contributions made by Government. In the case of IDB, 51 per cent. of capital is subscribed by the Central Government and

---

[11] This limitation serves as a meaningful criterion for determining whether a particular economic activity should fall within the purview of the private or public sector. The specialized lending agencies can help private enterprises to expand but can in no sense serve as substitutes for that sharing of risks which is implicit in the provision of long-term equity capital.

the rest by banks, insurance companies and other investors. PICIC share-capital is entirely private, but with Government advances of Rs. 60 million (to date) ranking below capital.

On this capital base, the specialized agencies have borrowed large sums for relending. Where the need has been for long-term capital in the form of goods and services which can only be acquired abroad, funds have been raised outside the country either directly as in the case of PICIC or indirectly, through Government channels, as in the case of IDB. In the case of rupee loans, the main source outside of Government has been the banking system. ADB and its predecessors have depended for seasonal finance from the State Bank of Pakistan (*see* Ch. VI). IDB had at the end of June 1964 credit lines with the National Bank of Pakistan of Rs. 22·5 million and with the State Bank of Pakistan of Rs. 2·9 million against Government securities, Rs. 100 million against Government guarantee and Rs. 10 million under the Bill Discounting Scheme. The housing agency had sold debentures worth Rs. 79·2 million, of which Rs. 25 million were held by the State Bank of Pakistan in June 1964; it had borrowed Rs. 36·4 million from the National Bank and Rs. 35·0 million from the Central Government.

Recently the two specialized 'banks' began to seek deposits. The Industrial Bank is mainly interested in long-term deposits for periods of three years and longer and has been permitted to offer rates $\frac{1}{2}$ to 1 per cent. higher than presently allowed on time-deposits by the commercial banks. At the end of June 1964 it had attracted long- and medium-term deposits of only Rs. 1·05 million and was convinced that 'there is hardly any scope for obtaining deposits of this nature in the present state of the money-market'. The Agricultural Bank accepts deposits of all kinds at selected branches, but by the end of June 1964 had raised no more than Rs. 6·6 million.

The apparent failure to secure larger resources from the market, and the dependence on low-interest rate loans from the banking system has several implications for the working of the specialized institutions. For one thing, it can become a severe limitation on the operations of the specialized agencies. It has already curtailed HBFC lending and may well eventually affect the two specialized banks. Secondly it renders these operations subject to the exigencies of Government finance and the success or otherwise of its borrowing operations. The raising of long-term credits from the Central Bank is directly inflationary by itself, and may indirectly be so when credit is obtained from the commercial banks. Finally the provision of low-interest loans secured from Government or the banking system obscures the point that the specialized financing institutions are also meant to serve as instruments of capital accumulation.[12] If they have failed to perform this function the reasons are manifold: legal restrictions applicable to potential sources of funds (e.g. insurance companies) the lack of capital market intermediaries, a desire to avoid competition with Government borrowing programmes and thereby weaken its monopolist hold on the capital market, and most important, a whole complex of policy attitudes and arguments favouring the adoption of a low-interest rate lending policy by the specialized agencies. This last has set an immediate limit to the rates which these agencies could afford to pay in order to attract market savings. To start with, the statutory agricultural agencies were required to charge no more than 4 per cent. on loans to co-operatives and 5 per cent. on loans to individuals. PIFCO loans were offered at $4\frac{1}{2}$ per cent. up to 1952 and 5 per cent. right through to 1959. The rate for HBFC loans was originally fixed at 6 per cent. but later reduced to 5 per cent. The 'subsidy' to borrowers implicit in such low rates was explained on the ground that there would be an insufficient demand for their funds from the private sector, or at least that it would be insufficient if the specialized institutions were to charge rates of interest high enough to cover their administrative costs, to provide for bad debts and to reflect the 'true' cost of capital. This presumption in turn involved another, namely, that the productivity of capital was very low in the country. There is an element of plausibility in the case of agriculture although the potential for raising yields per acre on given crops or the cash returns that ensue from shifting from lower-value to higher-value crops would appear to belie these presumptions. In large-scale industry, the productivity of investment has been considered to be as high as 30 per cent. The massive boom in residential construction (especially luxury housing) partly financed by HBFC, would indicate high rates of return on such investment. The Second Plan document argues the case for

[12] SFP, Ch. 3, Para. 103.

higher interest rates on the general grounds that it would attract savings, bring about selectivity in investment and help to develop a more freely operating capital market. In the specific case of the specialized institutions, it is pointed out that they have not served as instruments of capital accumulation; loans made by them 'at low rates of interest have meant that prices have not reflected a real scarcity of capital and insufficient margin has been left for an adequate volume of savings to be generated.'[13]

The effect of pronouncements made in the Second Plan and in the Report of the Credit Enquiry Commission (paras. 167–9 and 460), has been to produce a distinct movement towards higher interest rates. The example of PICIC has been instructive in this respect for it has convincingly argued that if capital abroad could not be raised at a lower rate than 6–7 per cent., it could not possibly afford to relend it except at $6\frac{1}{2}$–$7\frac{1}{2}$ per cent. In 1959 the PIFCO lending rate was raised to 6 per cent. and its successor, the IDB, charges $2\frac{1}{2}$ per cent. over bank-rate, with a minimum of $6\frac{1}{2}$ per cent. for rupee loans and $7\frac{1}{2}$ per cent. for foreign currency loans. The Agricultural Bank now enforces a two-tier rate, viz., 6 per cent. for long-term loans and 7 per cent. for short- and medium-term loans. The rate on HBFC loans was restored to 6 per cent. in 1959 and raised by another $\frac{1}{4}$ per cent. in 1961. This general rise in rates should place the specialized agencies in a stronger position for attracting deposits or selling bonds and debentures and in other ways discharging more effectively their intended dual role as purveyors of credit and mobilizers of capital.

[13] Ibid.

VIII

PRICE TRENDS

A N analysis of price trends presents unusual difficulty in Pakistan. No official index of wholesale prices was available until recently. There are retail prices for individual commodities but without proper weightage or a common base, their interpretation is hazardous at best. Official cost of living indexes for industrial workers in selected centres are published but these are based on commodity weights obtained from a family budget inquiry conducted in five selected centres in 1943–4; their reliance on controlled prices detracts from their significance over extended periods when prices of most essentials were controlled. More recently, a consumers' price index for clerical employees in Government and commercial establishments has been computed with a 1956 base for Karachi. The Institute of Development Economics has prepared a general price index for the period 1951–2 to 1960–61.[1] The Central Statistical Office released in 1963 a wholesale price index with 1959–60 as base. (Table 35.)

TABLE 35

WHOLESALE PRICE INDEXES

Year	East Pakistan	West Pakistan	All Pakistan
1956–57	100·92	90·03	95·37
1957–58	96·02	95·38	95·62
1958–59	94·53	92·80	93·94
1959–60	100·00	100·00	100·00
1960–61	102·83	104·77	102·99
1961–62	106·78	104·65	105·88
1962–63	106·16	102·86	104·80
1963–64	102·55	106·35	107·62

Source: Statistical Bulletin, Central Statistical Office, March 1965 issue.

[1] Institute of Development Economics, Karachi, as published in *Pakistan Development Review* (Vol. I, No. 1 and Vol. II, No. 1).

186

Another set of problems inheres in geography. There are two distinct price areas; each province constitutes a predominantly two-crop economy; rice/jute prices dominate in East and wheat/cotton prices in West Pakistan. Inflationary pressures generated in the eastern province tend to remain confined to it.[2] The same is less true of the other province because of the much larger flow of goods from it in inter-wing trade.

Physical separation makes it impossible to evaluate the precise impact of common forces on regional prices. For example, movements in the balance of payments can only be discussed in all-Pakistan terms because there are no data on each province's global payments position, i.e., including its external accounts with the other province. Similarly, the effects of public sector deficit financing cannot be allocated because there is no estimate of the provincial distribution of Government receipts and disbursements. Private sector credit expansion is also non-allocable because in a branch-banking system, the points at which credit is granted may not coincide with the places at which it is utilized. Although foreign trade movements, budgetary deficits or credit changes appear small in relation to movements in national income, their impact on the monetized sector of the economy can be fairly substantial if the subsistence component of the national product (e.g., food consumed directly on the farms) is deducted. The discussion in the next section attempts to describe in a general way the role of some of these common forces on the price level while the following two sections focus more sharply on the price experience in each province.

All Pakistan. In a predominantly agricultural country with a majority of the population living on low incomes, the food-grains position has the the greatest relative effect on prices in general. Price expectations tend to change quickly with the state of the harvests. A short-fall in production tends to have an immediate upward effect on prices through a more than proportionate decline in marketable surpluses. Small farmers naturally defend their own consumption while larger farmers might shift rapidly from money balances to speculative cereal stocks in the hope of selling at higher prices. In the urban areas, inelastic food demands are maintained in the face of rising food prices partly by reducing consumption of non-food items and partly by the

[2] SFYP, Chapter 3, para. 41.

activization of 'precautionary' cash balances. Thus a given initial rise in food prices can be sustained and even furthered by rapid adjustments in (real) cash-holdings.[3]

In a largely subsistence economy, supply factors have a close bearing on prices. But to the extent that a surplus arises, market demand factors become important. With two major export crops in jute and cotton, changes in international demand conditions are significant. A period of high and rising export prices will result in larger incomes for growers (unless intercepted by export taxes) and for the entire chain of tenure middlemen and marketing intermediaries through whose hands the crops pass. Foreign influences also work through import prices, through changes in foreign exchange reserves and in the flow of aid.

While relative prices may move without reference to over-all monetary forces a general price-level change emanating from internal demand conditions is apt to be directly related to the manner in which domestic spending is financed. Credit creation by the banking system, whether to finance private or Government spending, will generate pressures on prices, other things remaining equal, if the resulting increase in liquid balances is in excess of the *real* requirements of the community for production growth or other transaction purposes. The Second Plan document states that the correlation between the increase in deficit financing, and the increase in general prices has been 'far less obvious' in the past than between the latter and the supply position of foodgrains.[4] This statement is not inconsistent with significant correlation between either independent variable and the price level. Most importantly, in an open economy the effects of inflationary financing will be reflected not only in price changes, but in the balance of payments also as excess monetization may be absorbed by larger imports financed by the use of reserves. Even in an economy that is seemingly insulated by import and exchange controls, the first effects of excessive monetization may be reflected in an intensification of quantitative restrictions and in related price increases.[5] If price-controls and rationing are

[3] Cf. Porter, 'Income-Velocity and Pakistan's Second Plan', *The Pakistan Development Review*, Vol. 1, No. 1. The de-stabilizing influences of cash balance adjustments need not become cumulative if succeeding crops are favourable.

[4] SFYP, Chapter 3, para 41.

[5] In fact, the balance of payments can never be completely insulated from

effectively enforced, inflationary pressure may become evident in shortages, queues and longer delivery dates and in an accumulation of idle money balances. While most of these symptoms of inflationary pressure are not quantifiable, some reference to them is appropriate to give support, where possible to inferences derived from price data.[6] Table 36 assembles some series that are pertinent to an understanding of the over-all price situation.

TABLE 36

SELECTED DATA RELATING TO PRICE MOVEMENTS
(In millions of rupees)

Year	(1) Institute of Dev Economics 1951–52 =100	(2) Total Monetary[1] Financing	(3) (4) of which absorbed by[2]		(5) (6) Unit value (1948–49=100)		(7) National Income Deflator 1949–53 =100
			Price Increases	External Deficit	Imports	Exports	
51–52	100·0	291	256	32	94·6	111·5	103·9
52–53	105·3	684	−182	767	77·9	65·8	101·3
53–54	87·5	−79	−239	−60	85·4	64·0	96·1
54–55	70·2	−305	−751	259	81·2	67·1	81·8
55–56	88·3	602	983	−453	118·3	81·3	94·3
56–57	115·1	986	543	212	143·6	91·0	115·4
57–58	111·4	534	250	238	153·1	90·1	113·2
58–59	118·0	801	679	125	154·9	82·5	113·6

[1] Defined as the sum of (1) internal credit monetization (i.e. increase in banks' domestic assets *less* increase in banks' domestic liabilities other than money), (2) external credit monetization (i.e., net external borrowing by the non-banking sector and excluding net unilateral transfers from abroad) and (3) changes in monetary liquidity (i.e., the monetary ratio or income-velocity).

[2] The residual absorption of monetary financing is in the requirements resulting from production growth.

Source: See fn. 1, p. 186 for Col. (1), Parvez Hasan, fn. 6, p. 189 for Col. (2) (3) and (4), Central Statistical Office for Col. (5) and (6) and Porter for Col. (7).

Pakistan inherited an inflationary situation from the undivided subcontinent. The methods adopted for financing World War II had caused a sharp rise in liquidity, although the full effects were

internal conditions; excess demand will absorb potential export or generate a demand for 'essential' imports which the controllers must satisfy.

[6] For an attempt to quantify the effects of monetary financing on production growth, balance of payments deficit and price changes, *see* Parvez Hasan, *Deficit Financing and Capital Formation—the Pakistan Experience, 1951–59* (Institute of Development Economics, Karachi, 1962). Columns 2, 3 and 4 in Table 36 in text show monetary financing as computed by Hasan and his estimate of the amount absorbed by price changes and external deficit respectively.

suppressed by extensive price-controls. The inflationary movement gathered momentum in the wake of the economic dislocation associated with the Partition. The transport system was strained to breaking-point by heavy refugee movements, staff difficulties and fuel shortage. Hence essentials could not be distributed while a virtual breakdown of credit facilities greatly hindered the working of the remnants of the distributive organization. The disruption of trade channels was greater on the side of imports than of exports so that a massive surplus emerged in external accounts. The pressure was intensified by deficits in Government budgets. Substantial emergency expenditures had to be incurred for refugee rehabilitation, for establishing a central administration and for defence purposes. A wholesale price index then available (1939=100) rose from 306·5 in August 1947 to 372·5 at the end of 1948, the sharpest increase being in prices of food-grains and cotton manufactures.

Growing anxiety at the rise in prices led to the tightening of controls on prices and distribution of essential consumption articles. More useful was the inauguration of a liberal import policy late in 1948 which became gradually effective in 1949 as credit facilities, internal trade channels and transport services revived. The external accounts moved into deficit and by the middle of 1949, the wholesale price index had declined to 344·2. (At this point the publication of this index was discontinued.)

A healthy disinflationary trend was apparently converted into a sharply deflationary one following the non-devaluation of the Pakistan rupee in September 1949. The export sector went through an inevitable process of adjustment, as internal prices were forced into line with the higher external value of the rupee *vis-à-vis* the currencies of its major trading partners in the Sterling Area. An index of the unit value of exports in rupee terms declined from 108·5 (1948–9=100) in mid-1949 to 79·3 in mid-1950. The trade deadlock with India intensified this movement. Landed costs of goods imported from devaluing countries fell, but by less than expected, while internal market prices changed little if at all due to the simultaneous reimposition of a restrictive import policy, increases in customs duties in the 1950–51 budget and the smuggling of imported goods to India because of the large difference in prices. On the whole the decline in export incomes, the emergence of a large deficit in external accounts and good food crops led to lower prices through 1950.

As the effects of the Korean War began to press on international commodity markets, prices of Pakistan's raw material exports rose sharply. Within a period of nine months, i.e., from the last quarter of 1950 to the middle of 1951, foreign exchange reserves rose by Rs. 642·4 million. While the internal expansionary effects of the external surplus were deliberately offset by raising export duties and thus making for a large budgetary surplus at the Centre, it was found difficult to maintain stable prices, especially after the resumption of trade with India in February 1951. Most important was the deterioration in the food situation, which brought about a sharp rise in prices. The major depressing factor derived from the external sector as imports rose rapidly under the stimulus of incomes swollen by the boom in export markets. On the whole, 1951–2 was a period of rising prices.

There followed three years of declining prices, although there is some inconsistency among the various indicators in the earlier phases. The contractionary forces were clear enough: there was a drop of 44 per cent. in export prices between 1951–2 and 1954–5 as market conditions for Pakistan's staples deteriorated unrelievedly. Import prices declined much less so that the adverse movement in terms of trade pumped real incomes out of the economy. Although the decline in external reserves was gradually brought under control through savage import cuts, food-grains aid had begun to flow into the country in response to the crop failures of 1951 and 1952 (*see* Chapter III *supra*). Although deficit financing in the Government sector reached high levels, it was offset in at least two years by a net contraction in credit to the private sector and in a marked fall in income-velocity (or a rise in the monetary ratio) as idle balances were built up in the wake of the import restrictions. This represented a forced postponement of expenditures and thus directly relieved the immediate price situation. While prices of imports naturally rose, the rapid growth of domestic industrial capacity helped to moderate the pressure on manufactured goods towards the latter part of this period. While stringent controls were imposed early in 1953 on prices and distribution of essential textiles and other consumer goods, domestic industrial production had risen sufficiently in the next two years, to make possible the removal of controls on cotton yarn in November 1954 and on cloth in January 1955. Finally, bumper harvests were reaped in 1953–4 throughout the country, making for lower prices and plentiful cereal supplies through the middle of 1955.

Thereafter, a sharply rising price trend set in. The devaluation of the Pakistan rupee at the end of July 1955 brought a rise in the rupee value of exports and imports, as seen in columns (5) and (6) of the last Table. The external accounts registered a heavy surplus, as shown by an accumulation of reserves by roughly Rs. 400 million (after adjusting for the rise in the rupee value of foreign assets). Credit expansion to the private sector rose as deficit financing to Government fell; even so, gross bank lending was somewhat higher than in the preceding year.[7] The food situation, however, remained the dominant factor in raising prices.

The floods that visited both provinces in 1955 and recurred periodically thereafter set in motion an upward leverage on prices which persisted for several years. While an emergency flood relief programme was initiated by the United States to be followed by large and growing aid shipments of food-grains[8] its major result in this period was to hold prices from rising much faster rather than stabilizing or rolling them back.

This was partly because other factors were simultaneously stimulating larger food consumption. Deficit-financing operations of Government rose sharply from Rs. 161 million in 1955–6 to Rs. 416 million in 1956–7 and Rs. 679 million in 1957–8.[9] Credit to the private sector expanded less from Rs. 100 million in 1955–6 to Rs. 237 million in 1956–7 and then fell sharply to Rs. 42 million in the following year. Equally significant was an apparent reversal in the money-holding pattern of the community. While in the earlier years (i.e., through 1954–5) there is evidence that the money/income ratio rose (income-velocity of money fell), it tended to decline steadily thereafter.[10] This dishoarding of

[7] Hasan, op. cit., p. 17.

[8] Food imports rose from 4,000 tons in 1954–5 and 48,000 tons in 1955–6 to 648,000 tons of wheat and 515,000 tons of rice in 1956–7, 692,000 tons of wheat and 394,000 tons of rice in 1957–8 and 904,000 tons of wheat and 219,000 tons of rice in the fifteen months ending June 1959.

[9] These figures are net of accumulation of counterpart funds, (see Notes to Table 15 in Chapter IV supra).

[10] For some of the pitfalls in estimating and interpreting this ratio, see Parvez Hasan, op. cit., pp. 20–24.

money balances added to the inflationary potential of the money creating operations of Government deficit spending. While the growth of production especially in large-scale industry, did provide some offset and both aid and loan-financed import surpluses were sustained, the main force of the massive monetization of this period spent itself in raising the general price-level.

The Government which assumed power late in 1958 moved vigorously to reverse the expansionary fiscal policies of earlier years. While the immediate effect of the heavy penalties imposed under the Martial Law for hoarding and profiteering was to bring about a sharp break in prices, especially of imported consumer goods, this was almost entirely at the expense of inventories. As part of its stocktaking of the nation's economic situation, a severely restrictive import policy was imposed for a major part of 1959 so that depleted inventories could not be reconstituted and localized shortages emerged as prices of most essentials remained strictly controlled. With food-grains production continuing to stagnate and with the momentum of earlier expansionary policies still too great to be arrested immediately after the reversal of such policies, the price level moved up in 1959–60 after an artificial respite in 1958–9. The establishment of a Bonus Scheme, involving an implicit system of multiple and depreciated exchange rates, brought larger rupee incomes to exporters and raised prices of items imported under the Scheme. More significant, however was the effect of the Scheme in diverting a variety of consumer and intermediate products (like cotton yarn and textiles) from domestic consumption to the export market leading to higher prices for them at home. Meanwhile, prices of the two major export commodities also rose under the impact of rising international prices. The external sector was thus a net expansionary influence on prices, although imports began to flow more freely from 1960 onwards as larger amounts of quickly usable non-project commodity aid became available. A policy of gradual relaxation of direct controls over the economy was inaugurated. A deliberate attempt was made to improve the terms of trade of agriculture. With the return of the food-grains trade to private hands, the Government release price for wheat was raised to Rs. 18 per maund. With continued drought, food prices rose appreciably following decontrol. Price and distribution controls on cotton textiles were lifted in January 1961, leading to only small price increases as production rose. In a sense, the price increases of 1960–62 signified the removal of conditions of repressed inflation and excessive liquidity. The inflationary inheritance of the past appeared to have worked itself out by the middle of 1962.

A degree of stability in prices appears to have been achieved during the past two years. Under an expanded Public Law 480 programme, it was decided to stockpile large quantities of food-grains in the country as a permanent buffer against price pressures caused by crop failure. At the same time, domestic food-grains production, after stagnating for many years, began to move up sharply. The 1960–61 crops were better than expected but in 1961–2, truly bumper crops were harvested in both provinces. The Plan target of 15·9 million tons by 1964–5 was virtually achieved in that year. At the same time, the level of imports started to rise from Rs. 3,188 million in 1960–61 to Rs. 3,819 million in 1961–2 and reached Rs. 4·5 billion in 1963–4. This meant that import requirements for industry were being met and, indeed, large inventories accumulated at all points in the marketing system. While industrial and agricultural production is forging ahead and large import surpluses can be financed by the flow of aid, Government financial policies have tended to exacerbate the massive expansion of liquidity emanating from credit expansion to the private sector. While the large stocks of cereals now held in the country have greatly increased the capacity to resist inflation, there is need for caution if pressures on prices are not to re-emerge.

1. WEST PAKISTAN

1. *August 1947 to December 1948.* Agricultural production declined during this period. The wheat surplus of the 1947 season had already been exported to India before the disturbances started. New crops were poor, owing to bad or late sowings and harvesting. Crops were damaged by excessive rains and a growing wheat shortage developed following disastrous floods in the Indus Basin in 1948. An active balance of trade developed, although its exact size could not be determined because of the absence of statistics for trade with India. The inflationary pressures were intensified by deficits in provincial budgets. The relief and re-

habilitation of over six million refugees necessitated heavy expenditures, whereas it took time before the refugees could render productive service to the community. The total deficits on revenue account in West Pakistan during the period August 1947 to March 1949 amounted to Rs. 120·9 million and expenditure in the capital budgets was partly financed by depleting cash balances.

2. *January 1949 to August 1949.* The tide began to turn late in 1948. Price-controls on essential goods and laws against profiteering and black-marketing were enforced with vigour. A liberal import licensing policy was inaugurated in August 1948 and a deficit of Rs. 407·6 million in the balance of trade was recorded in the year ending June 1949. Favourable developments also occurred on the food front. Increased production of wheat during the wheat year May 1949 to April 1950 provided a surplus of 426,115 tons for export.

3. *September 1949 to June 1950.* Following the trade deadlock with India, cotton prices fell from Rs. 533·9 per bale in the middle of 1949 to Rs. 475·8 a year later. Meanwhile the easy wheat situation resulted in continued pressure on food prices. Rationing in the large cities was maintained, mainly to dispose of Government stocks, but free market prices fell below controlled prices. Working-class cost of living indexes published by the Central Ministry of Labour with 1948–9 as the base year, declined and were 93 by the middle of 1950 at Karachi and even lower in other centres (Table 37). Since these indexes are heavily weighted for food, the decline was largely a reflection of lower food prices.

4. *July 1950 to December 1951.* A rising price trend commenced with the outbreak of the Korean War. A short-fall in the American cotton crop brought a sharp rise in the internal prices of cotton from Rs. 488 to Rs. 935 per bale. The Government sought to offset the strong inflationary impact by successively raising the export tax on cotton from Rs. 60 per bale to Rs. 300, and by imposing an *ad valorem* export duty of 25 per cent. on wool. The food situation during this period also deteriorated. Anticipations of a lower wheat crop combined with the lower output of the *kharif* grains (bajra and jowar) caused hoarding and prices rose sharply. The balance of trade in West Pakistan showed a surplus of Rs. 427·7 million during 1950–51 despite liberal imports.

5. *January 1952 to June 1953.* Recessionist influences began to

appear in the world textile market during 1951 and intensified pressure on cotton prices, which declined to Rs. 503·6 per bale by the end of 1952, compared with almost double this value at the height of the Korean War boom. Foreign quotations for key imports, particularly textiles and yarn, were continually being reduced and up-country traders withheld purchases, awaiting a further decline in prices. However, the growing scarcity of food resulting from the failure of both the *kharif* and *rabi* crops of 1951–2 brought a sharp rise in food prices. Food prices were temporarily stabilized as there were heavy imports of food-grains late in 1952.

6. *July 1953 to June 1955.* Wheat and other U.S. aid supplies began pouring into the country after August 1953 and prices fell. However, the effects of severe import restrictions applied in the second half of 1952 began to be evident as prices of imported consumer goods rose sharply. The interpretation of available statistics for this period is rather difficult owing to the extensive controls on prices and distribution of imported cotton textiles and a wide range of other imports.

TABLE 37

PRICE TRENDS IN WEST PAKISTAN

	Wholesale Prices 1948–49=100		Cost of Living Indexes 1948–49=100		Consumer Price Index 1956=100	Institute of Development Economics Index 1951–52=100
	Wheat	Cotton	Karachi	Lahore	Karachi	
1950–51	67·6	124·4	96	82	91	
1951–52	96·5	109·7	100	93	96	100
1952–53	141·8	76·7	107	99	98	114·2
1953–54	107·7	85·2	111	101	98	98·8
1954–55	83·6	92·1	107	96	97	81·7
1955–56	94·4	106·9	107	94	100	93·2
1956–57	112·3	111·1	113	102	107	112·0
1957–58	108·6	101·6	123	111	110	109·4
1958–59	107·2	98·2	118	103	106	117·0
1959–60	116·5	102·7	125	111	115	121·2
1960–61	131·7	113·6	127	118	116	133·7
1961–62	131·6	108·9	130	124	117	n.a.
1962–63	122·8	103·1	128	120	119	n.a.
1963–64	n.a.	n.a.	132	127	120	n.a.

Source: Central Statistical Office and fn. 1, p. 186.

By the middle of 1954 the rapid increase in prices of manufactures was moderated. Negotiations between Government and
private interests produced price reductions in cement, petroleum
products and other commodities, while Government on its own
initiative reduced prices of steel and coal, of which it was the chief
importer. Meanwhile, indigenous production of cotton yarn and
cloth rose swiftly and it was possible to remove controls on yarn
in November 1954 and on cloth in January 1955. The announcement of substantial U.S. non-project aid for financing imports
of essential consumer and investment goods produced a favourable effect. Prices of coarse and medium varieties of cotton textiles declined as the country had attained self-sufficiency. Most
important, however, was the continued decline in food prices.
Bumper harvests of wheat were a million tons higher in 1953–4
and *kharif* food-grains were plentiful, leading to a considerable
decline in food-grain prices throughout West Pakistan in the
following year.

7. *July 1955 to September 1958.* This was a period of almost
continuous pressure on prices. The devaluation raised agricultural incomes as it raised rupee prices of cotton, wool and other
export products. For the same reason import prices rose. There
were recurrent floods from 1955 through 1957 which affected
food production and led to shortages which were partially
alleviated by large imports after the middle of 1956, at an annual
rate of about three-quarters of a million tons. Despite this, the
wholesale prices of wheat rose continuously and in 1956–7 were
over a third higher than in 1954–5. The adverse effect of high
food prices is clearly reflected in the rising cost of living indexes.
Imports of other consumer goods were severely restricted and the
inflationary financing of budgetary deficits was more heavily felt
in this province because of the larger expenditures of the Central
Government. There was a heavy decline in the cash balances of
the provincial government in 1956–7. In the following year some
decline in wholesale prices occurred as export prices receded.
The wholesale price of cotton declined by roughly 10 per cent.
and wheat prices were lower as imports were stepped up to
almost a million tons a year. The consumer was, however,
afforded little relief, for as value of exports continued to decline
import restrictions were tightened further and domestic industry
was able to reap large profits. The budgets for 1958–9, both at

the centre and in the provinces, introduced several new taxes, but since the dependence on the banking system was not correspondingly reduced, the over-all effect tended to be inflationary.

8. *October 1958 to June 1960.* The promulgation of Martial Law led to a precipitate decline of prices in the urban areas as punitive regulations against hoarding and profiteering brought stocks of consumer goods into the markets. The cost of living index in Karachi, for example, declined from 128 in September 1958 to 112 in January 1959. This was a temporary respite, however, for once the available supplies were exhausted, price-controls became nominal. Shortages prevailed as imports continued to be severely restricted while the new Government undertook an inventory of the country's foreign exchange position. Not until April 1960 were new licences first issued, and then at levels below the issuances in the tight 1957–8 year. In 1958–9 there was a deficit of Rs. 581 million in foreign trade, and a surplus of Rs. 401 million in trade with East Pakistan; hence the general trade deficit was reduced to Rs. 180 million as compared with Rs. 440 million in 1957–8 and Rs. 529 million in 1956–7. In 1959–60 imports were rising sharply but exports also moved up under the stimulus of the bonus scheme, expecially for cotton textiles and yarn, which by this time had become significant factors in the export trade. This led to higher prices in the provinces for these and other manufactures being exported.

Meanwhile the régime began to move away from controls. In May 1960 the marketing of domestic wheat was decontrolled and the Government raised the price at which it would release imported wheat from Rs. 14 to Rs. 18 per maund in the market. With a drought curtailing the local crop, food prices rose by as much as 40 per cent. soon after decontrol. However, sales of imported wheat gradually rolled prices back to roughly 20 per cent. above those prevailing before decontrol. In the two years ending June 1960 the level of wheat imports was stepped up to about 900,000 tons a year.

9. *July 1960 to December 1961.* The picture was mixed and prices in general moved up at a much slower rate than in the preceding period. The policy of decontrol was extended to cotton textiles in January 1961 and most other consumables were freed of control during the year. There was some rise in prices, but the industrial production rose with the liberalization of

imports of raw materials, spares and fuel, so competition increased in the domestic market. The foreign trade deficit tripled in 1960–61 (to Rs. 1,633 million) as compared with 1958–9, for imports rose to Rs. 2,173 million, partly because of larger wheat imports. While this was to some extent neutralized by a larger surplus in trade with the western wing, the global deficit on trade account was still in excess of Rs. 1·25 billion. This factor helped to finance the sharp rise in development spending.

10. *Since January 1962*. An improved food-grains harvest in 1960–1, large imports of wheat in 1960 and 1961 and the bumper crops of 1961–2 brought prices under distinct pressure. Government had to reduce the release price for imported wheat to Rs. 14 per maund in 1962 in order to move accumulated stocks. Prices continued to drop as a large harvest of 1962 came in and as Government purchases were not forthcoming (in part because of over-extended storage facilities). Domestic wheat prices dropped below the support levels in some producing areas. Meanwhile the global trade deficit continued at the level reached in the preceding year. Existing manufacturing capacity was being more fully utilized than at any previous period, and new capacity has been coming into operation. While domestic credit has been expanded largely in the private sector at a rapid rate, it has apparently been absorbed by the larger flow of aid and the growth of transactions in the province.

2. EAST PAKISTAN

1. *August 1947 to August 1949*. During this period the demand for jute was sustained and prices remained high. A heavy volume of exports produced an active balance of trade with foreign countries of Rs. 1,101·6 million in 1948–9. The provincial budget was in heavy deficit on revenue account, as initial expenses in establishing a new administration were heavy. Rice crops were below normal, and food prices therefore ruled high. A factor which intensified the inflationary pressures was the presence of many minority traders and professional men who may have made substantial one-way remittances of capital and profit to India in the form of unrequited exports (there being no exchange control in force with India during this period.)[11] The reason for the

[11] Dr. A. Sadeque in *Economic Emergence of Pakistan*, Vol. I, Dacca Economic

phase of higher prices persisting longer than in West Pakistan could therefore be found in the difficult food situation and in the apparent failure of the liberal import policy to take effect, owing to lack of adequate port facilities, inadequacy of means of communication, and dislocation of the distributory mechanism.

2. *September 1949 to February 1951*. Just as inflationary pressures had been more intense in East Pakistan and had lasted longer than in the western wing, so the downward trend appeared to be sharper and more drawn out. The main cause for this was the heavy decline in raw jute prices following the trade deadlock with India. The price of jute dropped almost a third compared with the previous year (Table 38). While a substantial quantity of jute was smuggled to that country, there was a sudden withdrawal of Indian buyers from the open market. Credit facilities from Indian banks which had hitherto provided the bulk of jute financing for purchase, movement, processing and even export, were also immediately restricted, thereby intensifying the pressure on prices. The establishment of the National Bank of Pakistan in November 1949 improved the situation and some relief was also available with the signing of the short-term barter agreement with India in April 1950.

Meanwhile food prices began to fall as a result of successive good crops of rice which transformed the food situation. By the middle of 1950 rice prices were at their lowest level since Partition. It was also suggested that at least a part of the sharp fall in rice prices could be attributed to the shrunken purchasing power of the jute growers. The over-all balance of trade surplus (i.e., including West Pakistan) was reduced to Rs. 90·8 million in 1949–50. The new jute season beginning June 1950 brought little improvement in prices paid to growers but there was a distinct tendency for wholesale prices to recover during the remaining period following the outbreak of hostilities in Korea.

3. *March 1951 to January 1952*. The re-entry of India into the market after the resumption of trade in February 1951 intensified the rise in jute prices, as Indian mills tried to cover long-deferred requirements, while non-Indian customers bought a record

---

Publications, Series No. 1, 1956. Dr. Sadeque develops the thesis that a large unrequited export balance was the primary cause of inflation in East Bengal, not only in this but also in subsequent periods. For a penetrating review of this thesis *see Pakistan Economic Journal*, November 1954, pp. 396–405.

TABLE 38
Price Trends in East Pakistan

Year	Rice		Jute		Working-Class Cost of Living Narayanganj (1948-49 =100)	Gov't Employees Cost of Living Dacca (1954-55 =100)	Institute of Development Economics Index (1951-52 =100)
	Harvest (1951-52=100)	Wholesale	Harvest (1948-49=100)	Wholesale			
0-51	—	83	63	101	98	—	—
1-52	100	100	85	101	105	—	100
2-53	88	101	34	47	109	—	96
3-54	59	76	50	65	102	—	76
4-55	50	54	52	67	88	—	59
5-56	82	86	62	82	105	100	83
6-57	105	116	82	98	109	108	118
7-58	117	117	68	91	116	116	113
8-59	109	125	54	82	117	111	119
9-60	152	132	64	99	123	117	125
0-61	116	121	170	181	123	116	119
1-62	n.a.	122	62	129	128	120	n.a.
2-63	n.a.	109	n.a.	115	132	n.a.	n.a.

Source: Central Statistical Office and fn. 1, p. 186.

quantity for stock-piling purposes. The early part of the 1951–2 season maintained the bullish trend, jute export prices reaching a peak of Rs. 238 per bale in July–September 1951. Rice prices continued to maintain a steady level. The over-all balance of trade surplus rose to Rs. 703·6 million in 1950–1, but was lower at Rs. 295·4 million in 1951–2.

4. *February 1952 to June 1953.* As the 1951–2 jute season progressed, it became apparent that Indian purchases of raw jute in Pakistan markets were declining, as were those of non-Indian manufacturers. The result was a sharp decline in raw jute prices to Rs. 108·2 per bale, less than a year after they had touched their post-Partition peak. A price-support programme was inaugurated, but difficulties in absorbing jute offerings in the internal market and selling them overseas led to a reduction in the support price from Rs. 23 to Rs. 17 per maund (bottom quality) in the middle of 1952, while the export duty was cut to less than half. This revived demand to some extent, but a large crop in 1952–3, coupled with a large carry-over, led to a decline in domestic market prices and distress sales were reported at the lowest prices since Partition. Rice prices were steady and the reviving foreign demand for jute towards the end of the season brought an improvement in its price.

5. *July 1953 to June 1955*. A growing shortage of manufactured goods was the major price influence in the eastern wing as it was in the west. However, since many of the new industries (especially cotton, textiles, soap, hosiery goods, etc.) were located in the western wing, the slight offsetting relief provided to the population of that wing was either absent or took much longer to be realized, as manufacturers turned to East Bengal for markets only after conditions became more competitive in West Pakistan. Hence the period of rising prices lasted longer. A rice deficit persisted until almost the end of 1953 and prices remained fairly high until the arrival of a bumper *aman* crop. Rice prices declined and the province was able to build up an emergency reserve and to declare a surplus of 59,000 tons for export, the first time in its history. The removal of the jute licensing fee of Rs. 2·5 on exports to India and the expectation of a smaller crop revived overseas demand and prices ruled somewhat higher. With the coming of floods—the worst the province had experienced—prices rose.

As the floods receded and conditions returned to normal, the price level might have been expected to decline. Rice prices were brought down as the underlying situation (despite a smaller crop) was one of surplus. Jute prices, however, continued to rise until early in 1955 and then relapsed in expectation of a bumper crop. A rising supply of manufactured goods began arriving from the western wing, and while scarcity of foreign goods continued, it was alleviated to the extent of flood-relief aid (mainly drugs and textiles) distributed by the U.S.A. The budgetary factor remained inflationary, the revenue deficit in 1954–5 being slightly less than in fiscal 1953–4, while large disbursements for state trading were financed by increasing the floating debt owed to commercial banks. The surplus in trade was higher in 1954–5 at Rs. 315·1 million compared with the past three years.

6. *July 1955 to June 1958*. This was a period of rising prices, as in the rest of the country. In addition to the effects of devaluation, growing restriction of imports and enlarged deficits on Government accounts, the province suffered from recurrent floods which sharply reduced rice production in 1955–6 and again in 1957–8. With hardly any imports of rice in the former year, prices rose sharply. The better crops of 1956–7 had a moderating tendency in the succeeding year, and imports of rice at an annual rate in

excess of half a million tons were received in both years. Coupled with a subsidy on rice (cf. Chapter X), the net effect was to hold retail prices roughly unchanged for two years. Jute prices, after rising through 1956–7, took a downward turn in 1957–8 as floods early in the season accelerated disposals by cultivators. There was a sharp rise in cloth and yarn prices, however, so that cost of living indexes show a rising trend throughout the three years, while the wholesale price index turned down in 1957–8.

7. *July 1959 to June 1960.* Prices were somewhat erratic in this period, although at the end of the period the levels were somewhat higher than at the start. With the removal of the subsidy on rice, prices rose a little in 1958–9. The crops in that year were again badly damaged by floods, but the effect fell more sharply on internal prices in the following year. Cost of living indexes therefore were either unchanged or declining in the earlier year, and rising markedly in the latter year. Cloth prices as well as other consumer prices were brought down by price controls and their effective enforcement by the new régime. The normal global surplus of the eastern province was converted into a deficit of Rs. 74 million in 1957–8 but in the following year a large surplus of Rs. 214 million was recorded as exports of many manufactured goods from West Pakistan found more profitable outlet in foreign markets, as a consequence of the Bonus Scheme. Raw jute prices were lower in 1958–9, owing in part to larger supplies and a sharp reduction in Indian offtake. In the following year prices improved as production fell and domestic consumption moved up decisively, while jute manufactures were exported at high profits.

8. *July 1960 and after.* There has been a tendency for the price level to stabilize, although the factors responsible for this have been changing. In 1960–61 raw jute prices reached unprecedented levels, following a very short crop resulting from flood damage. The effect of this tended to be neutralized, however, by a perceptible reduction in rice prices as a massive crop of 9·5 million tons was harvested. Jute prices subsided to more normal levels in 1961–2 as a larger crop was marketed. In the case of rice, the level of output remained high but prices did not decline, and this despite a cut in the price of wheat from Rs. 18·50 to Rs. 12·50 per maund in April 1962. Apart from some doubts as

to the accuracy of the data on rice production in the province,[12] failure of rice prices to soften is attributed to the sharp rise in development expenditures in the province, which have increased incomes of classes with a high income-elasticity of demand for food-grains. The high jute prices of 1960–61 would have brought larger money incomes to farmers and stimulated their consumption. As for wheat, it is claimed that the effect of lower prices may have been confined to urban areas where a significant increase in consumption may have occurred at the lowest income levels. The provincial finances have also been greatly strengthened while the growing tempo of foreign aid is clearly reflected in a large global deficit of Rs. 208 million on trading account in 1960–61 and a virtually balanced position in 1961–2. The over-all stability may conceal, however, a rising trend in certain strategic costs, e.g., construction costs are said to have risen by 19 per cent. since 1958 in Dacca, with wage-rates of construction labour going up as much as 35 per cent. in the same period.[13]

---

[12] The marketable surplus may have risen much less than the increase in production because of larger consumption at the farms, i.e., a larger rice crop may generate part of its own demand.

[13] *Economic Survey, 1961–62*, Finance Department, Government of East Pakistan, p. 30.

IX

FEDERAL FINANCE

UNTIL July 1962 Pakistan followed, with some adjustments, the basic pattern of public finance inherited from undivided India. The Centre was responsible for foreign affairs, defence and communications, with concurrent responsibilities in most other fields. The provinces were primarily responsible for law and order, agriculture and social services. Revenue resources were placed under four heads:

(a) taxes levied and retained by the Centre included customs duties on imports, taxes in income and capital of corporations, and receipts from public undertakings administered by the Centre, e.g., railway, posts and telegraphs.

(b) taxes levied by the Centre but divided between the Centre and the provinces included export duties, excise duties (with some exceptions) and taxes on personal incomes other than agricultural.

(c) taxes levied and retained by the provinces included land revenue and irrigation charges, taxes on sales, succession duties on agricultural property, taxes on agricultural incomes, duties on goods and passengers carried by inland waterways, tolls, excise duties (on items exempted from central excises), taxes on employment and professions, mineral rights and entertainment.

(d) taxes levied by the Centre but distributed to provinces, included stamp duties, terminal taxes on movements of goods and passengers by rail or air, succession duties (except on agricultural property). These taxes were provincial sources of revenue but levied by the Centre in the interest of uniformity.

The Niemeyer Award of 1937 spelled out the distribution of revenue from divisible taxes. Provincial shares were prescribed out of the divisible pool of income-tax collections, and the province of Bengal received 62·5 per cent. of proceeds from the jute export duty. In addition, the Award provided for annual subventions to the provinces of the North West Frontier and Sind of Rs. 10 million and Rs. 10·5 million respectively.[1]

Partition led to urgent needs for additional revenues at the Centre. A new administration had to be established and the provinces had to be assisted in caring for an influx of millions of refugees. Defence expenditures rose as relations with India deteriorated following disputes over Kashmir and other matters. Pakistan had to defend the Durand Line which divided the tribal areas in the north-west from Aghanistan. The railways, which had operated on a separate budget since 1921, were included in the general budget. They were overburdened with surplus staff while earnings were impaired by ticketless refugee travelling on a vast scale. 'Strategic' railway lines in the Frontier Province were a net liability, the entire burden for which (about Rs. 12·4 million annually) fell on Pakistan.[2]

While central responsibilities were mounting, revenues were adversely affected by the prevailing economic dislocation. Collections from direct taxes were less than half of what had been expected on the basis of Pakistan's share of undivided India's population. This was in part due to arrears left behind by the evacuees and by the fact that these taxes were collected at the head offices of firms, many of which remained in India. Similarly, central excise duties were collected at points of manufacture in India, although part of their consumption markets were in Pakistan.

The 1948–9 budget imposed new taxes to raise Rs. 101·6 million. The provincial share in income-tax was suspended. The sales tax was temporarily transferred from the provincial list to the Centre. Development grants to provinces were suspended. However, the subvention to the N.W.F.P. was continued, as was East Pakistan's share in the jute export duty. It was agreed that the provinces should leave the raising of public loans to the Centre, which would relend to the provinces.

Following the improvement in the Centre's finances in the wake of the Korean War, the provinces requested a greater share in available revenues. The Central Government responded by

---

[1] The subvention to Sind was discontinued in 1940.
[2] The Partition settlement sought to compensate Pakistan for this liability by reducing the capital-at-charge for the 'strategic' lines.

making *ad hoc* grants totalling Rs. 137 million in 1950–1 and 1951–2. The Raisman Award of 1952

(a) assigned half of the net proceeds of taxes on personal incomes to the provinces, with East Pakistan receiving 45 per cent. of the provincial share after some adjustments;

(b) confirmed the transfer of the sales tax to the Centre but assigned roughly half of the net collections within their respective territories to the provinces.

(c) assigned half of the net proceeds of central excise duties on tobacco, betel-nuts and tea to the provinces on the same percentage basis as prescribed for income-tax.

(d) fixed the basic rate of export duty on jute at Rs. 4 per bale, with 62·5 per cent. of the net proceeds allotted to East Pakistan.

(e) raised the subvention to the N.W.F.P. from Rs. 10 million annually to Rs. 12·5 million and provided for a subvention to be given to the province of Baluchistan, when formed.

Federal Finances and the Constitution of 1962. The Constitution made substantial changes in the distribution of revenue sources and responsibilities. All activities not enumerated in the Third Schedule fall within the competence of the provinces. The Schedule enumerates 49 heads in respect of which the central legislature has exclusive jurisdiction. The most important of these are defence, external affairs, national economic planning and co-ordination, foreign exchange, banking, insurance, shipping, aviation, nuclear energy and mineral oil and natural gas production and/or regulation. The railways become provincial responsibilities. The Pakistan Industrial Development Corporation, which pioneered industrial investment in the public sector, has been bifurcated and assigned to the provinces. Many establishments and institutions in the field of agriculture, education and health have been transferred. Provision is also made for delegation of powers to the provinces even in respect of functions within the executive authority of the centre.[3] To enable the provinces to discharge their enlarged responsibilities they have received powers of taxation in respect of all sources other than those specified in Section 43 of the Third Schedule which covers

[3] *See* Article 143.

(a) customs duties, (b) excise duties, including salt but excluding alcoholic liquors, opium or other narcotics, (c) corporation taxes and taxes on income other than agricultural income, (d) estate and succession duties, (e) taxes on capital value of assets not including taxes on capital goods or immovable property, (f) taxes on sales and purchases, (g) terminal taxes on goods and passengers carried by sea or air and taxes on their fares and freights, and (h) taxes on mineral oil, natural gas and minerals for use in the generation of nuclear energy. Even the central taxes are subject to sharing with the provinces on the recommendations of a national finance commission as approved by the President and subject to review every five-year Plan period. A national Finance Commission was appointed in 1962 and under its recommendations, which replace the Raisman Award from 1962–3, the new allocations to the provinces are as follows:

(a) Fifty per cent. of net collections of income-tax, including corporation tax but excluding the tax on federal emoluments;
(b) Sixty per cent. of the net collections of sales tax and central excises on tea, tobacco and betel-nuts; and
(c) The entire collections of export duty on raw jute and cotton.

The central budget through 1964–5 may be examined in the framework of the above allocation of revenues. There are in effect two budgets—Revenue and Capital. The Revenue budget covers such expenditures as are of a current, recurring and administrative nature and is financed through taxation, surpluses of public enterprises and other current receipts. The Capital budget covers expenditures leading to the creation of 'concrete assets of a material character' or loans and advances to the provinces and local bodies for the same purpose. It is financed chiefly by borrowing, and this is justified by the consideration that expenditures are incurred for asset-building. Foreign aid, both grants and loans, has become an important means of financing the capital budget in recent years. Other financing items for the capital expenditure are transfers to various funds from revenue,[4] the accumulation of various types of deposits left with the

---

[4] Transfers to these funds are shown as an expenditure item in the Revenue budget so that there is, in effect, a larger surplus in that budget than is shown on an accounting basis.

TABLE 39

SHARING OF TAXES COLLECTED BY CENTRE
(In millions of rupees)

	CENTRAL EXCISE			SALES TAX			INCOME-TAX			CUSTOMS		Total Collections of Shared Taxes	Amount paid to Provinces
	Centre	E. Pak.	W. Pak.	Centre	E. Pak.	W. Pak.	Centre	E. Pak.	W. Pak.	Centre	E. Pak.		
1948–49	53·4	0·8	1·6	41·7	18·0	17·4	65·9	—	—	329·2	62·5	590·5	100·3
1949–50	51·5	1·0	2·2	89·4	18·0	34·5	115·5	—	—	422·5	40·5	775·1	96·2
1950–51	67·2	0·8	2·9	71·1	18·0	49·6	132·4	—	—	776·2	67·2	1,185·4	178·5
1951–52	70·9	0·7	3·3	145·1	32·0	73·9	172·3	—	—	821·5	60·0	1,378·7	168·9
1952–53[1]	69·9	12·1	13·7	130·1	27·4	63·0	175·9	14·0	15·8	658·9	43·2	1,224·0	189·2
1953–54	131·6	15·6	18·0	86·5	19·3	52·2	180·7	14·8	16·8	361·0	40·0	936·5	176·7
1954–55	115·5	13·9	16·1	106·0	20·3	64·9	194·1	16·8	19·4	416·1	39·7	1,022·8	191·1
1955–56	135·0	14·6	18·1	137·2	20·2	73·8	214·2	19·9	23·1	557·9	58·1	1,272·1	227·8
1956–57	144·9	17·5	20·4	132·3	25·2	100·9	211·4	19·7	22·9	469·6	45·1	1,209·9	251·7
1957–58	193·7	18·4	21·4	142·7	25·9	99·9	240·4	20·7	24·1	420·5	43·3	1,251·0	253·7
1958–59	264·1	25·1	29·2	170·2	36·2	127·5	234·4	37·8	43·8	493·6	51·7	1,613·6	351·3
1959–60	287·4	21·6	25·2	164·2	33·7	111·1	304·8	24·4	28·3	509·3	47·5	1,557·5	291·8
1960–61	343·4	27·7	30·0	243·6	55·0	168·5	324·4	27·0	31·6	585·0	35·5	1,871·7	375·3
1961–62	339·3	31·5	38·5	242·6	62·1	175·3	373·7	35·2	40·5	670·3	66·2	2,075·2	449·3
1962–63[2]	409·0	52·8	44·9	215·8	139·7	167·1	277·2	123·3	107·8	676·6	45·8	2,300·3	772·7
1963–64RE	601·8	60·5	51·7	273·0	186·8	220·2	297·2	147·5	129·9	747·0	45·9	2,800·6	881·6
1964–65BE	684·0	62·9	53·6	294·5	201·4	237·1	332·6	163·7	149·2	819·0	46·4	3,084·1	954·0

[1] Raisman Award redistributing revenues put into effect from 1952–3;

[2] Recommendations of Finance Commission implemented from 1962–3 (*see* text); West Pakistan also received a share in Customs revenue as total receipts from jute *and* cotton export duties will be distributed exclusively between the two provinces in the ratio of their population (54:45); payment to West Pakistan was Rs. 41·9 million in 1962–3; Rs. 39·1 million in 1963–4 and Rs. 39·6 million in 1964–5. However, figures for 1964–5 do not adjust for tax changes in that year's budget.

Source: Explanatory Memorandum, 1962–63, Govt. of Pakistan.

Treasury under court orders, pre-payment of taxes, earnest monies paid by contractors,[5] recoveries of loans granted in earlier years and the sale proceeds to the public of shares in state industrial undertakings. The commercial operations of Government, e.g. food-procurement, provide net financing in years when sales-proceeds exceed purchases. The residual item is the cash balances of the Government. While it is convenient to examine Revenue and Capital budgets separately, a correct appraisal of central finances requires their combined study.

In view of the constitutional changes affecting the Central Government's share various tax-heads, trends in total revenues collected by the Centre and shared with the provinces are examined before reviewing Central budgets. Table 39 shows the four tax-heads in this category. Customs revenues are the largest source and in the five-year period preceding the First Plan ('pre-Plan' hereafter), contributed more than the other three tax-heads combined. The share declined from 57 per cent. to 39 per cent. in the First Plan period as customs receipts declined and other tax collections rose. Since customs revenues are affected by market conditions for major export products and by the level and composition of imports, the decline reflected the shrinkage in the value of foreign trade, especially exports, in the First Plan period. Export taxes which exceeded half of customs revenue in the boom year 1950–1 had declined to less than one-third by 1957–8 and this trend has continued. Rates of export taxes have been lowered to maintain farm incentives; the tax was cancelled in the case of wool (from 29–4–52), hides and skins (from 1–4–55), *Comilla* cotton (from 12–8–62) and tea (1–7–63). In the case of tea and the staple varieties of cotton, collections dwindled as exportable surpluses were curtailed by rising domestic consumption in the face of stagnant output. While cotton production moved up from 1962–3, rates of duty have been progressively reduced (*see* chapter 1) leaving the jute export duty as the predominant source of revenue. However, in the 1964–5 budget, taxes on both jute and cotton were cut by one-half, and collections may perhaps be down to no more than Rs. 50 million henceforth.

Import duties have risen in recent years, raising over-all

---

[5] The Treasury in effect acts in a banking capacity and receives deposits which it uses much as would a commercial bank.

customs revenue from an average annual rate of Rs. 550 million in the First Plan to Rs. 775 million in the Second Plan period. However, the increase has been less than proportionate to the rise in imports from an average of Rs. 1·9 billion in the First Plan to Rs. 3·6 billion in the four years of the Second Plan ending 1963–4. This reflects in part changes in the structure of imports and in part shifts in the manner of financing imports. Growing production at home of items on which tariffs were 50 to 80 per cent. or higher and their replacement by industrial raw materials and capital goods on which tariffs are 5 to 15 per cent. has led to a net loss of revenue from any given level of imports. Cereal imports pay no duty. The financing of substantial imports through grants from the U.S.A. has not been reflected in customs receipts as import taxes must be credited, under U.S. laws governing grant aid, to the counterpart funds. In 1961–2, the amounts so credited were around Rs. 100 million but this figure has declined sharply as commodity aid has been shifted from grants to loans on which no counterpart deposit obligation applies. With emphasis on the development of a capital goods industry, higher rates of duty are likely. Already this has occurred to some extent in 1964–5 in the context of liberalization of imports of raw materials and capital goods. To reduce the strain on foreign exchange resources following the removal of import licensing on these items 'regulatory' duties were levied at rates of 5 to 10 per cent. *ad valorem*.[6] The 1964–5 budget estimates placed import revenues, before new taxation, at Rs.819 million; after taking account of 'regulatory' duties, collections may exceed Rs. 900 million. Even so, customs taxes yield only 30 per cent. of total revenue from shared taxes at the present time.

Sales tax is next to customs and its growth over the years is perhaps a better measure of the over-all growth of tax revenue, whether derived from imports[7] or domestic output. The tax is payable on an *ad valorem* basis and the general rate has risen from 10 per cent. to 12½ per cent. (in 1961–2) and 15 per cent. (in 1963–4). In 1964–5 a one per cent. increase was made for the

[6] The effective taxation of such imports increased by more than this as sales tax rates were raised through a one per cent. surcharge and a 2 per cent. fee levied on letters of credit, the opening of which was made obligatory. Moreover, sales tax is levied on the duty-paid value of imports.

[7] Sales tax collections on U.S. grant-financed imports were not credited to counterpart funds.

specific purpose of refugee rehabilitation. Lower rates apply to a few items and total exemption is given in the case of many items of essential use such as foodstuffs, salt, edible oils, handloom cloth, ready-made garments and utensils. Establishments with a turnover of Rs. 60,000 or less are also exempted. Collections have risen from an annual average of Rs. 191 million in the pre-Plan period to Rs. 281 million in the First Plan and Rs. 577 million in the Second Plan period. In fact, during the last period, collections have risen at a rate of about 25 per cent. a year to an estimated Rs. 733 million in 1964–5 to which about Rs. 40 million may be added if the rehabilitation surcharge is included.

Central Excises have shown the highest rate of increase, however, of the four taxes under review, their average yield having risen more than fivefold between the pre-Plan and the Second Plan period to Rs. 566 million. Compared to 1959–60, collections have more than doubled—from Rs. 334 million to about Rs. 800 million in 1964–5 budget estimates or at a higher rate than the target of 60 per cent. increase in industrial production in the Second Plan. However, excises are confined to a narrow range of goods. Petroleum and its products account for about 38 per cent. of collections in the latest year, followed by tobacco (22 per cent.), cotton and jute textiles (12·5 per cent.) and sugar (9 per cent.) or an aggregate of over 80 per cent. from these items alone. Other commodities subject to excise include tea, cement, matches, salt, vegetable products, soap and steel products. In many instances, excises have failed to compensate for the lag of customs revenue. This is illustrated by cotton textiles where gross yield (about Rs. 90–100 million currently) is less than the loss of revenue from displaced textile imports (on which peak collections were Rs. 172 million in 1951–2). The loss is greater if account is taken of export duty collections on raw cotton which would otherwise have been exported, and holds true even if direct taxes paid by the textile industry were taken into account. While the range of industrial production has expanded enormously, new excises have been imposed on less than a dozen items. Administrative limitations have been a deterrent to the extension of excises to domestic production in small and widely dispersed units. However, the gradual shift from physical checking by excise staff posted at the factory gate to reliance on documentation may enable a larger revenue potential to be tapped. While collections in 1964–5 may exceed Rs. 850 million, including changes in that year's budget, extension of excises is inevitable if the Government is to capture its appropriate share of a growing industrial sector. Excises are also needed to restrict domestic consumption, releasing some of the output of new industries for export.

The fourth category of shared taxes covers income and corporation taxes. Personal incomes up to Rs. 6,000 per annum are exempted and thereafter the tax rate rises progressively to a maximum marginal rate of 75 per cent. The high exemption limits restricts income-tax to less than one per cent. of the population. Collections have risen from an annual average of Rs. 150 million in the pre-Plan period to Rs. 246 million in the First Plan and Rs. 370 million in the Second Plan period. Corporate taxes are currently levied at rates ranging from 45 to 60 per cent., depending upon (a) the size of the company (b) the place where dividends are declared and (c) the degree of concentration in share-holding. The basic rate for Pakistan-based companies is 50 per cent. with a rebate of 5 per cent. for industrial companies with incomes up to Rs. 50,000 a year and a surcharge of 5 per cent. for closely held companies, i.e. family corporations and others where majority ownership is in the hands of 19 shareholders or less. For companies declaring dividends outside Pakistan, the basic rate is 60 per cent. As for intercorporate taxation, the basic rate is 20 per cent. for companies established before Independence and for all commercial companies. For industrial companies established after Independence, the basic rate is 15 per cent. except that the tax is reduced to 10 per cent. for a Pakistani parent company holding not less than one-third of the shares of a subsidiary Pakistani company. Collections were small in the pre-Plan years (an average of Rs. 37 million a year), reflecting the marked aversion to corporate forms of enterprise among the new entrepreneural class (*see* Chapter 7). In the First Plan period, the average collections were Rs. 68 million and are expected to be Rs. 122 million in the Second Plan period. Even though collections in 1964–5 are expected to reach Rs. 165 million, these are relatively small in relation to the level of corporate profits earned in recent years. The major explanation lies in the liberal tax incentives granted to industry. Total exemptions are granted from taxes on industrial income for varying periods (from two to six years) depending on the location of industry, with the most underdeveloped regions receiving the largest tax holiday. In addition, industries based on indigenous raw material and a list of 30 other industries also qualify for these exemptions, including basic manufactures, transport vehicles and electric appliances and units which export at least 30 per cent. of their production.[8] After the tax holiday period expires, full depreciation allowances are permitted on the original value of capital assets. Whether all this adds up to an unnecessarily low level of taxation on corporate enterprises is examined in a later section of this chapter.

Other taxes which are shared with the provinces are the Estate Duty and the Wealth Tax. These are included under 'income-tax' in Table 39 from 1962–2 onwards. The estate duty has been levied since 1950; the duty relating to agricultural land is paid to the provinces. Similarly, in respect of the wealth tax levied from July 1, 1963, the tax relating to immovable property is paid to the provinces, after deduction of collection charges. While the revenue from estate duty is currently at the rate of Rs.2 to 3 million, the wealth tax may yield up to Rs. 25 million in 1964–5 of which Rs. 10 million would be payable to the provinces.

Central Budget

Total collections from shared taxes have moved up decisively in the Second Plan period to an average rate of Rs. 2,426 million per year as compared with Rs. 1,380 million in the First Plan period and Rs. 1,150 million in the five years preceding the First Plan. The share of the Central Government in these taxes has risen at a lower annual rate from Rs. 970 million in the pre-Plan to Rs. 1,105 million in the First Plan and Rs. 1,750 million in the Second Plan period. The years in which changes occurred sharply are 1952–3 when the Centre's percentage share declined from 85 to 81 reflecting the application of the Raisman Award and again in 1962–3 when the decline was from 78 to 69 per cent. In

[8] Moreover, a rebate of 15 per cent. has been granted since 1964–5 in tax payable by export houses which are incorporated and 10 per cent. in all other cases. In the case of manufacturers who are also exporters a rebate of 10 per cent. is given on taxes attributable to export sales if they range between 20 to 30 per cent. of total sales, rising to a rebate of 20 per cent. where export sales exceed 30 per cent. The value of export sales is reduced by the amount of export bonus earned and no rebate is allowed on raw jute and manufactures, tea and cotton.

that year, the Centre may have lost roughly Rs. 200 million in revenues on the basis of its 1961–2 share. The complete transfer of export duties and the sharing of the corporation tax (including business profits tax) may have cost Rs. 80–85 million. Another Rs. 50–60 million was foregone through the inclusion of Karachi in the 'divisible pool' for computing the sharing of income-tax collections and a similar amount from the reduction of one-fifth in the Central share in sales tax. However, the net loss in overall revenues would appear to have been less because of inter-related increases in non-tax-heads (*see* below). Meanwhile, the buoyancy of revenues led to a resumption of the growth of Central receipts from the shared taxes and in 1964–5 estimates, Rs. 2 billion are expected (*see* Table 40).

Other tax sources are of relatively minor significance. They include taxes and duties levied in connexion with the rehabilitation of displaced persons, provincial sources of revenue from what were until 1962 centrally-administered areas (Karachi) and the tax imposed on gifts after 8 June 1963.

Non-tax receipts cover the profits of the railways until 1961 and other commercial departments (Posts, telegraphs and telephones), interest receipts on loans extended to provincial governments, local bodies, etc., However, the transfer of the railways to the provinces is not a net loss to the Centre, as instead of paying profits the railways now provided a fixed return of 4 per cent. on the total investment of the Central Government. This accounts for part of the increase under 'Debt Service' in 1961–2. A much larger rise in 1962–3 is attributable to the resumption of payment of interest on loans granted to the provinces by the Centre. This resumption was in accordance with a formula laid down by the Finance Commission and incorporated in the *Consolidation and Repayment of Loans Order, 1962*. Similarly, interest receipts accrue from investments in PIDC and other transferred institutions. Total receipts under Debt Service have risen faster than corresponding payments and the net excess has helped to compensate for some of the loss of revenue from shared taxes. In 1964–5 interest receipts constituted a little over one-half of non-tax revenue of Rs. 825 million. Next in importance are Defence Service receipts (Rs. 90–100 million currently) consisting of sales of obsolete stores and supply of civil end-use items by ordnance factories. Other revenues include fees for various administrative

TABLE 40

Consolidated Central Budgets
(In millions of rupees)

	1948-49 1954-55	1955-56	1956-57	1957-58	1958-59 (Annual Rate)	1959-60	1960-61	1961-62	1962-63	1963-64 R.E.	1964-65 B.E.
A: Receipts											
1. Revenue account	1,448·3	1,749·4	1,636·6	1,816·2	2,446·9	2,444·3	2,192·2	2,626·7	2,455·5	2,951·3	3,278·9
1.1 Taxes	(1,127·4)	(1,435·8)	(1,331·4)	(1,525·0)	(1,567·0)	(1,887·7)	(2,094·7)	(2,198·5)	(2,138·5)	(2,662·2)	(2,973·7)
1.2 Commercial depts. (net)	920·3	1,113·2	1,021·8	1,048·3	1,112·2	1,326·2	1,572·4	1,752·9	1,633·1	1,999·5	2,236·7
1.3 Debt services	44·7	94·2	94·5	120·7	106·9	150·4	76·6	34·6	46·9	51·0	53·9
1.4 Administration receipts[1]	66·7	91·4	86·8	117·7	110·5	68·8	67·8	89·2	192·0	372·3	421·9
1.5 Extraordinary and 'other'[2]	73·0	110·0	94·2	121·4	137·3	170·6	194·0	143·1	208·7	186·6	208·8
2. Capital accounts	24·5	27·0	34·1	116·9	100·1	171·7	184·2	178·7	57·9	52·8	52·5
2.1 Accretions to reserve funds	(319·1)	(313·6)	(305·2)	(336·2)	(879·9)	(556·9)	(97·5)	(428·2)	(317·0)	(259·1)	(305·2)
2.2 Recoveries of loans and advances	156·0	129·7	136·3	132·2	409·9	154·3	201·1	396·0	91·8	132·0	176·2
2.3 Sale of PIDC assets and 'other'	54·7	72·9	72·4	130·6	90·1	107·1	7·0	123·5	179·2	122·4	127·3
2.4 Treasury depository functions (net)[3]	8·8	14·1	4·4	3·3	3·7	37·9	53·3	16·0	—	—	—
	47·1	−39·8	92·1	70·1	204·5	257·3	−163·9	−141·3	37·9	34·7	−1·7
2.5 State trading (net)	52·5	136·7	—	—	171·7	—	—	34·0	8·1	—	—
B: Expenditures											
3. Revenue account	1,704·6	2,140·0	2,284·2	2,993·0	2,910·7	3,501·5	3,601·4	3,863·8	4,411·4	5,645·5	6,455·9
3.1 Defence services	(1,115·9)	(1,433·4)	(1,330·7)	(1,521·8)	(1,565·2)	(1,733·8)	(1,775·7)	(1,885·9)	(1,805·2)	(2,465·9)	(2,785·5)
3.2 Civil administration[4]	655·3	917·7	800·9	854·2	797·3	959·9	1,005·3	1,010·1	954·3	1,228·8	1,296·5
3.3 Debt services	249·8	351·3	348·2	397·9	411·0	493·7	475·1	507·8	495·9	595·0	690·4
3.4 Adjustments and provinces	62·8	93·7	125·5	121·3	135·4	202·1	182·8	202·4	241·7	318·2	414·3
3.5 'Other'	36·5	48·9	23·0	36·8	31·6	42·3	26·9	24·7	47·5	47·1	37·5
	111·5	21·8	33·1	111·6	189·9	35·8	85·6	80·8	65·9	276·8	396·8
4. Capital account[5]	(588·7)	(706·6)	(935·5)	(1,471·2)	(1,345·5)	(1,767·7)	(1,826·7)	(1,917·9)	(2,606·2)	(3,179·5)	(3,670·4)
4.1 Defence	122·5	103·4	−23·2	−110·5	40·0	43·6	39·0	13·8	6·4	661·1	—
4.2 Direct development outlay	170·2	379·3	405·3	643·6	663·8	908·5	612·1	732·0	470·1	214·7	939·9
4.3 Loans to local bodies	23·5	38·2	34·4	82·9	75·7	105·5	56·8	80·0	90·6		277·5
4.4 Assistance to provinces	209·1	377·1	340·0	628·2	563·7	563·9	990·4	1,019·9	1,942·3	2,387·2	2,315·7
4.5 State trading (net)	62·3	—	172·6	196·6	—	33·4	52·1	53·9	57·6	16·3	17·6
4.6 Repayment of external debt	1·1	11·5	21·3	30·4	32·3	45·4	41·1			74·9	82·8

	256·3	390·6	647·6	1,176·8	463·8	1,057·2	1,409·2	1,177·1	1,955·9	2,694·2	3,177·0
C: DEFICIT (B–A)	256·3	390·6	647·6	1,176·8	463·8	1,057·2	1,409·2	1,177·1	1,955·9	2,694·2	3,177·0
D: FINANCE OF DEFICIT											
5. Internal debt (net)	(232·4)	(138·6)	(877·2)	(912·1)	(339·0)	(211·3)	(351·5)	(144·2)	(340·2)	(506·6)	(331·8)
5.1 Permanent debt (net)	170·1	55·3	183·1	175·7	78·5	212·0	174·7	22·8	28·9	351·8	195·0
5.2 Unfunded debt (net)	32·5	80·3	97·3	58·4	121·1	93·8	80·4	100·9	105·7	97·8	99·7
5.3 Floating debt (net)[6]	29·8	3·0	596·8	678·0	148·5	−94·5	96·4	20·5	205·0	57·0	37·1
6. Foreign aid and loans (gross)	(19·1)	(14·5)	(39·1)	(64·7)	(506·5)	(691·1)	(1,002·2)	(1,094·2)	(1,618·5)	(2,237·6)	(2,744·0)
6.1 External debt	18·1	14·5	34·3	36·7	411·5	225·8	349·8	432·3	948·9	1,731·9	2,485·2
6.2 Foreign debt repayable in Rs.[7]	—	—	—	—	—	51·7	81·3	123·0	158·8	160·0	140·0
6.3 Local currency grants	—	—	—	—	94·9	413·6	374·1	425·1	339·1	101·4	−80·9
6.4 Other grants	1·0	—	4·8	28·0	—	—	195·0	113·8	171·7	244·4	199·6
7. Use of cash balances (increase—)	79·1	142·4	−158·2	270·6	−354·7	202·0	74·5	−155·6	13·2	−53·3	102·7
E: Difference between (D–C) = Remittance[8] and transfer items (net)	−54·9	−4·9	−110·5	−70·6	−26·9	−47·2	−15·9	94·3	−16·0	−3·2	0·5

[1] Includes receipts for services rendered and stores sold by civil departments, defence services and 'miscellaneous' heads.

[2] Includes 'Currency and Mint' receipts.

[3] Covers all deposits lodged with the Central Treasury including interest-bearing tax deposits, non-interest bearing balances in reserve and depreciation funds, court and revenue deposits, etc.

[4] Includes direct demands on revenue (i.e., tax-administration expenses), civil administration (proper), currency and mint, civil works, pensions, stationery and printing and contributions to the special fund for rehabilitation (of refugees).

[5] Excludes non-cash disbursements of Rs. 47·7 million in 1948–9 for Government subscription in capital and reserves of State Bank, Rs. 542·9 million in 1949–50 and Rs. 148·5 million in 1950–51 transferred in the form of *ad-hocs* to the State Bank to cover rupee losses in book-values of Indian and sterling assets following non-devaluation of Pakistan rupee, Rs. 78 million in 1950–51 as subscription to IBRD and Rs. 320 million to IMF. In 1955–5 Rs. 104·6 million were paid to IMF and IBRD to cover the short-fall in dollar-value of Pakistan's subscriptions following devaluation of Pakistan rupee in 1955–6. Other non-cash disbursements were Rs. 16·1 million in 1952–3 and Rs. 44·6 million in 1958–9.

[6] All non-cash disbursements have been adjusted by reducing 'floating debt' figures on the assumption that the same were 'financed' by issue of *ad-hocs*. Similarly non-cash receipts in the form of *ad-hocs* of Rs. 354 million returned by the State Bank following the rise in the Pak-rupee value of its foreign assets have also been adjusted against 'floating debt'. This item thus covers only receipts from sales of Treasury bills to the market and *ad-hoc* sales to the State Bank for actually financing Government operations; the latter amounted to Rs. 50 million in each of the three years 1953–54, 1954–5 and 1955–6, Rs. 600 million in 1956–7, Rs. 675 million in 1957–8 and Rs. 115·3 million in 1958–9. In 1959–60, *ad-hocs* to the extent of Rs. 100 million were retired by the Government.

[7] Covers loans of 'counterpart' and other local currency funds accumulated from sale of U.S. P.L. 480 and other commodity assistance.

[8] Transfer and remittance heads cover accounting adjustments.

Source: Annual Financial Statements, Government of Pakistan.

services rendered by Government departments and miscellaneous sources. The latter include profits on coinage, Government's share in the profits of the State Bank of Pakistan (Rs. 50–60 million), fees realized under the Imports and Export Control Act (Rs. 10–11 million) and a development surcharge on petroleum products designed to absorb for the State certain reductions in prices of products granted by the international oil companies and designed to yield Rs. 60–70 million currently. (Receipts in 1961–2 were Rs. 92·2 million as they included realization of arrears for the period since August 1959.) Together the non-tax sources provided Rs. 634 million annually in the Second Plan years against Rs. 451 million in the First Plan period. In 1964–5 the share of non-tax heads was 28 per cent. of total Central revenue of about Rs. 3 billion.

Turning to central expenditure, it may be recalled that Central Government responsibilities have largely related to defence, foreign affairs and communications, various social services being the responsibility of the provincial or local bodies. Hence false conclusions on the proportion of the country's revenues absorbed by defence may result if attention is focused on central finances. Thus it is not unusual to find defence expenditures constituting more than one-half of revenue expenditures, although it cannot but be regarded as unfortunate that so much of a poor country's meagre tax revenues should be spent for non-development purposes. In the earlier years, through 1953–4, substantial expenditures on defence were debited to capital account; in 1952–3 there was peak spending of Rs. 211·2 million in addition to Rs. 783·4 million in the revenue budget for a total of Rs. 994·5 million as against receipts on revenue account of Rs. 1,334·3 million. Total defence expenditures were at a level of Rs. 1,000 million in the five years ending in 1962–3 which was probably less in real terms than the pre-1955 spending, because of the devaluation of the rupee in that year. More significant is the fact that the level of spending had apparently stabilized after 1957–8, so that the proportion of growing resources claimed by defence must have been declining in the 1958–63 period.[9]

[9] This may in part be related to the U.S. military assistance programme. Deliveries of equipment and stores under the programme are nowhere shown in the budget, nor the use of counterpart funds to defray local currency expenditures related to it. These expenditures do not represent a claim on domestic

Civil administration, as shown in Table 40, includes a number of heads. These are firstly, expenses involved in the collection of taxes. These constitute a 'direct demand on revenue' and at Rs. 40–50 million amount to less than 2 per cent. of gross collections made by the Central Government (i.e., including the provincial share). The general day-to-day internal administration accounts for roughly Rs. 70–80 million until 1962–3 and Rs. 100 million thereafter. Another Rs. 75 million is paid by way of subsidies and welfare expenditures in the tribal areas of the North West Frontier which have been regarded from the outset as a central responsibility analogous perhaps to Defence. 'External Affairs' account for Rs. 30–35 million and include contributions to U.N. agencies. Expenditure on 'beneficent departments' covers, in addition to direct spending on health, education and other social services in centrally administered areas, grants by the centre to universities, hospitals and cultural institutions throughout the country. However, more than half of the outlay of Rs. 90–105 million under this head relate to two central responsibilities—civil aviation and broadcasting services. The rest of the expenditure is by way of miscellaneous public services or represents transfers to various funds. To illustrate, in 1961–2 there were transfers to the Petroleum Products Development Surcharge Fund (Rs. 92·2 million), to the Refugee Rehabilitation Fund (Rs. 27·6 million), to the Central Road Fund and others. This is expenditure only in a nominal sense for it reappears as a receipt on the capital budget (*see* later discussion).

The third major head of expenditure on revenue account is Debt Service. It has almost quadrupled in the last decade as more internal loans have been floated and external credits received. It covers only interest charges plus a flat appropriation of Rs. 20 million annually to a sinking fund for reduction of debt[10] (raised to Rs. 50 million in 1964–5). Its share in total expenditure rose from 8·8 per cent. in the First Plan to 12·7 per cent. on the average of the Second Plan years and was estimated at 15 per cent. in 1964–5.

---

resources in an aggregative sense. There was, however, a sharp stepping-up in the rate of domestic spending to Rs. 1,250–1,300 million from 1963–4, reflecting in part salary increases.

[10] Repayments of principal by the Centre are shown as expenditures in the capital budget, just as recoveries of principal from other agencies are shown as a receipt item.

Grants-in-aid to the provinces fluctuate annually between Rs. 25 and Rs. 50 million and include subventions to the West Pakistan Government (Rs. 12·5 million) paid prior to integration to the N.W.F.P., grants for flood relief measures, etc. The residual item of expenditure is hard to describe. In some years when it has been notably high (1950–51 to 1952–3), the explanation is found to lie in the use of this head to accommodate the funding of special receipts which accrued to Government through exceptional circumstances. In the past few years the item accommodates identifiable development expenditure in the revenue budget. The amounts involved have risen from relatively modest sums to Rs. 166 million in 1963–4 and are estimated at Rs. 288 million in 1964–5. Moreover, these sums are net of expenditure financed from foreign aid. On a gross basis, the amounts were Rs. 479 and Rs. 646 million respectively. Foreign aid grants were available, for the most part, to finance the Works Programme for Rs. 300 million in 1963–4 and Rs. 400 million in 1964–5.

Finally, 'other' expenditure on revenue account includes losses on state trading in food-grains of about Rs. 110 million in each of the last two years; the losses result from the subsidy on imported wheat of about Rs. 150 million offset by profits on rice during these years.

Turning to the capital budget, the receipts side displays large fluctuations attributable to two items. State trading transactions provide net receipts in certain years as commodity stockpiles accumulated under price support programmes are sold. Hence these receipts are not profits, since the entire operation is expected to be conducted on a non-profit basis. In the past decade there have been 4 years when net receipts have accrued from this source. The other fluctuating item is treasury depository receipts. As explained above, the Treasury serves as banker for a larger number of local bodies, semi-public agencies and individuals. In some years the net outcome is an inflow of cash—in others an outflow, but in either case the amounts involved tend to fluctuate. Table 40 shows this item on the receipts side because in the last decade there were 4 years of cash outflow while in other years there have been net accretions although the amount of receipts has varied from Rs. 38 million in 1962–3 to Rs. 257 million in 1959–60. Recovery of loans and advances is the third receipt item. Since 1953–4 it has ranged around an average Rs. 85–90 million a year. In 1960–1 however, there was a sharp drop as repayment of loans by the provincial governments were temporarily suspended pending a review of federal-provincial financial relationships by a national finance commission. After the *Order* of 1962, receipts rose to Rs. 125 million on the average of the last two years. Sale of PIDC assets covers disinvestment by Government under its declared policy of transferring to the private sector any industrial unit which it may have undertaken to build because private capital was not adequately forthcoming at the time. The only stable receipt item is the accretion to reserve funds which as explained above are transfers from Revenue or from the earnings of the commercial departments for building up depreciation and replacement reserves and for funding budgetary allocations which are not expected to be disbursed within the year. The amounts involved averaged roughly Rs. 200 million until 1960–1. The large increase in 1961–2 represents the proceeds of the petroleum products surcharge mentioned above. The subsequent decline reflects the transfer of the railways and other agencies to the provinces under the 1962 Constitution. Excluding state trading receipts, the Capital Budget may be said to have contributed between Rs. 250 and Rs. 300 million to the financing of capital expenditures in the last few years.

Apart from defence outlays in the earlier years, the Capital Budget is almost exclusively related to spending on development, whether directly by the Central Government or through loans and other forms of assistance to the provinces[11] and local bodies. Table 41 shows the direct capital outlay of the Centre in Part A of the Table, while Parts B and C show the provincial outlays which are substantially financed through the central budget. A sectoral analysis of these outlays is deferred to Chapter XI. Commencing in 1953–4 repayment of foreign loans has gradually become an important item of capital expenditure. It was Rs. 61·2 million in 1961–2 and has risen sharply in subsequent years. Finally, there are net expenditures on state trading for purposes mentioned above.

[11] This is not strictly true in all years. Thus in 1953–4 loans of Rs. 153·2 million were advanced to provincial governments to enable them to repay their immediate outstanding liabilities to the banking system. In 1956–7 Rs. 130 million was sanctioned for flood relief.

The over-all deficit shown in line C of Table 40 is defined as that portion of total expenditures which must be financed either through internal borrowing or through foreign aid and residually through the use of Government cash balances. There is no normative connotation attached to the deficit as here defined. It could be argued that foreign aid financing is merely the counterpart of equipment and other materials secured by the Government from abroad and that but for the availability of such assistance, capital expenditures (and hence the deficit) would have been correspondingly lower. This is not quite the case, as

TABLE 41

DIRECT CAPITAL OUTLAY

(In millions of rupees)

	Annual Average		
	Pre-Plan (5 Years)	First Plan	Second Plan
A: CENTRE			
Railways	91·9	163·7	232·9[1]
Industry	51·1	181·7	76·4
Posts and telegraphs	17·0	50·1	90·9
Civil works	19·6	33·3	34·0
Civil aviation	8·0	20·0	31·4
Irrigation	0·3	11·6	146·6
Other	20·4	112·5	207·8
B: EAST PAKISTAN			
Railways	—	—	167·8[1]
Civil works	37·7	38·9	140·1
Irrigation	11·3	53·5	—[2]
Industry	2·2	2·7	19·5
Town development	—[3]	8·2	41·4
Electricity	—[3]	13·1	—[2]
Other	6·6	12·3	21·0
C: WEST PAKISTAN			
Railways	—	—	189·7[1]
Civil works	35·0	80·7	142·8
Irrigation	90·2	158·7	173·4[2]
Industry	3·2	—2·8	29·7
Town development	4·6	7·3	14·0
Electricity	32·1	69·3	72·1[4]
Other	2·1	9·7	41·3

[1] Railways were transferred from the Centre in 1962–3.
[2] Expenditure transferred in part or wholly to provincial Water and Power Development Authority and Agricultural Development Corporation.
[3] Included in 'Other'.
Source: Explanatory Memorandum for 1964–5, Government of Pakistan.

will be explained later, especially in respect of the use of the proceeds of aid sold to the private sector. Similarly, in the case of internal borrowing, this source of financing can be regarded as a normal factor in the growth of the community's debt as the economy grows. While borrowing for the purpose of adding to capital assets appears justified, the form of borrowing is of great importance. To the extent that domestic public debt is held by non-banking sources it is not likely to be directly expansionary. It does raise the question of the share which the public sector should have relatively to the private sector in the voluntary savings of the community. However, most of the internal public debt is known to be held by the banking system (line 5.1 in Table 40) and under certain conditions this can have inflationary consequences. This would be 'deficit finance' proper in the sense of net creation of new spending power. This would happen, e.g. on the assumption of a perfectly elastic supply of credit so that net subscriptions to Government loans do not reduce the ability of the banking system to provide finance to other borrowers. This again would be based on two possibilities: (a) that a corresponding increase in banking deposits occurs when Government spends the amounts borrowed and the recipients 'bank' it, or (b) that the banking system is highly liquid and tends to be conservative in its lending policies, so that in the absence of Government loans it would have preferred to hold cash rather than lend elsewhere. While neither assumption would have applied fully to Pakistan in the years from 1952–3 to 1957–8 when Government borrowing from the banking system was expanding rapidly, there is little doubt that this manner of financing was directly expansionary and had undesirable consequences.[12] To the extent that money-creation through the budget was in excess of the amount of savings which the community was prepared to hold willingly in the form of cash balances, the economy was subjected to inflationary pressures. These were translated into balance of payments deficits (discussed in Chapter III) or into price-level increases (*see* Chapter VIII). As quantitative restrictions on imports, physical allocations of domestic output or price-controls

---

[12] These comments do not apply to the years 1948–9 to 1950–51 because a substantial part of the sale of Government bonds in this period either added to Government cash balances or was in replacement of Indian rupee securities previously held by financial institutions.

and rationing pre-empted avenues for spending, excess liquidity accumulated and inflationary pressures were suppressed but not eliminated.[13]

The government that came to power in October 1958 declared that its budgetary policy would seek to balance claims and resources without resort to inflationary financing. It was greatly assisted in implementing this policy by a massive rise in foreign assistance financing from 2·2 per cent. of total central expenditures (i.e., line 6 as % of line B in Table 40) to 17·4 per cent. in 1958–9 (annual rate). The relative share of external resources has risen progressively and is estimated at 42·5 per cent. in 1964–5. The share of internal (non-borrowed) resources has declined correspondingly from 84·1 per cent. to 50·8 per cent. since 1958–9. While the availability of external resources enabled the Central Government to reduce its dependence on inflationary financing, it left unsolved the fundamental problem which such financing has posed—the lack of adequate domestic savings for the public sector. This problem was in some ways intensified by the rising magnitude of aid itself and by the Government's desire to absorb it expeditiously. The willingness to raise taxes was weakened by the apparent lack of need for larger internal resources. In 1962–3 the share of domestic sources in the financing of the budget deficit declined not only relatively[14] but even absolutely.

It was recognized that the failure to mobilize internal resources for financing growing deficits was hardly consistent with the objective of achieving viable development. In 1963–4, a series of tax measures were adopted. Three new direct taxes were imposed on wealth, capital gains and gifts respectively. On net capital assets in excess of Rs. 400,000, a tax was levied at the rate of 1 per cent. on the first Rs. 1 million and at 1½ per cent. on addi-

[13] For two interesting studies of the subject, see Mahbub ul Haq and Khadija Khanam, *Deficit Financing in Pakistan, 1951–60*, Monograph No. 4, Institute of Development Economics, Karachi, 1961 and Parvez Hasan, *Deficit Financing and Capital Formation—the Pakistan Experience, 1951–9*, Special Publications, Institute of Development Economics, Karachi, 1962.

[14] In percentage terms, the share of foreign resources has been rising steadily since 1958–9. The budget figure (line 6, Table 40) is not comprehensive, however, for it does not show foreign aid in the revenue account; in that account it shows mainly under defence and technical assistance schemes. The amounts of the latter are substantial, e.g. Rs. 196·9 million in 1960–1, Rs. 388·6 million in 1963–4 and Rs. 420·9 million in the 1964–5 budget estimates.

tional amounts. Agricultural assets were generally exempted and the exemption was extended in the subsequent year to the assets of private companies; to compensate for the latter exemption, the maximum rate was raised to 2 per cent. on net capital assets in excess of Rs. 3·4 million. A tax on capital gains was levied at the rate of 20 per cent. for companies and registered partnerships and in all other cases one third of the capital gains was added to other income to be assessed at the income-tax rate appropriate to the tax-payer. Gains in respect of immovable property were exempted. A tax on gifts was applied on a graduated basis ranging from 5 per cent. on the first Rs. 50,000 to 30 per cent. on gifts about the value of Rs. 2 million. In addition, the corporate tax rate on closely held companies was raised 5 percentage points above the level for more widely held companies. Indirect taxes were also raised by widening the coverage of excise duties and by increasing rates on existing items; the general rate of sales tax was increased from $12\frac{1}{2}$ to 15 per cent. and customs duties on furnace and diesel oils were raised substantially to bring them in line with higher excises. It was expected that these measures would raise an additional Rs. 300 million in revenue. In the event, collections proved more buoyant and as much as Rs. 400 million were secured. In 1964–5 there were additions to indirect taxes, including the imposition of regulatory duties up to 10 per cent. *ad valorem* on imports which were liberalized and the general rate of sales tax was raised one percentage point for financing the rehabilitation of refugees arriving in East Pakistan. These taxes are estimated to yield Rs. 150 million or more. The total collections from additional taxes imposed during the Second Plan period are estimated at Rs. 1,850 million.

The potential for raising tax revenues is by no means exhausted. The Taxation Inquiry Committee (1960) made a number of recommendations which are still to be implemented, with benefit both to revenue and to equity. In the field of central direct taxation these include lowering the exemption limit for personal income-tax from Rs. 6,000 to levels less out of line with average family incomes in the country, the raising of minimum rate of estate duty and the reduction of tax incentive for new industry. There is enough protection to the domestic industry through the exchange system, import restrictions and tariffs to make it perhaps unnecessary to offer incentives through the tax system except in special cases such as to attract industries to less developed regions. Finally, large disparities in consumption standards follow from inequalities of income and wealth and there may even be scope for taxes on certain expenditures to restrict conspicuous consumption without damaging incentives to work or save. The relationship of financial resources to public sector development programmes as a whole is examined in Chapter XI.

X

PROVINCIAL FINANCE

THE revenue resources available to the provinces and the constitutional responsibilities governing their pattern of expenditures, together with the changes introduced in 1962–3, have been discussed in the previous chapter. The arrangements established by the Government of India Act, 1935, prevailed with few changes until 1962. The Raisman Award did increase the share of the provinces in taxes collected by the Centre, but its keynote was that the scheme of divison of revenues should conform more closely to the Act of 1935. The Unification of West Pakistan Order of 1955 changed the administrative organization of the western wing, but it did not modify the fundamental structure of provincial finance. The Constitution of 1962 assigns much greater responsibilities to the provinces, and a larger share has been assigned to them from central revenues. The distribution of the divisible pool between the two provinces is on the basis of population except in the case of the sales tax, where only 70 per cent. is distributed on the basis of population and the rest on the basis of incidence.

The structure of the provincial budget is similar to the central, with revenue and capital accounts. The former cover administrative services and are financed from provincial taxes, assignment from central revenues and other receipts, including grants-in-aid for specific purposes from the Centre, interest income and fees for services rendered. The latter cover expenditures leading to the creation or purchase of capital assets and are mainly financed through market loans or assistance obtained from the Central Government. Although included in capital accounts, state trading transactions stand somewhat apart. Although expected to be self-liquidating over a period of years, the state trading accounts fluctuate considerably from year to year. An excess of disbursements over receipts is normally reflected in a rise in the debt to the banking system, especially the 'floating debt'.

1. EAST PAKISTAN

On Partition, East Pakistan acquired more than two-thirds of the population of undivided Bengal, but enjoyed less than a third of its revenue. The Permanent Settlement of 1793 froze the Government's share in the produce of the land. To offset this handicap, the province was given a two-thirds share in the central export duty on raw jute in 1937. Its difficulties were aggravated by the award of the Arbitral Tribunal which transferred to it 64·8 per cent. of the liabilities of the undivided province. Its share in the assets of the latter (amounting to Rs. 127·2 million) was not received from West Bengal, nor were large sums due from the Government of India on account of lands and buildings requisitioned during the Second World War.

Revenue receipts in the first seven and a half years ending 1954–5 averaged Rs. 196·9 million, of which about 37 per cent. derived from the province's share in central taxes.[1] Provincial taxes were Rs. 95·7 million and all other receipts accounted for less than Rs. 30 million yearly. In 1952–3 the province secured a larger share in other central taxes, which partly offset the decline in its share of the jute export duty from Rs. 60 million in 1951–2 to a little over Rs. 40 million in 1954–5. However, the dependence on the jute tax rendered the provincial revenues vulnerable to changes in the export market for the province's major cash crop.

From 1955–6, provincial taxes and revenues moved up decisively, averaging Rs. 163·3 million per year in the First Plan period. The largest improvement was under land revenue, which accounts for roughly half of provincial taxes (line 1.2). In 1956–7 all rent-receiving interests were acquired by the Government under the State Acquisition and Tenancy Act of 1950. The revenue demand rose 50 per cent., but collections simultaneously declined to 40 per cent. of demand.[2] There was a sharp rise in 1958–9—on an adjusted annual basis, as the martial law régime moved to collect both current demands and arrears. This level

---

[1] References to line numbers in this section pertain to Table 42 unless otherwise stated.

[2] *Report*, Taxation Enquiry Committee, Vol. I, Para. 619. The proportion of collections to current demand was 96 per cent. in 1950–1.

has been improved upon in subsequent years as the revenue administration has been tightened.

In the Second Plan period, revenue from provincial sources averaged Rs. 354·4 million, of which land revenue contributed Rs. 125 million. There remains scope for further increases in land revenue, as agricultural prices have moved up sharply since 1940 while the effective rates of rent are on a pre-war basis, except for a 25 per cent. development cess imposed in 1959. The average rate of rent was estimated at Rs. 3·75 per acre, but actual rents may range from Rs. 0·75 to Rs. 15 per acre. While part of the difference may reflect different grades of soil, fertility and productivity, it is mostly an arbitrary outcome of historical factors. A cadastral survey, the preparation of up-to-date records of rights and the organization of technically efficient revenue departments are pre-conditions for the fixation of fair rents which bring higher revenues as well as imparting equity to the land tax system.[3]

Other provincial taxes (line 1.3) are stamp duties (including court fees) and registration fees which together provide roughly Rs. 50–60 million yearly. The province levies a tax on net agricultural income at progressive rates, but more than 80 per cent. of the proceeds (Rs. 10 million a year) are paid by the tea-estates on the 60 per cent. of their total income which is assumed to be non-agricultural in origin. (The rest is charged to central income-tax.) Provincial excises contribute Rs. 10–12 million and the remaining receipts are derived from the motor-vehicles tax, entertainment and betting taxes, urban immovable property tax, and an internal tax on jute, which together yield Rs. 20–25 million yearly.

The most important source under non-tax receipts (line 1.4) after 1962–3 is interest receipts (over Rs. 100 million annually) as Government has transferred more funds to autonomous bodies like WAPDA. Improved collections of land revenue also account for higher receipts on interest on arrears. Another head of growing importance is forests, which has yielded Rs. 15 million annually in recent years. It represents mostly the proceeds of timber and other produce removed from Government

---

[3] The problems involved in meeting these pre-conditions are truly enormous. There are as many as 75 million plots of land. It is necessary to prepare records in respect of location, ownership, productivity and rent, respecting each plot. (ibid., para. 621).

	1947–48 to 1954–55 (Annual Rate)	1955–56	1956–57	1957–58
A: Revenue Accounts				
1. Receipts	196·9	288·4	303·8	314·1
1.1 Taxes from Centre	72·7	122·5	117·6	123·2
1.2 Land revenue	31·2	50·8	51·5	67·5
1.3 Other taxes	64·5	59·0	64·8	71·5
1.4 Non-tax heads	26·8	56·1	65·3	44·4
1.5 Grants-in-aid from Centre	1·7	—	4·6	7·5
Expenditures	216·7	285·1	338·5	325·5
2.1 Direct demands on revenue	17·1	30·1	44·7	44·4
2.2 Civil administration	83·6	123·2	182·3	165·8
2.3 Beneficent depts. and civil works	53·8	61·4	44·9	54·6
2.4 Development	23·8	35·6	37·5	46·4
2.5 Debt service	7·5	29·8	22·0	4·5
2.6 Other	30·9	5·0	6·6	9·8
3. Surplus/Deficit (−) (2−1)	−19·8	3·3	−34·7	−11·4
B: Capital accounts				
4. Receipts	13·7	−20·7	12·7	110·4
4.1 Accretions to reserve funds	2·4	17·5	24·7	3·7
4.2 Deposits and remittances (net)	1·4	−44·2	−14·6	98·9
4.3 Recoveries of loans and advances	9·9	6·0	2·6	7·9
5. Expenditures	67·4	62·4	157·3	249·2
5.1 Development outlay—direct	42·8	34·9	94·9	205·8
5.2 Loans and advances for development	14·4	11·5	41·2	27·8
5.3 Repayment of loans	9·7	15·4	20·5	14·9
5.4 Other	0·5	0·6	0·7	0·7
5.5 Less—likely short-fall in development expenditures				
6. Deficit (5−4)	−53·7	−83·1	−144·6	−138·8
7. State trading (net)	−7·1	−16·7	−37·9	−78·1
C: Combined deficit (3+6+7)	−80·6	−96·6	−217·3	−228·3
D: Financing of deficit				
8. Debt raised in the province	16·3	−12·7	−40·5	71·5
8.1 Permanent debt (net)	4·4	—	—	—
8.2 Unfunded debt (net)	1·1	4·1	4·5	6·0
8.3 Floating debt (net)	10·8	−16·8	−45·0	65·5
9. Loans from Centre	66·4	91·8	127·0	210·7
10 Utilization of cash balance (−means increase)	−2·1	17·5	130·8	−53·9

Source: Explanatory Memorandum, Budget of the Central Government for 1964–65.

42

BUDGETS
rupees)

1958–59 (Annual Rate)	1959–60	1960–61	1961–62	1962–63	1963–64 B.E.	1964–65 B.E.
418·3	397·9	447·7	706·1	738·6	1,003·5	1,063·0
137·4	136·1	151·9	194·6	368·0	381·3	480·9
104·4	93·5	108·3	145·5	76·6	145·0	150·0
86·1	100·1	107·3	117·8	119·8	113·6	120·0
81·5	55·0	75·8	87·9	73·9	159·3	179·5
8·9	13·2	4·4	160·2	100·4	204·3	132·0
416·8	378·9	470·9	559·5	639·5	917·1	1,054·5
50·3	57·0	60·0	60·7	73·9	100·9	109·4
155·5	139·9	154·2	122·3	128·0	129·6	141·5
64·8	72·1	139·8	161·7	165·2	280·7	189·3
54·6	74·1	109·8	169·4	137·0	280·7	352·4
86·5	23·6	4·6	7·6	81·8	188·1	225·2
5·1	12·1	2·4	39·8	53·6	42·8	36·7
1·5	19·0	−23·2	146·6	99·1	86·4	8·5
53·8	−13·6	136·9	52·1	136·2	100·9	117·1
92·5	21·1	−9·0	2·8	31·4	37·1	28·2
−49·9	−40·5	127·4	−1·3	81·0	33·4	10·5
11·3	5·8	18·5	50·6	23·8	30·4	78·4
220·2	243·0	361·7	513·4	771·7	1,243·2	1,729·2
173·4	141·2	132·9	221·9	219·0	514·6	566·8
34·2	101·0	208·9	287·7	521·9	941·7	1,123·4
12·0	—	—	—	28·7	32·7	36·8
0·6	0·8	19·9	3·8	2·1	1·9	2·2
					−247·7	−400·0
−166·4	−256·6	−224·8	−461·3	−635·5	−1,142·3	−1,212·1
32·0	2·9	−95·7	181·5	10·6	−57·2	81·0
−132·9	−234·7	−343·7	−133·2	−525·8	−1,113·1	−1,122·6
−8·2	79·7	65·5	−109·5	104·2	48·5	−216·0
—	15·0	2·7	−1·0	30·0	—	45·0
5·4	3·7	6·8	7·7	7·8	8·5	9·0
−13·6	61·0	56·0	−116·2	66·4	40·0	−270·0
141·2	219·5	252·1	294·0	511·3	1,111·2	1,228·6
—	−64·5	26·1	−51·3	−89·7	−46·6	110·0

forests which are quite extensive in the province. Electricity schemes yielded about Rs. 10 million until 1959–60 from sales of power, when the receipts were transferred to WAPDA. Grants-in-aid from the Centre (line 1.5) include normal allocations from refugee rehabilitation and national road funds, and exceptional grants for flood and cyclone relief. There is a sharp rise in 1961–2, following the decision to show all foreign aid grants passed on by the Central Government in a separate revenue account. Mainly for this reason, total revenues, which had taken a decade to double from the 1948–9 level, doubled again by 1961–2. By 1964–5, revenues were about Rs. 1,000 million of which roughly 60 per cent. were transfers from the Centre.

Expenditure consistently exceeded revenues in the first decade, except for two years, when there were small surpluses. Through 1954–5 heavy expenses were entailed by the need to organize a new government and to extend its functions in the face of exceptional problems relating to border control, civil defence, anti-smuggling operations and after 1950 to settlement of refugees; the influx resumed from 1963.

The cost of the collection of revenues (line 2.1) has constituted a relatively high proportion of expenditures in the revenue budget, at least through 1960–61. Collection costs have constituted as much as one-third of provincial tax receipts in recent years. This is largely attributable to the high cost of the Revenue Department, which, apart from collecting rents from occupiers who became tenants of the State, is responsible for reorganizing the estates acquired under the tenancy reform legislation, and for the survey and settlement work connected with assessment of compensation and fixation of rents. If compensation to large holders whose interests were acquired is added, the cost is more. Actual payments for compensation were minor, but they have risen from Rs. 7·4 million in 1960–61 to Rs. 15·5 million in 1961–2 and Rs. 35·4 million in 1962–3. These payments are being phased at Rs. 40 million a year since 1963–4 so that the net contribution of land revenue to financing the budget is likely to be but a small fraction of receipts under this head for the next five years.

Civil administration (line 2.2) has been a heavy burden on the revenues, absorbing over 40 per cent. through 1959–60. The cost of the police establishment has hitherto called for the largest expenditure of funds. It showed a steady rise until 1957–8 when the cost reached a peak of Rs. 61·4 million. Since then it has tended to decline in percentage terms. Beneficent departments and civil works (line 2.3) expenditure were more or less stationary in the earlier years, but have shown a continuous rise after 1955–6, as public welfare services have been expanded under the stimulus of the five-year development plans. The rise is even more impressive under education and public health, if development spending financed from revenues (line 2.5) is included.

From an average of Rs. 50 million in the First Plan period, the annual rate of development spending (line 2.4) in the revenue account has risen to Rs. 166 million in the Second Plan period; in 1964–5, this item was budgeted at one-third of total expenditure.

Debt Service (line 2.5) covers payment of interest plus appropriations for reduction of debt. Repayment of principal is shown in the capital account. Debt service should ordinarily be expected to register a steady increase, in line with the growing public debt incurred for development and other purposes. In fact, it has tended to fluctuate in response to the exigencies of provincial finance. With expenditures on an inflexible upward course, and revenues less elastic, the province incurred substantial deficits on revenue account in most years (line 3). By 1957–8 the net aggregate of deficits had reached Rs. 201·3 million—financed mainly by depletion of cash balances and by the growth of short and medium-term debts owed to the Central Government and the banking system.[4] In 1958–9 the finances improved as arrears of revenue were realized, and debt service payments rose to Rs. 108·1 million. With this temporary gain in revenues exhausted, debt service again declined. From 1958–60 a moratorium was granted by the Centre to both provinces on loans owed to it and the only payments shown in recent years are for interest paid on banking loans and appropriations to sinking funds against market loans.

It is in this context that the recommendations of the National Finance Commission must be set. Apart from the general desirability of using the mechanism of public finance to bring about

[4] From a positive opening balance of Rs. 48·7 million in 1948–9, there was a decline to a negative opening balance of Rs. 115·6 million in 1957–8. The negative balance represented an overdrawn position at the State Bank of Pakistan, i.e., a forced loan from the banking system. In addition, there was a net increase of floating debt, i.e., credits from the commercial banks, by Rs. 85·6 million over the same period.

transfers of resources from relatively developed to less developed parts within a federal estate, the Commission had to find a solution for the specific financial problem of East Pakistan. The application of the principle of sharing the divisible pool of central taxes in the ratio of population (except for sales tax) was distinctly beneficial to that province. Its only loss was that its share in the jute export duty was reduced from 66 to 54 per cent., but as an offset it received a share in the cotton export duty. As against Rs. 194·6 million in 1961–2, the assignment from central revenues rose to Rs. 368·1 million in 1962–3. Simultaneously, it was decided that half of central loans (other than foreign loans) outstanding against both provinces on 1 July 1962 would be written off and the recovery of the balance made in 25 annual instalments with interest at $3\frac{1}{2}$ per cent. per annum. Foreign loans would be recovered at the same rate and in the same number of instalments as specified in the original agreement with the foreign lending agency. This formula reduced East Pakistan's indebtedness to the Centre at one stroke by about 40 per cent. It has been possible, as an outcome of these developments, to resume the debt service in 1962–3 at a level of Rs. 82 million as against Rs. 7·6 million in the preceding year. In 1964–5 debt service was estimated to absorb one-fifth of total expenditure in the revenue budget.[5]

Turning to the capital budget, the most important item is the direct capital outlay of the provincial government on development, as shown in part B of Table 41. For many years the outlay was heavily weighted towards 'Civil Works' as public buildings had to be constructed to accommodate the Government and other institutions at Dacca. There has been a gradual re-orientation in favour of commercially remunerative schemes, e.g., power, irrigation and, more recently, agricultural and industrial development. In addition to the direct outlay on capital account of the provincial government, there have been development loans to local bodies and autonomous corporations (cf. line 5.2) such as the East Pakistan WAPDA, the Inland Water Transport Authority and the Agricultural Development Corporation, which

[5] This includes the payment of a fixed 4 per cent. return by the Pakistan Eastern Railways for credit to the Central Government on their past investments, and interest charges on foreign loans obtained by the railways up to 30 June 1962. The province receives these sums from the railways as a revenue item and merely passes them on to the Centre.

organizations have now become the main executive agencies of the provincial government. Thus, in the Second Plan period the allocations for the provincial government (excluding PIDC, railways and other central projects to be transferred under the new constitution) amount to Rs. 4,540 million.

The province has depended heavily on Central Government loans for financing its development expenditures. In the years ending 1954–5 the direct capital outlay averaged Rs. 42·8 million yearly (line 5.1) and development loans from the Centre were Rs. 29·2 million (part of line 9). In 1953–4 a market loan of Rs. 33·4 million was raised. In the First Plan period, development loans from the Centre aggregated Rs. 734·2 million. This covered the entire direct development outlay of the Government and left Rs. 45 million for relending to the autonomous agencies. A market loan of Rs. 15 million was raised in 1959–60. Unfunded debt contributed Rs. 25 million in the Plan period. The remaining indirect expenditure was met out of accretions to reserve funds.

The Second Plan allocation for the provincial government was Rs. 5·52 billion. Amounts spent up to 1962–3 were Rs. 2·31 billion. In 1963–4 and 1964–5, gross allocations of Rs. 1·71 billion and Rs. 2·05 billion were provided. However, short-falls of Rs. 130 million and Rs. 400 million respectively were indicated in these years, giving aggregate spending of Rs. 5·54 billion in the five-year period. Transfers from the Centre by way of loans and grants were estimated at Rs. 4·36 billion or a little under four-fifths of total Plan outlays. Most of the financing from provincial sources has occurred recently. In 1963–4, this contribution was estimated at Rs. 150 million; it was hoped to raise it to Rs. 370 million in 1964–5.

The capital accounts also accommodate state trading transactions and loans by the provincial government not directly related to development. The provincial government has been a consistent operator in the market for food-grains and has at various times been responsible for trading in imported cement, textiles, iron and steel. Official policy of all Pakistani governments to date has been to leave to the private sector all functions which can be adequately performed by private enterprise. However, imports of food have been on Government account since World War II. The great importance of holding down the cost of living for the poorer sections in the urban areas and ensuring stability in the face of fluctuations in the local production of food-grains has led to the continued activity of Government in the food-grains trade. Since 1959, however, the provincial government has sold food-grains to wholesalers at the main commercial centres, while keeping prices and distribution under control through releases of grain from its own stocks if prices rise. The import of coal and coke, and sometimes of cement, is justified by a different rationale. The railways, Public Works Department, and other Government bodies are the chief consumers of these commodities, and they wish to secure the economies of bulk buying without intermediaries. These transactions are assumed to be run on a 'no-loss-no-profit' basis, i.e., the cost of establishment together with the value of purchases is presumed to be passed on to the consumer through sales at prices which cover all costs. There are large fluctuations in the net value of transactions. This represents in part changes in the value of stocks—of which an accumulation would show up as net disbursement, and vice versa. These fluctuations would be expected to be offsetting and to leave no net disbursement figure over an extended period of time. However, there is a persistent tendency for net disbursements to exceed net receipts, at least through 1957–8, and especially between 1953–4 and that year. This reflects the payments of subsidy on rice with a view to stabilizing internal prices for the consumer in the face of rising external prices for rice, which the province must import from abroad. Through 1957–8 there was a loss of Rs. 108 million in the sale of rice, and although this was partly recouped through profits from the sale of other commodities (e.g., sugar, cement, iron and steel) and partly from grants from the Central Government, net losses nevertheless have been substantial. The losses were absorbed from 1958–9 onwards; the large net disbursement in 1960–1 (Rs. 95·7 million) reflects accumulating stocks which were sold in 1961–2, reversing most of the outflow of Rs. 71·8 million. The State trading accounts also include the cost of construction of new godowns, although expenditures are offset in part by central grants and loans for the purpose. Subsidies on sale of American wheat are substantial but have been absorbed by the Central Government.

The provincial government also functions as a lender to cultivators under various laws (*see* Chapter VI), to its own employees and to others, especially in times of emergency, such as floods. Here again its operations have not been self-financing and recoveries were consistently below advances. From 1947 to 1956–7 the Government had advanced Rs. 80 million more than it collected and the rate of recovery continued to decline until the latter part of 1958–9 when the exclusion of political influence temporarily improved collections. Net expenditures on State trading, money-lending and other non-development operations have been financed in part from central loans, expecially at times when the financial situation was becoming unmanageable, as in 1953–4 and again in 1957–8. To the extent that such loans have been scaled down, the deficits on these accounts have really been met from deferred grants by the Centre. In some years, the function of the Government as banker has provided net receipts (line 4.2). A more consistent source—although a fluctuating one—has been the accumulation of various funds, e.g., for depreciation of assets of public undertakings and repayment of debt or deposits with special funds set up for purposes jointly undertaken with the Centre (line 4.1). Larger receipts in some years reflect such special deposits in funds for flood relief, refugee rehabilitation and social uplift.

2. WEST PAKISTAN

This province was established on 14 October 1955 by the merger of the former province of the Punjab, Sind, and the North West Frontier with the Princely States and the centrally administered territories in Baluchistan and the frontier regions. Of the ten states that acceded to Pakistan at Independence, six (Kalat, Makran, Las Bela and Kharan in Baluchistan and the riverine states of Bahawalpur and Khairpur) lost their identity in the merger, although their ex-rulers were confirmed in their titles, privileges and immunities and granted substantial privy purses. Four small states in the north (Amb, Dhir, Swat and Chitral) survived and were administered as special areas in a manner similar to the neighbouring tribal areas. The Governor of the province, as the representative of the Central Government, exercises executive powers in these areas, but central and provincial laws do not apply except by express sanction of the Central Government.

	1947–48 to 1954–55 (Annual Rate)	1955–56	1956–57	1957–58
A: Revenue accounts				
1. Receipts	370·7	510·6	613·1	610·7
1.1 Taxes from Centre	55·9	115·6	147·9	149·4
1.2 Land revenue	41·8	75·5	117·5	119·5
1.3 Other taxes	56·2	71·6	78·7	91·7
1.4 Irrigation receipts—(net)	77·6	57·8	48·3	47·3
1.5 Grants-in-aid from Centre	11·9	21·4	67·2	35·1
1.6 Other	127·2	168·7	153·5	167·7
2. Expenditure	374·5	477·3	548·1	614·7
2.1 Civil administration	101·8	122·8	136·7	156·4
2.2 Direct demands on revenue	52·3	30·5	38·6	38·4
2.3 Beneficent depts. and civil works (incl. interest on capital outlay of irrigation)[1]	132·6	200·3	217·6	256·0
2.4 Debt service	27·6	55·8	70·2	68·7
2.5 Irrigation (excl. interest charges)	8·2	20·3	28·0	31·7
2.6 Other	52·0	47·6	57·0	63·5
3. Surplus/Deficit (−)	−4·0	33·3	65·0	−4·0
B: Capital accounts				
4. Receipts	67·7	−43·6	−147·0	27·7
4.1 Accretions to reserve funds, deposits and remittances (net)	61·0	−49·0	−169·6	15·2
4.2 Recoveries of loans and advances	6·7	5·4	22·6	12·5
5. Expenditures	199·8	340·2	300·3	321·3
5.1 Development outlay—direct	134·6	202·8	237·1	273·2
5.2 Loans and advances for development	23·6	28·7	35·9	25·2
5.3 Repayment of loans	31·6	106·7	24·3	19·1
5.4 Other (including 'contingency item')[2]	10·0	2·0	3·0	3·8
6. Deficit (5−4)	−132·1	−383·8	−447·3	−293·6
7. State trading (net)	4·5	110·6	45·3	−22·4
C: Combined deficit (3+6+7)	−140·6	−239·9	−337·0	−320·0
D: Financing of deficit				
8. Debt raised in the province	1·1	−34·5	20·6	33·6
8.1 Permanent debt (net)	7·5	14·8	19·0	−1·8
8.2 Unfunded debt (net)	0·7	6·1	7·2	6·4
8.3 Floating debt (net)	−7·1	−55·4	−5·6	29·0
9. Transfers from Centre[3]	129·1	313·3	152·0	391·4
10. Utilization of cash balance (−means increase)	13·2	−38·9	164·4	−105·0

Source: Explanatory Memorandum, Budget of the Central Government for 1964–5.
 [1] Includes development expenditures (in million rupees): 1961–2–82·2; 1961–2–110·3; 1962–3–157·2; 1963–4 (R.E.)–338·3 and 1964–5 (B.E.) 461·4 respectively.

43

Budgets
rupees)

1958–59 (Annual Rate)	1959–60	1960–61	1961–62	1962–63	1963–64 R.E.	1964–65 B.E.
704·7	804·9	823·2	933·2	1,251·3	1,528·0	1,647·3
156·1	163·0	233·1	243·6	355·0	439·0	473·1
142·8	138·6	133·6	116·0	145·5	74·6	78·2
119·3	122·9	134·6	141·1	203·4	221·4	250·3
40·6	85·6	108·0	100·4	51·3	138·3	137·6
39·2	31·2	23·7	131·2	222·3	289·2	328·2
206·7	263·0	189·2	200·4	273·8	365·5	385·9
702·6	654·3	686·6	781·9	996·8	1,307·5	1,547·7
174·7	174·1	167·3	181·2	219·5	227·6	243·2
45·0	48·5	45·7	50·7	68·4	59·6	62·0
324·6	311·6	368·3	425·0	559·6	754·9	938·9
67·4	22·8	29·3	30·0	67·5	194·3	224·7
32·8	27·9	16·5	22·2	11·3	7·7	8·0
58·2	69·4	59·5	72·5	70·5	63·4	70·9
2·1	150·6	136·6	151·3	254·5	220·5	99·6
40·1	135·1	84·3	147·4	−21·2	237·3	353·0
20·5	119·3	67·5	124·6	−38·0	193·1	296·0
19·6	15·8	16·8	22·8	16·8	44·2	57·0
477·7	495·9	508·9	459·7	765·4	1,428·9	1,575·1
398·3	300·6	357·5	232·9	354·4	683·0	938·8
53·4	188·9	147·2	225·2	357·1	669·7	805·1
21·4	1·4	—	−1·4	40·0	0·9	1·8
4·6	5·0	4·2	3·0	13·9	75·3	−170·1
−437·6	−360·8	−424·6	−312·3	−186·6	−1,191·6	−1,222·1
−28·1	−21·7	38·4	229·1	96·5	−43·3	23·6
−463·6	−231·0	249·6	−390·1	−435·6	−1,014·4	−1,098·9
172·8	0·7	34·0	149·0	−84·1	40·7	68·3
40·1	50·2	18·0	23·4	12·8	19·9	46·2
11·9	11·3	13·6	16·0	19·1	20·8	22·1
120·8	−60·8	2·4	109·6	−116·0	—	—
208·8	209·2	295·6	226·9	570·2	1,034·7	948·1
81·9	21·9	−80·0	−25·8	−50·5	−61·0	81·9

² Adjusted for anticipated short-fall of Rs. 300 million in 1964–5.
³ Includes grants, etc., from the Centre of Rs. 112·7 million and Rs. 52·8 million in 1963–4 and 1964–5.

The data in the consolidated Table 43 are not strictly comparable for different years. Up to 1954–5 they comprise the accounts of the three ex-provinces only. The year 1955–6 includes five and a half months of the post-integration period, so it is only from 1956–7 onwards that data for the whole of West Pakistan are included. Other breaks in the series arise from the merger of Karachi, formerly the federal capital, into the province in 1961–2, and the constitutional changes described in the preceding chapter which became effective with the 1962–3 budgets.

The former Punjab was by far the most important unit, accounting for about 60 per cent. of the over-all revenues prior to 1955–6. Sind accounted for another 26 per cent. The former Frontier Province was the weakest financially and required a subsidy from the Centre which was raised from ten to twelve and a half million rupees annually in 1952–3. The average yearly revenue for the pre-integration period, as shown in line 1 of Table 43[6] was much lower than in recent years. The massive exchange of populations immediately following Independence disrupted economic life and severely limited collections at the same time that large expenditures were essential for the rehabilitation of several million refugees. In succeeding years, revenues rose as tax arrears were realized and refugee farmers settled down to cultivate their new lands. A rise in central revenues between 1950 and 1952, in the wake of the commodity boom, brought a corresponding improvement in the share paid to the provinces from the divisible pool. Land revenue also showed some improvement in the Sind region, because of the sliding scale of assessment which made it responsive to the sharp rise in cotton prices in 1950 and 1951.[7]

Provincial receipts declined in 1952–3 despite the larger assignments of central revenue under the Raisman Award. From Rs. 386 million in that year, revenues gradually rose to Rs. 510 million in 1955–6 as sales of newly irrigated lands increased with the completion of pre-Independence irrigation projects and new taxes were imposed. The first complete year of integration

[6] All line references in this section pertain to Table 43.

[7] Under this system standard rates of tax are worked out per acre for each crop for each assessment circle, but these rates are only used as the basis of assessment in a scale which is related to the average market price of the produce over the immediately preceding harvesting and marketing periods for a given crop. See later discussion on changes in assessment practices.

(1956–7) recorded an improvement of over one-fifth in revenues. In addition to the subvention for the ex-Frontier province, it was decided to make an annual grant of Rs. 10·2 million to West Pakistan to cover net expenditures in Baluchistan and in the Frontier tribal areas previously administered by the Centre. Collections of land revenue rose because this was the chief revenue source in the ex-Princely States. The new province also received grants-in-aid from the Centre to meet some of the losses sustained in the most destructive floods in that region in historic times. The strain on provincial finances increased when the Centre decided to reduce development loans. To meet the short-fall, additional taxes were imposed in 1958–9, including a cess on the major cash crops—sugar-cane, oil-seeds and cotton. The integration of the rates of taxation for motor vehicles and urban immovable property also brought larger revenues as rates were levelled upwards. Stamp duties, entertainment and betting taxes were raised. Collections improved further following the imposition of martial law.

Revenues have continued to rise owing partly to larger assignments of central revenues, and in 1962–3 revenues were in excess of Rs. 1·25 billion. Assignments of central revenues amounted to Rs. 355 million in that year, as the province received a larger share under the Finance Commission's recommendations. However, the province benefited less than East Pakistan, because the population criteria worked against it, although the incidence of tax collection was much higher. The other factors in the increase in revenues in recent years are (1) the merger of Karachi, (2) the receipt of interest from the Pakistan Western Railway on its capital-at-charge, and (3) the decision in 1961–2 to show all foreign aid grants in the revenue budget. (The latter two are reflected in the rise under item 1.6 which covers debt service, foreign grants, fees charged by the beneficent departments for services rendered and extraordinary receipts from the sale of land brought under irrigation, etc.)

An interesting change within the structure of revenues may be noted. Receipts from land revenue (line 1.2) after reaching a peak of Rs. 142·8 million in 1958–59 have declined to Rs. 78·2 million in 1964–5. On the other hand, net receipts from irrigation works (line 1.4) have risen from Rs. 50·1 million to Rs. 137·6 million. These are largely compensating movements, and derive from the application of the 'Punjab System' to the ex-Sind areas. Under the former, land revenue was separate from water rates, which represent a service charge for the supply of irrigation water. In the Sind region both land revenue and water rate were combined into a single assessment rate and shown under land revenue. Now that the rate has been bifurcated, the water-rate component is shown under the heading 'Irrigation—Net Receipts', which has become the most important revenue head in the budget. This is not evident from line 1.4 of Table 43, because the receipts are shown there on a *net* basis—i.e., after deducting the working expenses of the canals, the establishment charges of the Irrigation Department and the interest on capital invested in the canal system. In 1962–3 working expenses were estimated at Rs. 51·1 million and interest at Rs. 95·2 million, so that gross irrigation receipts were roughly twice the figure for net receipts. It is notable that in addition to direct receipts of water charges, the irrigation works receive a portion of the collections of land revenue, on the principle that but for the construction of canals, the land would have yielded very little in crops or revenue.

Turning to expenditure met out of revenue, the cost of administration (line 2.1) absorbed over 27 per cent. of the total in the pre-integration period. The police establishment absorbed between Rs. 50 and Rs. 60 million yearly, while the administration of justice, jails and convict settlements cost about Rs. 20 million per year. If the cost of tax collection is added to that of the civil administration, the proportion of revenues absorbed rises to over 41 per cent.

In order to collect the land revenue, it was necessary to maintain a large collection establishment, reaching down to every village. The Revenue Department is also responsible for the management of Government estates, survey and settlement operations, consolidation of holdings, and land records and registration. Its officials also dispense flood relief and administer *taccavi* loans, and as a result this department, more than any other, personifies the omnipotent and paternalistic '*sarkar*' to the mass of the peasantry. Another department which collects considerable revenue is the Forest Department, but its annual cost of Rs. 10 to Rs. 15 million absorbs almost all the revenues obtained from the 4 per cent. of the provincial land area covered by forests under its administration.

After general administration, the 'beneficent departments' come next in importance, accounting for over 35 per cent. of expenditures met from revenues until 1954–5. In contrast to East Pakistan, this head covers not only education, health and agriculture, but also includes civil works and miscellaneous public improvements.

Debt services appear to absorb less than 7½ per cent. of revenues on the average during the pre-integration period, although by 1954–5 the percentage had risen to about 10 per cent. In addition to interest payments on various loans raised in the market or taken from the Central Government after Independence, the debt service includes the entire liability in respect of the pre-Partition debt of the undivided Punjab (Rs. 314·8 million) which was laid upon the Pakistani province pending its division with the province of the same name in India. While no agreement on the division has been reached, payments of interest plus repayment of principal on maturing loans had amounted to Rs. 136·7 million by 31 March 1956, of which Rs. 71 million represented liquidation of debt. The integrated province assumed a liability of Rs. 243·8 million on the pre-Partition debt, Rs. 166·3 million of market loans raised by the integrating provinces and Central Government loans of Rs. 866·3 million.

Following the unification, expenditures rose but on a different pattern. The total expenditure on administration rose in 1956–7 by Rs. 22 million, compared to the previous year, but this was substantially accounted for by the enlarged territorial responsibilities of the province. The privy purses of the ex-rulers of the Princely States alone accounted for Rs. 5·5 million. The expenditure, including direct demands, stabilized in the region of Rs. 220 to Rs. 230 million, the increase after 1956–7 being mainly in the police and in frontier regions, where public services were expanded to bring them in line with the standards prevailing in other areas. The increase after 1961–2 is due mainly to the merger of Karachi with the province and after 1963–4 to the increase in pay and emoluments of public servants.

In contrast to slow growth under administrative expenditure is the rapid expansion under the 'beneficent departments'. In the five years ending 1959–60, the outlays rose to roughly 43 per cent. of total expenditures met from revenue. Education and health services advanced rapidly to reduce the arrears of neglect in the less developed regions and to meet the rising demands elsewhere. This trend has accelerated and the Second Plan outlay averaging Rs. 610 million a year is roughly twice the outlay in the First Plan years. In 1964–5, these expenditures were budgeted at Rs. 939 million or about two-thirds of the total budget.[8]

Another heading which has shown substantial increases after unification is debt service. The average service burden in the First Plan period was Rs. 75·5 million as against Rs. 34·1 million in the five years preceding, and this was despite the moratorium on central loans which applied after 1958–9. With the resumption of payments in 1962–3, the debt service has risen to Rs. 225 million by 1964–5. This includes interest payments relating to the railways, PIDC and the Karachi Development Authority. The liability would have been greater but for the reduction of total debt of the province as it stood on 30 June 1961, at Rs. 2,219·3 million by a half, excluding the pre-Independence debt and foreign loans. In addition, loans of Rs. 176·8 million for flood relief and rehabilitation have been converted into grants and the same principle is to apply to borrowings of Rs. 258·2 million which were spent in the earlier years on the construction of link canals. Together, this reduced the debt by Rs. 1,340 million to Rs. 879·3 million. However, in the years 1961–2 to 1963–4 Central loans amounted to Rs. 1,760 million and Rs. 895·9 million were expected in 1964–5, so that the debt liability has risen by double the amount of the cancellations granted by the Central Government. The debt service is thus bound to absorb a growing proportion of revenue in coming years, although this must be set against the income from productive investments which have been financed by the loans.

The Irrigation head (line 2·5) covers outlays which are not set off against the gross income from 'productive' irrigation projects (viz., working expenses, the establishment cost) or included in the debt service. For the most part, it represents expenditures on maintenance and repairs of canals for which capital accounts are not kept.

Miscellaneous expenditures (line 2.6) cover a variety of transactions, such as grants to local bodies, to the basic democracies,

[8] However, this includes development expenditures averaging Rs. 230 million a year in the Second Plan period and Rs. 461 million in 1964–5 which may have been booked under other heads prior to 1960–61.

donations for charitable purposes, superannuation allowances and pensions, etc. This item also accommodates emergency operations, since refugee rehabilitation was a major item in earlier years and flood relief in recent years. From roughly 50 million a year through 1954–5, expenditures have risen to Rs. 60 million in the First Plan period and are currently at an annual rate approaching Rs. 70 million.

Expenditures charged to revenue exceeded receipts in most of the earlier years. Through 1954–5 the accumulated deficits amounted to Rs. 31·6 million. Except for a minor deficit in 1957–8 (Rs. 4 million) there have been large surpluses in the post-integration period. The surpluses from 1959–60 to 1961–2 are suspect in the sense that they were made possible by the moratorium on debt service on Central loans.

In the pre-integration period the annual development outlay averaged Rs. 135 million (line 5.1) with another Rs. 24 million spent indirectly (line 5.2).[9] This average conceals a substantial rise over the years. from Rs. 129 million in 1950–1, the first 'normal' year, to Rs. 255·2 million in 1954–5. Direct outlays almost doubled in the First Plan period, to an annual rate of Rs. 250·7 million, while indirect spending almost tripled to Rs. 58 million annually. Irrigation projects have claimed half to three-fifths of the direct capital outlay in this period. This is inherent in the arid geography of most of West Pakistan. In the earlier years, a high proportion of funds was spent on the construction of feeder links to protect against sudden interruptions of supply from headworks in India, by connecting areas dependent upon them to the headworks situated in Pakistan. The rest of the irrigation outlay has been on a series of barrages at Thal, Kotri, Taunsa and Gudu. Their construction, along with the digging of canals and the colonization of lands commanded by the barrages, have dominated the capital budget. More recently there have been growing expenditures on anti-salinity control.[10]

[9] However, part of this indirect outlay, at least through 1957–8, may not be strictly for development, as it covers *taccavi* loans to agriculturists. To the extent that the loans were made under emergency situations, i.e., for refugee and flood relief operations, no productive use was expected. Even where the purpose was ostensibly productive, the funds may have been misapplied (*see* discussion of *taccavi* in Chapter VI above).

[10] The capital outlay on irrigation in the Second Plan period (averaging Rs. 175 million yearly) is only a partial figure as substantial funds have been transferred to the Water and Power Development Authority (WAPDA) and the

Electricity schemes, which were next in importance to irrigation works, until 1958–9 were transferred to the WAPDA budget except for a payment of Rs. 72·1 million in 1961–2. Civil works constitute the third important head of capital expenditure and cover construction of educational and medical facilities as well as roads and Government buildings (see Section C in Table 41). Town development schemes have ranged between Rs. 5 and Rs. 15 million a year as several satellite towns have been constructed to rehabilitate urban refugees and to provide housing and develop plots for the rapidly-growing population in urban areas.

The Second Plan allocation for execution by West Pakistan authorities was Rs. 6,230 million. In the first three years, Rs. 2,657 million were actually spent. The 1963–4 revised estimates are placed at Rs. 1,390 million. The 1964–5 budget provides for Rs. 1,950 million or an aggregate of Rs. 6 billion. However, there is expected to be a short-fall of as much as Rs. 300 million in the last year. Not included in these figures is the provision for the rural works programme undertaken in the province from 1963–4 onwards for which Rs. 250 million was budgeted in the Plan period. Unlike East Pakistan, more funds are spent directly by the provincial departments than through special agencies. However, this may in part reflect a greater reliance on internally generated resources or independent borrowing by WAPDA.

The financing of capital outlays is partially dependent upon provincial resources. Apart from recoveries of loans and advances by the Government, the only other source is the accrual of deposits in the provincial treasury's function as banker. This is an intermittent source, however, and in years like 1956–7 and 1962–3 there have been large withdrawals. This in part reflects deposits of amounts received from the Centre for specific purposes (and therefore funded) and withdrawals from the funds in subsequent years as actual spending is processed through the accounting system. In the pre-integration period there were capital receipts averaging Rs. 61 million a year. In the First Plan period there were net withdrawals averaging Rs. 33 million a year, so that capital expenditure led to substantial deficits on capital accounts,

---

Agricultural Development Corporation. In addition, the works connected with the Indus Basin Settlement are entirely outside the frame of the provincial budget because these are financed under a separate international agreement (see Ch. III).

averaging Rs. 377 million annually. In the Second Plan period there have again been net receipts averaging Rs. 31·5 million a year in recoveries of loans and Rs. 128·6 million through accretions to deposits, including fairly substantial accretions since 1962–3 for retirement of debt. Despite these, the deficits have mounted as development spending has risen. In 1962–3 the deficit increased sharply as a number of activities were transferred to the province, and for which loans were secured in corresponding amounts from the Centre.

State trading has also provided resources in some years, notably through 1956–7, but thereafter there were deficits which reflected in part losses of stockpiled grains due to floods. In the Second Plan period there have been net disbursements, especially in 1961–2. In particular, the raising of the price for sugar-cane paid to growers in 1962 has cut sharply into the profits which the Government used to realize from its participation in the sugar trade.

Combining the surplus and deficits on revenue, capital and state trading accounts, the residual deficit, as shown in Table 43, Section C, is financed through loans raised in the province or from the Centre. In some years cash balances decline, while in others the excess of debt items over the combined deficit, allows for an improvement in the cash position.

In the pre-integration period, debt raised in the province provided little net financing, as there were substantial repayments of principal by the Punjab on its inherited debt. In 1955–6 there was net retirement of floating debt following a large surplus on State trading account. In the remainder of the First Plan period provincial loans were floated and there were net receipts in three years, despite repayment of the pre-Partition debt. In the Second Plan period loans floatations have averaged Rs. 24 million a year. There has been little *net* use of floating debt through 1963. Unfunded debt contributed less than a million rupees annually in the early years, but it has provided amounts increasing from Rs. 6·1 million in 1955–6 to Rs. 22·1 million in 1964–5.

Loans from the Centre have been the main financing item in recent years, as in the case of East Pakistan. In some years the development loans, including the share given to the province out of postal savings and for agricultural improvement, have almost exactly equalled the development outlay in the provincial budget.

In other years, notably 1955–6 and 1957–8, as well as in the pre-integration period, large loans were received for non-developmental purposes, such as refugee rehabilitation, flood relief and the funding of accumulated short-term liabilities of the provincial government, either to the banking system or to the Central Government.[11] Over the Second Plan period transfers from the Centre have almost equalled net deficits as defined in Section C of Table 43.

3. AN OVER-ALL VIEW

A major conclusion of the preceding survey is that the provinces are heavily dependent on transfers from the Centre. Their revenue accounts are substantially financed by assignments from central tax heads and grants-in-aid for schemes of development as well as to meet emergency situations such as flood relief or refugee rehabilitation. Their capital outlays are similarly supported by Central loans. This dependence is to some extent inherent in the dichotomy between financial powers and executive responsibilities in the Constitution. Provinces are made responsible for the greater part of public sector development; the Central Government has the most elastic sources of tax revenue. Moreover, foreign assistance is channelled through the Centre which also has access to central banking credit and to local borrowing from other financial institutions. While recognizing this fact, there is no gainsaying the need for additional sources of revenue.

The failure to raise taxes has meant greater dependence on loans from the Centre, thereby incurring a larger debt service burden, which must be met out of revenues. A recurring liability is also involved in the expansion of the 'beneficent' programmes. These engender current expenditures for the payment of salaries to teachers, medical personnel and technicians, for the upkeep of facilities constructed and similar purposes. A

---

[11] For example, in 1957–8 a loan of Rs. 48·8 million was secured in order to transfer to the Central Government the evacuee property receipts which apparently the provincial government had realized on behalf of the Centre, but had utilized for its own expenditures. The fact that the Central loan was large enough to meet the current deficit and allow an improvement in cash balances, as in 1955–6, 1957–8 and in 1961–2 may reflect no more than the fact that the assistance has to be assured in order to permit the provincial government to retire its borrowings at the State Bank, as reflected in negative cash balances.

majority of the population is too poor to pay for public amenities like elementary education or rural health centres, so these services must be heavily subsidized, if not rendered without charge. The community must pay for them through taxation.

The expenditure of the general administration has been held in fairly tight control, and this is commendable in principle. However, this has involved holding down the emoluments of public servants to levels that bore little relation to their responsibility or their powers. Following the implementation of the recommendations of a high-level Pay Commission in 1963, there has been a decisive rise in the cost of administration.

While the increased assignments of central revenue starting with 1962–3 provide some net relief (i.e., net of larger debt service and the establishment costs of responsibilities transferred from the Centre) and additional revenues may be expected from the existing tax rates, there is undoubtedly need for tapping new sources to meet rising expenditures on both revenue and capital accounts. Table 43 shows the yield of the provincial taxes in recent years. It is evident that land revenue and irrigation yield by far the largest returns. The yield from agricultural income-tax is surprisingly low and in East Pakistan it relates almost exclusively to that part of the income of tea-estates which is arbitrarily designated as being agricultural in origin. In effect, incomes originating in agriculture are not taxed directly. It has been contended that land revenue and irrigation receipts (net) do constitute taxation of agricultural income which is already burdensome because of the absence of any exemption limits and the lack of progressivity in rates. It has also been argued that agriculture tends to be taxed in many other ways, through export duties, through an exchange system which undervalues the foreign exchange earned from agricultural exports, through a system of official price and distribution controls, and through import policies which admit food-grains and agricultural raw materials at low tariffs or none. The total effect of these policies has been to penalize agriculture by moving the internal terms of trade against it. These are weighty arguments, but they leave unresolved the question whether the taxation of agriculture is adequate, even after account is taken of indirect taxation, e.g., excises and sales taxes levied on goods consumed in the agricultural sector and the transfer of incomes from the agricultural

TABLE 44

MAJOR PROVINCIAL REVENUE SOURCES

(In millions of rupees)

	East Pakistan			West Pakistan		
	1960–61	1961–62	1962–63	1960–61	1961–62	1962–63
Land revenue	108·3	112·6	125·0	133·6	68·3	78·6
Provincial excise	10·7	10·5	12·0	20·7	32·7	35·4
Stamps	46·0	42·5	42·5	29·1	31·5	32·8
Registration	11·8	11·2	11·0	3·0	2·6	2·8
Motor vehicles	3·9	3·0	4·0	21·8	26·2	26·9
Forests	14·8	14·4	14·5	24·7	26·8	28·4
Entertainment[1]	6·5	9·3	9·3	15·9	25·8	26·8
Electricity duties	1·1	1·2	1·2	0·8	2·9	0·1
Tobacco vend. fees	—	—	—	0·4	0·5	0·5
Jute taxes[2]	6·9	7·8	7·8	—	—	—
Urban immovable property	1·1	0·9	1·0	12·0	16·0	18·2
Other	4·6	2·6	4·3	5·2	2·1	7·0
Sub-total—taxes	215·7	216·0	232·6	267·2	235·4	257·5
Net irrigation receipts	—	—	—	108·0	161·2	162·9
Debt services	6·2	34·0	58·5	19·4	47·8	134·2
Sale of land, etc.	—	—	—	37·8	56·3	57·2
Service departments[3]	36·5	25·3	41·1	78·2	92·1	70·7
TOTAL	258·4	275·3	332·2	510·6	592·8	682·5

[1] Includes betting taxes.
[2] Includes receipts under the East Pakistan Jute Dealers Registration Act.
[3] Covers Receipts of Civil Administration, Beneficent Departments, Civil Works and Miscellaneous Public Improvements.

to the non-agricultural implicit in the exchange rate system. With almost 50 per cent. of national income originating in agriculture, a low burden of taxation on the sector substantially lowers the State's share in the GNP. It is estimated that in 1964–5 the Government was capturing only about 9 per cent. of the GNP in taxes. The Third Plan Outline suggests a target of 11 per cent. and the Perspective Plan establishes a long-run goal of capturing about 20 per cent. of the GNP in the form of taxes by 1985.[12] A target of this magnitude is wholly unattainable unless ways and means are found to capture some of the increase in agricultural productivity that is bound to result from the process of economic development. Within the agricultural sector itself there exist

[12] Outline of the Third Five-Year Plan (1965–70), Government of Pakistan (August 1964) p. 55.

great inequities in the distribution of income and wealth; e.g., no more than 2 per cent. of land owners command almost one-fourth of the total cultivated area. The improved taxation of this group would not only have desirable redistributive consequences but may even have the effect of forcing them to more efficient use of land. It is important that a system of taxation be devised that would be more efficient in allocative terms, and which would minimize inequities which undoubtedly prevail at the present time, while also providing an elastic source of revenue from the land. In a predominantly agricultural country, this sector must be taxed.

The Taxation Enquiry Committee of 1959 recommended that central income-tax be assessed on all incomes with proceeds from agricultural incomes being paid to the provinces after deducting the costs of collection. It rejected earlier arguments that land revenue was a fair basis for assessment of tax on agricultural income. The long period of thirty to forty years or more which has elapsed since the last assessments make the present rates quite untenable as a measure of ability to pay at the present time.[13]

The commutation prices adopted at most of the settlements represented an average of the Depression years of the 1930's and hence were very low. Prices have risen steeply since then, especially during the war years, but except for the ex-Sind areas, where the sliding scale assessment prevailed, the prices used for computing land revenue are unchanged. The objective of attaining uniformity of tax incidence throughout the province has been met by levelling down the ex-Sind rates instead of by levelling up rates elsewhere. Thus, in 1957, ceilings were fixed in the ex-Sind areas, to the rates which could be applied regardless of price rises. Moreover, all districts of West Pakistan were not assessed at the same time, so that the Government's share in the 'net assets' is still not uniform. The levy of surcharges on the

---

[13] *See* Table in para. 641 of this *Report*, op. cit. Local cesses, at varying rates, have been levied from time to time in certain parts of West Pakistan for the benefit of local bodies, refugee rehabilitation, education, road maintenance, etc. A development cess at a uniform rate of 25 per cent. of basic rates was levied in the Northern region of the province in June 1959 (raised to 35 per cent. in June, 1963). But the basic rates are low: in 1954–5 the average land revenue per acre of cultivated area in the ex-Punjab ranged from under half a rupee in Mianwali (where the last settlement was in 1929) to Rs. 5·62 in Lyallpur, where the settlement was made in 1936.

basic rates in areas where settlements are overdue has reduced this inequity somewhat, but it has by no means eliminated it. In East Pakistan permanent settlement is being liquidated, perhaps too slowly, but a most effective impediment to realistic assessment is the legal bar to enhancement of rent rates beyond 25 per cent. every 30 years, under the State Acquisition and Tenancy Act, 1949. This not only prevents Government from collecting a fair share from cultivators, but is bound to perpetuate inequities, at least for a long period.[14]

The situation with regard to irrigation water rates (*abiana*) in West Pakistan is similar. Water rates are virtually unchanged from 1924 in the ex-Punjab[15] and since 1931–6 in the ex-Frontier areas. On the other hand, the cost of maintenance as well as expansion of the canal system has risen substantially. The rules promulgated under the Canal and Drainage Act of 1873 gave secondary importance to the cost of water supply in the fixation of rates. The Taxation Enquiry Committee enunciated the principle that water rates should be so fixed as to cover full costs. It also recommended the elimination of the practice of crediting about 80 to 85 per cent. of land revenue receipts from canal irrigated land to the Irrigation Department. It regards the theory behind it as 'obviously fallacious' because water rates are a service charge with a determinable cost and should not be confused with land revenue, which is a tax or a quit-rent.

[14] Para. 625, *Report*, op. cit. A similar bar was applied in the ex-Punjab areas under a 1928 law.

[15] The only changes in the ex-Punjab areas were (a) doubling of water rate on gardens in 1954, (b) 50 per cent. increase in inundation canals in 1953, and (c) the levy of charges for supply of additional water in the non-perennial areas. (*Report*, op. cit., para 682.)

XI

DEVELOPMENT PLANNING

THE subject of economic planning was widely discussed in the subcontinent during the Second World War. Public agencies prepared schemes for absorbing defence personnel to be demobilized at the end of the war. The development under way at the time of Independence consisted mostly of these post-war projects, while private investment was in a state of virtual suspension owing to the events leading to Partition. The creation of Pakistan imparted a sense of urgency to the need for forging a national economy out of the two parts comprising the new state.

To start with, the Central Government appointed a Board in 1948 to co-ordinate schemes for development in the *public* sector. The Board was unable to exert much influence as it was frequently bypassed both by applicants and by sanctioning authorities. Its own approvals were given on an *ad-hoc* basis. Until its replacement by a Planning Commission in January 1951 the Board had approved all schemes 'in principle', involving an estimated outlay of Rs. 1,250 million. Following the establishment of a Commonwealth Consultative Committee to promote regional development in South and South-east Asia in 1950, Pakistan submitted a plan for the Committee which examined and incorporated it into the regional 'Colombo Plan', covering the six-year period commencing July 1951. Of the total investment of Rs. 3,050 million, a sum of Rs. 1,700 million was expected to be provided from internal rupee sources. Of the remaining Rs. 1,350 million, external aid was to account for all but the Rs. 150 million to be secured by running down the inherited sterling balances.

The Plan was a hastily prepared list of projects under execution or preparation, which might be completed within six years, if required financing were forthcoming. In some sections, including agriculture, only lump-sum provisions were made. Some important projects, such as colonization of Thal and the generation of power at Rasul, were outside the Plan.

The Korean War created unforeseen problems. While increasing

Pakistan's exports and capacity to pay for imports, it also interrupted the availability of many necessary items. Prices of capital goods rose and financial provisions in the Plan became clearly inadequate. The fear of a possible world war lent urgency to the early completion of some strategic parts of it. A 'Two-Year Priority Plan' was formulated in April 1951, emphasizing an accelerated pace of development in certain industries which would promote self-sufficiency in essential goods and services. Government decided to undertake from its own resources the entire outlay, if found necessary.

Before the implementation of the priority plan had proceeded far, another radical change occurred in the economic situation. The drastic decline in Pakistan's terms of trade at the conclusion of the Korean War coincided with a serious food shortage. As a result shrinking exchange earnings had to be diverted to cereal imports, leaving relatively little for the purchase of development goods. The food shortages emphasized the need for schemes for quickly increasing grain production. Substantial changes in the emphasis and direction of planning appeared inevitable.

A Planning Board was appointed in July 1953, charged with (a) reviewing development activity since Independence, (b) assessing the resources, material and human, which could be made available during the five years commencing 1 April 1954, (c) preparing a National Plan of Development based on the fullest possible utilization of those resources for implementation in a period of five years, and (d) making recommendations regarding the administrative machinery best calculated to assure the successful implementation of the Plan.

First Five Year Plan. The Board was unable to meet the deadline, but in May 1956 it released a draft Plan for 1955–60. The delays were traceable to lack of adequate planning arrangements at the Centre and in the provinces, paucity of statistics and well-prepared schemes and political turmoil. With five different governments between 1955 and 1958, the Plan was not formally approved until May 1958. This lack of political commitment prevented the Plan from functioning as an effective framework for the development that was under way.[1]

---

[1] For an incisive comment on the travails of planning in the years prior to 1959 *see* chapters 2 and 3 of Albert Waterston, *Planning in Pakistan*, published by the Economic Development Institute, IBRD, Johns Hopkins University Press, 1963.

Nevertheless the Plan must be credited with a profound impact on all subsequent efforts. It was the first exercise undertaken in Pakistan to assess expertly the total resources available for development, to determine priorities and to examine schemes in their light and to integrate them into an over-all programme. The Board laid out five objectives for the Plan: (a) to raise the national income, (b) to improve the balance of payments (c) to increase opportunities for useful employment (d) to extend social services and (e) to increase rapidly the rate of development in East Pakistan and in other relatively less developed areas. Of these, the first three were clearly primary objectives. In cases of conflict between the first and third objectives, preference was accorded to the former.[2]

The assessment of resources proceeded at two levels. First there was an aggregative examination of potential *real* resources, as expressed in monetary terms: here the objective to be achieved was financial balance, i.e., 'the avoidance of any serious excess or deficiency of claims in relation to the real resources which could be made available' Second: 'In addition to the requirements of over-all balance it was necessary to adjust the scale and the composition of the development programme to the limitations of supply of certain *specific* resources such as foreign exchange and entrepreneural organizational and technical capabilities.'

While private sector allocations represented only an estimate of what was expected to be achieved under the influence of appropriate Government policies, an attempt was made to allocate resources in the public sector programmes more or less on rational criteria. In allocating resources *at the margin*, three tests were applied. If it was proposed to increase the provision for any particular sector, the first question was: 'From what sectors would the resources be drawn, and what would be the effect of this transfer on the growth of national income?' This was the test of *efficiency* in the use of resources. The second question was: 'Did the administrative organization necessary for the proposed expansion of the particular sector exist?' This was the test of *feasibility* in execution. The third question was: 'If the proposed transfer of resources were carried out, how would it

---

[2] *See* David E. Bell, *Allocating Development Resources: Some Observations Based on Pakistan Experience*, in *Public Policy*, a yearbook of the Graduate School of Public Administration, Harvard University, 1959, pp. 84–106.

affect requirements for specific inputs, and were these input requirements consistent with the expected supplies?' This was the test of *consistency*.[3]

The size of the Plan was placed at Rs. 11,600 million. This included Rs. 1,500 million in public (budgetary) savings, Rs. 5,900 million in private savings and Rs. 400 million in foreign private investment. This left a gap of Rs. 3,800 million to be met through foreign aid and loans. It was emphasized that the achievement of the figure for domestic savings was not to be regarded as 'an automatic and assured by-product of economic growth'. The Plan required an incremental private savings ratio of 10 per cent. of the gross national product and an average ratio of 7 per cent. in the last year of the Plan, whereas the average ratio (gross) in 1954–5 was mistakenly assumed to be no more than 5 per cent.

The Board framed a development programme of Rs. 12,830 million—Rs. 1,230 million larger than the estimated available resources. This deliberate excess was based on the near-certainty that there would be a short-fall in expenditures in some sectors and over-programming of a modest nature was essential to prevent some resources from remaining idle. It was an ambitious Plan, embodying a diversified programme, parts of which required emphasis on sectors of social and economic life which either had been largely neglected, such as health and social welfare, or had received insufficient recognition, such as technical training.

On the basis of experience in the first two years, final spending targets were cut down to Rs. 10,800 million, with public sector outlays estimated at Rs. 7,500 million and private expenditures at Rs. 3,300 million. Table 45 gives certain details of sectoral allocations in the First Plan in comparison with earlier and later Plan periods:

[3] These tests were necessarily subjective in some cases and rather approximate in others because of formidable deficiencies in the data. Cf. Bell, op. cit. Also, Edward S. Mason, *Economic Planning in Under-developed Areas: Government and Business*, Fordham University Press, New York, 1958. For the industrial programme in the public sector, a more sophisticated technique of 'shadow prices' was used. *See* Gustav F. Papanek and Moin A. Qureshi, *The Use of Accounting Prices in Planning Organisation, and Programming for Economic Development*, Vol. VIII, U.S. Papers prepared for the U.N. Conference on the Application of Science and Technology for the Benefit of Less Developed Areas, Geneva, 1963.

TABLE 45

SECTOR ALLOCATION IN DEVELOPMENT PLANS
(percentages)

	Pre-Plan (1950–55)	First Plan	Second Plan Revised	Third Plan Draft
Agriculture	6	7	12	12
Water and power	13	—	19	17
Transportation and communications	14	17	18	17
Industry, fuels, minerals	36	31	27	29
Housing and settlements	22	20	15	11
Education and training	5	6	4	6
Health	3	2	2	2
Social welfare/manpower	1	—	—	1
Works programme	—	—	3	5
	100	100	100	100

Source: Outline, Third Five Year Plan (1965–70) Govt. of Pakistan, 1964.

Expenditures under the First Plan reached almost 90 per cent. of estimates, but the short-fall in real terms was larger.[4] National income rose about 13 per cent. against the 15 per cent. target. Population growth exceeded estimates a wide margin. The rise in per capita income was under one per cent. against a goal of 7 per cent. The foreign exchange gap widened as deteriorating terms of trade and smaller exportable surpluses reduced foreign exchange receipts by Rs. 1,100 million while aid inflows fell short by another Rs. 823 million, so that development imports fell below targets. The most striking short-fall was in the mobilization of domestic resources for capital formation. Against a target of Rs. 6,600 million for domestic saving, the actual amount in terms of 1955–6 prices was Rs. 4,680 million only. As shown in line 11 of Table 46, the rate of saving, in terms of 1959–60 prices, in the last year of the First Plan was actually lower than in 1954–5, so that the average rate of saving declined from 7·2 to 6 per cent. while the marginal rate of savings was negative. While the Plan had called for a surplus in Government current revenues over non-development expenditure of Rs. 1,000 million there

[4] In terms of 1955–6 prices on which the original Plan outlays were presumably based, there was a short-fall of roughly 30 per cent. in Plan implementation. *See* Mahbub ul Haq, *The Strategy of Economic Planning: A Case Study of Pakistan*, Oxford University Press (Pakistan Branch) 1963 (pp. 141–2).

was in fact a deficit of Rs. 28 million as non-development outlays rose excessively in the first three years of the Plan.[5] There was a decline in private savings compared to 1954–5, indicating that the private sector was not enabled to invest all its potential savings owing to a variety of economic controls, in particular controls that impeded its access to scarce foreign exchange resources. In fact the use of sterling balances accumulated during the commodity boom following the Korean war and the availability of deferred payment credits had made it possible for the private sector to import and invest at a higher rate in the five years preceding the First Plan. With these reserves and credit lines exhausted and with foreign assistance largely directed to public sector projects, it proved virtually impossible to find the complementary foreign exchange for private sector investments.

There was an excessive resort to borrowing from the banking system, leading to pressures on prices and on the balance of payments. Price rises, domestic and world-wide, led to much higher project costs so that actual outlays purchased less goods and services per rupee than expected. Naturally, financial implementation does not necessarily indicate effective expenditure, for money may be spent wastefully and expenditure in one sector may be rendered ineffective by failures in connected sectors. There was a serious lack of organizations with adequate staff to prepare or execute projects. Some projects suffered from faulty design and bad costing, with final costs approximately 160 per cent. above original estimates. Out of nine major irrigation projects scheduled for completion in the Plan period, only two were actually completed on time. Even this referred to completion in an engineering sense, e.g., an irrigation dam was ready but colonization measures were delayed or feeder channels were not yet built. Power generation units were in place but the construction of power distribution facilities fell behind so that capital assets built at great cost in scarce capital and foreign exchange resources remained unutilized. Finally, project costs increased because of administrative delays in the budgetary and sanctioning procedures used during most of the Plan period. Delays in

[5] The definition of public saving used in Table 46 is different from that used in the Plan as it includes total domestic resources mobilized by the public sector to finance public investment.

TABLE 46

CHANGES IN GROSS NATIONAL PRODUCT—COMPONENTS AND USES
(In millions of rupees except where specified)
Base: 1959–60 prices

| | 1949–50 | 1954–55 | 1959–60 | 1964–65 | Annual % Compound Rate of Growth | | |
					Pre-Plan	First Plan	Second Plan
GNP at factor cost	24,466	27,908	31,439	40,525	2·3	2·3	5·2
Population (millions)	79	88	99	112	2·2	2·3	2·6
Per capita income (Rs.)	310	317	318	362	0·4	—	2·6
Agriculture	14,669	15,654	16,753	19,895	1·3	1·3	3·5
Manufacturing	1,433	2,220	2,930	4,440	9·2	5·7	8·7
Services	8,364	10,034	11,756	16,190	3·7	3·2	6·6
Public investment[1]	310	610	1,710	3,070	14·5	22·1	12·4
Private investment[2]	780	1,470	1,290	3,070	13·5	−2·6	18·9
Changes in stocks	30	120	430	250	—	—	—
Gross investment	1,120	2,200	3,430	6,390	14·5	9·3	13·2
Gross savings	1,120	1,900	1,850	3,830	11·1	−0·4	15·6

[1] Includes rural works programme.
[2] Includes non-monetized investment.

Source: The Third Five Year Plan (March 1965) Chapter 1.

the approval of expenditures by the Ministry of Finance resulted in retarding work, as when funds were not forthcoming in time to take advantage of construction seasons. In other cases costs increased because of the deterioration of material or because supplies could not be obtained when needed.[6]

Agriculture had priority in the Plan, but results in that sector were very disappointing. Only 52 per cent. of planned financial outlay was actually spent. Perhaps the chief reason agriculture lagged was the shortage of trained technical and administrative personnel. Agricultural vocations have never appealed to the

---

[6] The dominance of the Ministry of Finance had consequences for the planning process which went far beyond project costs. In a sense it undermined the discipline of the Plan by rendering the planning function ineffective. The annual development programmes prepared by the planners were 'honoured in the breach as well as in the observance'. cf. Clair Wilcox, Chapter 3 of *Planning Economic Development*, Ed. Hagen, 1963.

urban-oriented educated classes from which trained personnel are recruited, and this indifference is compounded by inferior pay and living conditions. Cultural inertia inhibited acceptance of change by the poor and illiterate small landholders. Contributory factors were a complex of official policies concerning taxation, exchange rates, prices and marketing arrangements that damaged farmers' incentives and may have turned the internal terms of trade against agriculture.

In complete contrast was the success in industry where the private sector was able to exploit the internal market opportunities created by quantitative import restrictions. In the public sector, PIDC investment met most of the targets in jute, paper, cement, sugar and chemical industries although at much higher cost than anticipated. The growth in industrial production exceeded targets and industry contributed between 35 and 40 per cent. of the increase in national income in the Plan period. However, there was hardly any progress in small and cottage industries. In the allied sectors of fuels and minerals there was again little progress except for natural gas.

Improvements in transport and communications were less consistent. While targets in railways were largely fulfilled in both provinces and in West Pakistan in roads, inland transport in East Pakistan lagged. Progress in education and public health programmes remained well below targets. Private housing construction did well as to luxury dwellings, but public housing fell behind. In fact, private construction probably exceeded Plan targets, reflecting both the inducement to invest in real estate which is characteristic of inflationary environments, and the foreclosing of other investment opportunities by the shortage of foreign exchange.

Despite failure to reach targets in several sectors, accomplishments were not insubstantial compared with progress before 1955. Even in the lagging agricultural sector much was accomplished. After the establishment of a more stable Government late in 1958 many essential recommendations of the First Plan concerning land reform, administrative reorganization, removal of unnecessary and vexatious controls and restrictions on the private sector were rapidly implemented. Government and public both learned to attach importance to the discipline of the Plan.

Finally, the Plan period was useful in overcoming many complex problems arising from the introduction of large amounts of foreign aid for the first time into the economy. By 1960 a substantial aid pipeline was ready to flow and sufficient experience had accumulated in the techniques of administering a development programme in partnership with a plurality of lenders and donors.

Second Five Year Plan

In contrast to its predecessor, the Second Plan was prepared in time and received prompt approval of the Government. A statement of objectives was released in July 1959 and a more complete outline was prepared in January 1960. The 'final' Plan document was released in June 1960. The objectives of the Second Plan differed little from the First. Self-sufficiency in food replaced increased social welfare services in the high priority field, and there was a clearer recognition of possibilities of conflict between objectives. While the maximization of income was given most weight, planning decisions would perforce continue to be made on pragmatic considerations.

The Planning Commission estimated that Rs. 19,000 million were needed for the Second Plan, of which the foreign exchange component would be Rs. 6,500 million. A revision of the Plan became necessary within a year of its promulgation. The signing of the Indus Water Treaty in September 1960 called for supplementary investments in railway capacity and in other fields for implementing the billion dollar programme of works, the financing of which was accomplished outside the Plan. Plan targets were 're-costed' as block provisions in a number of programmes were replaced by detailed engineering and financial studies of projects. It was found that there had been an under-estimation of Rs. 1,250 million, chiefly in the cost of most water and power and some industrial projects. Moreover, the original Plan had been expressed in terms of 1959 prices. Following decontrol of foodgrains and the relaxation of many price controls, domestic prices and money wage-rates rose. International prices for machinery were also rising. Finally, some increases in the size of the Plan were made on the grounds that larger investment outlays (given the capital/output ratio) were needed if the target for a 2 per cent. per annum increase in per capita incomes was to be maintained in the face of the much higher rate of population growth revealed by the 1961 Census.[7]

The estimated cost of the revised Plan was raised to Rs. 23,000 million, the increase of Rs. 4,000 million being distributed as follows: under-provision of physical input—31 per cent.; price increases—43 per cent.; and increases in physical targets—26 per cent. The size of the Plan was frozen at this level and new projects were to be introduced 'only by substitution of existing projects and not by addition to the Plan'.[8]

The foreign exchange component of the revised Plan rose by Rs. 2,500 million; partially because the increase in cost was in sectors which were more 'foreign exchange intensive' (industry, water and power) and partially because import prices of investment goods had risen more than domestic prices as virtually all suppliers of aid 'tied' their assistance to purchases in their own countries. In 1963, a re-classification of imports led to a further raising of the foreign exchange component. Whereas previously all raw-material items were lumped together into a category of 'maintenance' imports, a distinction was introduced between imports used principally by the domestic capital goods industry and those used by consumer industries. On this basis, the foreign exchange component of investment outlays rose to Rs. 13,190 million or from 37 per cent. to 55 per cent. of total planned expenditure.

The revised Plan projected an increase of 24 per cent. in national income. Gross investment was expected to rise from about 10 per cent. by GNP in 1959–60 to 15–16 per cent. in 1964–5. This, however, did not take account of two other programmes which were to run concurrently with the Second Plan. The first was the Indus Basin Settlement Works on which Rs. 3·3 billion were expected to be spent in this period. The other was a programme of Rural Works consisting of labour-intensive, local community projects in the countryside for which

---

[7] According to the Census, population had been growing at an average rate of 2·1 to 2·2 per cent. per annum instead of 1·6 to 1·8 per cent. as assumed in the original Plan. Some experts have suggested that the actual rate of growth may have been even higher, e.g. not less than 2·6 per cent. in East Pakistan and 2·5 per cent. in the West. *See* Krotki: 'Population Growth, Size and Age Distribution', in Vol. III, No. 2 of the *Pakistan Development Review*.

[8] The Second Five Year Plan (Revised Estimates) Planning Commission, Karachi, November 1961.

TABLE 47

FINANCING OF INVESTMENT PROGRAMMES

(In millions of rupees)

	Second Plan		Third Plan Target
	Target	Revised	
A. Five Year Plan	23,000	25,530	} 52,000
B. Rural works programme	1,600	800	
C. Indus Basin	3,300	2,930	—[3]
Total	27,900	29,260	
A. Five Year Plan			
(a) Public sector	(14,620)	(14,030)	(30,000)
Revenue surplus[1]	1,920	2,163	8,600
Net capital receipts	1,400	1,546	2,100
Additional taxation	1,750	1,800	3,000
Local bodies	200	200	300
Deficit financing	nil	911	2,500[4]
Project aid	5,250	2,932	7,000
Commodity aid	3,500	3,306	5,500
PL 480 counterpart funds	600	1,172	1,000
(b) Private sector	(8,380)	(11,500)	(22,000)
Personal and corporate savings	6,180	9,620	19,000
Private foreign investment	600	450	700
Foreign exchange loans	1,600	1,430	2,300
B. Works Programme			
PL 480 counterpart funds	1,600	800	—[5]
C. Indus Basin			
Foreign exchange funds	2,240	1,750	2,730[6]
PL 480 counterpart funds	1,060	750	2,200[7]
Contribution by Pakistan[2]	—	400[2]	125[8]

[1] Including import taxes on commodity aid where applicable.

[2] Includes for Second Plan period, estimated refund of over Rs. 300 million by Pakistan to Indus Basin Development Fund (IBDF) for customs duties, sales and other taxes paid by the Fund.

[3] Total cost of Indus Basin programme to be executed in Third Plan period is not known at present.

[4] Includes Rs. 1,000 million of 'possible additional resources'.

[5] Included with Five Year Plan financing.

[6] Equal to total appropriations in foreign exchange committed by participating nations *less* estimated disbursements in Second Plan period.

[7] Figure mentioned in Table 7 Chapter 6 of Third Plan document.

[8] Covers only appropriation by Pakistan under original agreement less estimated disbursements up to mid-1965. Does not include refund of taxes to be paid by IBDF. Under supplementary agreement, Pakistan has made an open-ended commitment to defray rupee costs not otherwise met.

Source: The Third Five Year Plan, Chapter 5.

Rs. 1·6 billion of PL 480 rupee funds were earmarked. However, this use of counterpart was given lower priority to the Second Plan. If expenditure under these programmes is included, the gross investment target would approach 20 per cent. of GNP by 1964–5. The pattern of financing for the three programmes is shown in Table 47.

The over-all implementation of the Plan has been satisfactory as shown by GNP data in Table 46 and the revised financing estimates of Table 47. During the first four years, national income has risen by 23·0 per cent. and on the basis of evidence concerning agricultural production in 1964–5 the growth target of 24 per cent. for the Plan period is expected to be exceeded, by over 5 per cent. At 5·2 per cent., the annual compound rate of growth is double that of the First Plan. More significant is the decisive rise in per capita income in the face of an annual 2·6 per cent. population growth, in striking contrast with the virtual stagnation of the previous decade. In a sense, this represents a turning point in the growth of the economy as does the 3·5 per cent. annual rise in agriculture. It is notable that per capita incomes rose only when the growth rate in agriculture exceeded population growth. The growth in industry has accelerated after slowing down in the First Plan period with the large-scale manufacturing sector expanding at over 12 per cent. a year. The share of industry in GNP has risen to a level of about 12 per cent. while that of agriculture has fallen to 49 per cent. in 1964–5 as compared with 7 and 60 per cent. respectively in 1949–50. Economic growth still depends heavily from year to year on the vicissitudes of agriculture but there is apparently enough momentum in the other sectors to offset the effects of bad crops (as in 1962–3) and to impart a degree of stability to growth rates.

Fixed monetized investment is estimated to rise to 13·9 per cent. of GNP compared to 8·2 per cent. in the base year 1959–60. Including the Rural Works programme, the percentage increases to 14·8; if stock changes, Indus Basin works and non-monetized investments are added, the figure rises to 18·5 per cent. However, these extra-Plan additions carry an upward bias because their outlays are reckoned at current rather than 1959–60 prices. Even Plan outlays for 1964–5 may fall short of projections, especially in the public sector where actuals usually tend to remain below budgeted estimates. Despite these qualifications there is little question but that gross investment has accelerated quite sharply involving in current rupee terms an outlay in 1964–5 more than twice as large as in 1959–60. Investments in the public sector, on the basis of revised figures, are expected to miss the target of Rs. 14·6 billion by ½ billion. Performance in the private sector is expected to exceed targets. Against the projected outlay of Rs. 8·38 billion, the revised estimates are placed at Rs. 11·50 billion. This represents an aggregate outlay of Rs. 25·5 billion; however, if adjustment is made for intervening price increases, the outlay is probably not far in excess of the revised Plan of Rs. 23 billion which was valued in terms of 1960–1 prices.

The financing pattern that has emerged during the course of the implementation of the Plan has been encouraging. The original intention of financing roughly one-half of outlays from external sources was not realized mainly because of difficulties in attracting projects or utilizing the aid secured. The gap has been covered by a rise in domestic resources, which are now expected to provide 60 per cent. of a larger (monetary) outlay. The average rate of gross domestic savings is shown to have risen from 6 per cent. in 1959–60 to 9·5 per cent. in 1964–5, implying a marginal rate of savings of 22·8 per cent. over the Plan period. (The marginal rate is lower in terms of 1964–5 prices, being nearer to 21 per cent.) There is some obscurity as to the precise deviation of domestic savings data. In the case of public sector saving, the amount equals public investment minus foreign assistance in the public sector. It is not clear whether the same procedure is applied to determining private savings or whether the estimate is independently derived. The problem is important for at least two reasons. External resources have been made available to the Pakistan economy for both investment and other purposes (e.g., military aid). Unless *all* foreign assistance is deducted from the gross investment figures, the estimate of domestic saving is inflated.[9] Secondly if the concept of saving is taken to be the total mobilization of domestic resources, including borrowing from the banking system, the net result is to equate deficit financing with genuine saving. This presumption is certainly found in the case of public sector saving. While the

[9] Cf. John H. Power, 'Two Years of Pakistan's Second Plan', *Pakistan Development Review*, Vol. III, No. 1 (p. 130) for an analogous argument.

Plan had not provided for any deficit financing the revised estimate has Rs. 911 million and there are indications that the actual magnitude may exceed this figure. In the case of private savings, present estimates are about 54 per cent. above the original projections. Here again, there has been very heavy reliance upon bank credit for private sector activity, including investment. While the credit expansion has not produced any serious pressures as yet, reliance upon it for financing investment does raise doubts whether domestic resources are being mobilized in a manner that can be sustained indefinitely, i.e. whether the 10·3 per cent. estimate of gross savings in 1964–5 prices can be interpreted as a trend value of domestic saving effort.

The discussion up to this point has assumed that domestic saving and external resources were substitutes. In reality (as noted in Chapter III), foreign assistance functions in a dual capacity. By relieving the shortage of foreign exchange its function is complementary to domestic savings in an *ex-ante* sense. The fact that the level of investment outlays was maintained despite reduced availability of external assistance means either that it proved possible to transform larger domestic resources, at the margin, into foreign exchange or that the foreign exchange component of investment was reduced. Both factors appear to have been at play. Exports and invisibles rose at an annual rate of 7 per cent. against the target of 3·5 per cent. and are expected to aggregate to Rs. 13·4 billion compared with Rs. 11·3 billion originally projected. Imports and other payments reached Rs. 21·3 billion against the target of Rs. 22·2 billion. Hence, the over-all balance of payments gap has been reduced from Rs. 10·95 billion to Rs. 7·90 billion.

Before assessing sectoral performance under the Second Plan, progress in two general areas may be reviewed viz., employment and regional balance. The planners had assumed originally that some 2·5 million persons might enter the labour market during the period. Apart from proposing to create the 'maximum possible employment' to provide for additions to the labour force and to cover the backlog 'at least partially', there was no quantitative estimate of employment likely to be created by investment outlays.[10] The revised Plan took account of the higher

[10] The only exception was in respect of large-scale and medium-scale manufacturing where average daily employment was expected to increase from

population growth reported by the 1961 Census in relation to per capita incomes but made no reference to its employment implications. It did refer to the extra-Plan programme of Rural Works 'to put the under-utilized manpower of Pakistan to work on nation-building projects by the liberal provision of basic wage goods'.[11] In the event, the net addition to the labour force, on the basis of a more refined interpretation of intercensal growth, is estimated at 4·18 million. The employment potential of estimated investment expenditure and the expected increase in income during the Plan period in the non-agricultural sector is roughly estimated within a range of 1·12 million and 3·27 million, depending upon what numbers are used for evaluating labour productivity, which is taken as anywhere from Rs. 1,175 per additionally employed worker to Rs. 3,433; if the mid-point of the range is adopted, the resulting employment would be 1.67 million.[12] In addition, employment equivalent to 1·7 million man-years is estimated from new cultivated area (0·5 m.), yield improvement (1 m.) and livestock increase (0·2 m.) in agriculture.[13] While the Rural Works programme did not move as rapidly as expected, it was being stepped up in the later years of the Plan, especially in East Pakistan where Rs. 250 million was allotted for 1964–5 as against 150 million in West Pakistan. It has been estimated that it takes much smaller capital expenditure to extend employment opportunities through this programme— about Rs. 600 as compared with as much as Rs. 20,000 per additional worker in industry. Hence some abatement of the rural unemployment problem would have occurred, even though it cannot be precisely qualified. The Third Plan document asserts that 'a major success of the Second Plan was that for the first time the economy grew fast enough to absorb all the additions to the labour force.'[13] However, it also states that of the labour force of 37 million workers in 1965, over 20 per cent. would be idle if the rest were to be fully employed; the total number of persons affected is even larger as unemployment occurs in the form of

---

440,000 in 1959–60 to 620,000 in 1964–5 and by an even larger number in small-scale industries (cf., para. 154, Ch. 9, The Second Plan).

[11] Ibid., Revised Estimates (para. 56).

[12] Cf. S. R. Bose, 'Labour Force and Employment in Pakistan, 1961–86: A Preliminary Analysis', *Pakistan Development Review*, Vol. III, No. 3.

[13] *Third Plan*, Chapter 7.

under-utilization of available rural manpower. The problem is especially acute in East Pakistan where nearly two-thirds of the current unemployment is concentrated.

This brings us to the second general objective of the Plan, viz. the acceleration of development in underdeveloped regions of the country, especially East Pakistan. The regional question is one of unusual complexity and has a unique importance in Pakistan because a majority of the population lives in the less advanced region of the country. It is not possible in the small compass of this chapter to go in any detail into the regional dimensions of the problem of development.[14] Suffice it to note that the disparities go deep into historical conditions, the relative scarcity of fuel and other resources for industry, the difficulty of communications in a predominantly deltaic region, etc. As shown in Table 48, per capita incomes in East Pakistan were about 18 per cent. lower than in West Pakistan soon after Independence. The disparity increased in the decade ending 1959–60 to almost 32 per cent. as a larger flow of immigrant capital, enterprise and technical skills tended to go to the western wing. There seems to be evidence that a *net* transfer of resources from the poorer to the richer province occurred in this period, as indicated by its 'global' surplus in trade (i.e. foreign trade as well as trade with West Pakistan) at least through 1955–6.[15] In effect, the province was 'forced' to save through a pattern of output that was export-oriented and biased against consumption.

The First Plan emphasized the need for accelerating development in East Pakistan but proposed a per capita investment of Rs. 125 in East as against Rs. 225 in West Pakistan in terms of 1959–60 prices.[16] Actual performance turned out to be Rs. 80 against Rs. 205 and per capita income disparities increased; this was especially due to greater failure in private sector investment.

The Second Plan showed much greater awareness of the regional problem and proposed a sharp acceleration in the rate of investment in East Pakistan, especially in the public sector where

[14] For this, the reader is referred to Chapter 4 of Dr. Mahbub ul Haq's path-breaking study on *The Strategy of Economic Planning.*

[15] Whether there was also a net surplus in the balance of payments of East Pakistan cannot be determined because of lack of data on invisible transactions and on capital flows between the two provinces and with the rest of the world.

[16] Haq, op. cit., p. 130–1.

it set aside an allocation four times as large as the estimated actual expenditure under the First Plan.

The performance to date has been markedly successful. Public sector expenditures have risen at more than twice the rate of West Pakistan, from Rs. 675 million in 1959–60 to over Rs. 1·7 billion in 1963–4 (after adjusting for anticipated short-fall). In the case of private sector investment East Pakistan's share is tentatively estimated at approximately one-third of the total; even so, investment has more than doubled from Rs. 300 million in 1959–60 to Rs. 750 million in 1963–4. The over-all increase is about 160 per cent. as against 130 per cent. in the other province. This reflects the strengthening of the administrative base and the increased reliance on semi-public agencies in preference to the slower moving departmental machinery. Foreign consultants and construction enterprises have been injected on a growing scale into the preparation and execution of projects. While this method has its limitations, there is little question but that this has enabled the province to implement a much larger programme in the public sector than appeared feasible earlier. Helped by seasonable weather which has raised rice production to record levels in 1963–4, the investment activity has begun to show results. As shown in Table 48, the annual growth rate has risen from about 2 per cent. in the preceding decade to 5·4 per cent., allowing both a net improvement in per capita income and a rate of growth in 1963–4 slightly higher than in West Pakistan. Hence the basis is being laid for moving towards the national objective enshrined in Article 145, Clause 4 of the 1962 Constitution, viz., to remove disparity in per capita incomes between the provinces.

The sectoral distribution of the Second Plan (shown in Table 45) derived its logic from the emphasis on maximizing income and the subsidiary objectives of attaining 'self-sufficiency' in food-grains and maintaining the rate of growth in industry at levels experienced in the preceding decade. A 24 per cent. income growth, increases of 21 per cent. in food production, of 60 per cent. in large-scale and 20 per cent. in small-scale industry were the primary targets from which allocations for agriculture and industry were obtained. Allocations for infra-structure were dictated by the need for consistency with the primary targets. Allocations for housing and social welfare were kept low to

TABLE 48

REGIONAL GROWTH RATES
(In millions of rupees: 1959–60 prices)

	1949–50	1959–60	1964–65	Annual Compound Growth Rate	
				1949–50 to 1959–60	1959–60 to 1964–65
A. Gross national product[1]					
East Pakistan	12,360	14,945	19,455	1·9	5·4
West Pakistan	12,106	16,494	21,070	3·1	5·0
B. Per Capita Incomes (Rs.)					
East Pakistan	287	278	318	−0·3	2·7
West Pakistan	338	366	411	0·8	2·4
C. Public Sector Investment[2]					
East Pakistan	84	675	1,745[3]	23·5	20·9[3]
West Pakistan	238	1,195	1,755[3]	17·5	8·0[2]

[1] Non-allocable items allocated to provincial accounts in proportion to directly allocable items.

[2] Expressed in current prices and including recurring expenditures on development.

[3] Relates to 1963–64.

Source: The Third Five Year Plan, Chapter 1.

concentrate investments on projects with short-run productivity. The Second Plan did give emphasis to investment in human capital (education and training) which had been badly neglected. While financial allocations were made to reflect these principles, the physical content of the Plan itself could not fully reflect them for several reasons. Firstly, the planners had insufficient knowledge of the direction of private investment; the purpose of sectoral allocations was 'not to tie the private sector in a "straitjacket" but to provide guide-lines for private decision-making'.[17] Secondly, public sector investment was heavily weighted by unexpended appropriations for on-going projects, especially in the water and power sectors. Thirdly, project selection was inevitably influenced, if it was not determined, by the known capacity (or lack thereof) of various organizations to prepare and execute programmes.[18] Finally, with the Plan so critically depen-

[17] SFYP, Ch. 1, para. 43.

[18] 'There is nothing wrong about considerations of administrative feasibility influencing the choice of sectoral allocations so long as the planners keep on

dent on foreign assistance and with aid granted (at least in the earlier years of the Plan) on a specific project-by-project basis, any project which could not attract aid had little prospect of implementation.

TABLE 49

GOVERNMENT FINANCED DEVELOPMENT EXPENDITURE DURING 1960–70
(In millions of rupees)

Sectors	Second Plan Target	Implementation		Third Plan Target[1]
		Total	per cent of target	
Agriculture	2,515	1,918	76	4,670
Water and power	4,140	4,280	103	8,420
Industries, fuels and minerals	1,910	1,685	88	5,280
Transport and communications	2,725	3,069	113	6,300
Housing and settlements	1,885	1,809	96	3,030
Education	955	842	90	2,730
Health	370	357	96	1,330
Social welfare and manpower	120	70	58	240
Total	14,620	14,030	96	32,000

[1] Does not include Rs. 2,500 million for Works Programme; no adjustment is made for expected short-fall.
Source: The Third Five Year Plan, Chapter 4.

Within these limitations, Plan execution proceeded with a fair measure of coherence, although short-falls or excesses were evident in certain sectors in respect of the public sector programme for which data are shown in Table 49. The Plan was lagging distinctly in agriculture and in public industry while exceeding in water and power, transport and communications, with education and health not too far behind. These results are provisional as in the last two years the data are based on budget or revised estimates rather than on final accounts and there have been fairly steep increases in budget allocations under education and health in these years.

Implementation in the public sector has proceeded with greater assurance and care than in the First Plan period. Organizational improvements in planning, evaluation and execution have been

making a consistent effort to build up the capacity of deserving but administratively weak sectors and to contain the more aggressive but less deserving sectors. (Agriculture and education illustrate the former category and railways the latter in current situation of Pakistan.)', Haq, op. cit., p. 183.

made. Plan outlays have been directly tied to the budget on the one hand through the annual development programme and to the allocation of foreign exchange on the other. A Development Working Party, consisting of high-ranking representatives of various ministries and agencies concerned, prepares the annual programme. Since the Ministry of Finance is represented on the Working Party, it is charged with scrutiny and approval of all projects prepared for inclusion in the budget. It is therefore possible with some exceptions for the executing agency to make expenditures within budgetary limits without further reference to Finance. There has been a substantial delegation of powers from the Ministry to financial advisers attached to the executing agencies. The Working Party's insistence on adequate technical and financial preparation of projects has greatly improved the quality of project planning and designing. Similar Working Parties operate in the provinces. There is a growing tendency to engage well-known international engineering and consulting firms to supervise the technical preparation of projects.

An important reform has been the gradual decentralization of executive responsibility. A sharp distinction is increasingly made between policy formulation and executive determination, with the Central Ministries confining themselves exclusively to the former. There has been a corresponding decentralization from provincial government to divisional and district levels. Another major reform is the gradual shift of responsibility for execution from the traditional slower moving Government departments to semi-autonomous public authorities which operate with greater flexibility, energy and independence and develop an *esprit de corps*, so essential for efficient personnel development. Finally, the strong political leadership behind the Plan has facilitated the reorganization of administration, the rationalization of planning procedures and the pursuit of policies that inspire confidence in the private sector.

Performance within individual sectors can be judged from the degree of implementation of physical targets, as shown in Table 50. The outstanding success has been in agriculture where despite lagging outlays, targets for several crops have been met, if not exceeded. While this reflects to some degree the fortuitious intervention of seasonable weather conditions, there is reason to believe that an upward trend has replaced the virtual stagnation of earlier years. The target of a 21 per cent. increase in food-grains was attained but self-sufficiency has eluded the country as the target was set on the basis of a constant per capita intake of grains. The increase of money incomes in the course of development has resulted primarily in higher consumption of food. Judged in terms of the quantum of food imports, the country may have 'receded from self-sufficiency during the last decade'.[19] The production of cotton has moved up decisively to 2·4 million bales in 1963–4. Jute production has continued to fluctuate with changes in the jute/rice price ratio (*see* Chapter I) and with flood conditions, but given normal weather and reasonable prices there is little doubt that a larger production is attainable without difficulty.

In industry, the large-scale sector has registered over-all growth at planned rates and while targets in specific industries may not be reached, the momentum of the industrial programme has been well-maintained, thanks in part to the expansion of the market consequent upon the improvement in the growth rate in agriculture. There remain substantial doubts whether the thrust of industrialization to date has moved the country towards or away from economic viability[20] but at least a base has been laid from which movement in new directions can be launched. The private sector is primarily responsible for industrial growth and it has been greatly assisted by the progressive liberalization of imports and the removal of price and distribution controls. While the Industrial Investment Schedule which lays down specific targets for private industry has proved to be something more akin to a straitjacket than a guide-line, its recent revision is a hopeful augury as is the decision to review the entire array of economic controls still in existence.

In the Water and Power sector, results in raising irrigated area are likely to be substantially short of targets but colonization measures have proceeded with greater efficiency through the

[19] Cf. Annual Speech, Governor, State Bank of Pakistan (September 1964). The Governor states that 'inflexibilities in factor supplies continue to characterize agriculture. A real breakthrough is only possible if agriculture is accorded a larger share in the total investment programme and the administrative machinery is fully geared to the task.'

[20] Cf. John H. Power, 'Industrialization in Pakistan: A Case of Frustrated Take-Off' and A. R. Khan, 'Import Substitution, Export Expansion and Consumption Liberalisation: A Preliminary Report' both in *Pakistan Development Review*, Vol. III, No. 2.

TABLE 50
SELECTED PHYSICAL TARGETS OF SECOND AND THIRD PLANS

	Unit	Base Period Results[1]	Second Plan		Third Plan Target
			Target	Results[3]	
A. Agriculture					
Food-grains	ooo tons	(13,189)	(15,921)	(16,800)	(21,466)
Rice	,,	8,341	10,164	11,000	14,445
Wheat	,,	3,703	4,339	4,157	5,465
Jute	ooo bales	6,000	7,300	6,200	8,000
Cotton	,,	1,666	2,292	2,217	3,500
Tea	million lbs.	54	64	56	74
Tobacco	,,	223	255	233	273
Fruit and vegetables	ooo tons	4,358	4,898	4,450	5,815
Oilseeds	,,	935	1,230	1,171	1,806
Fish	,,	290	360	350	473
Fertiliser use	,,	31	204	194	476
Crop protection	ooo tons	1,280	4,700	n.a.	n.a.
Food-grains storage	ooo tons	1,663	1,841	1,726	2,070
B. Water and Power[2]					
Newly irrigated area	ooo acres	1,080	2,445	2,110	5,540
Improved area	,,	2,740	7,112	7,300	21,700
Power generating capacity (net)	ooo kw.	480	858	553	1,452
Transmission lines (11 kw. and over)	circuit miles	5,000	7,700	7,500	8,000
C. Industries, Fuels and Minerals					
Cotton yarn	million lbs.	380	520	520	720
Jute goods	ooo tons	250	380	365	800
Refined sugar	,,	150	300	312	640
Cigarettes	million units	9,000	15,000	18,500	30,000
Fertilizer (ammonium sulphate)	ooo tons	43.5	55.0	550	2,500
Cement	,,	1,050	3,000	1,600	6,000
Steel	,, ingot tons	nil	nil	11	1,200
Paper and board	,, tons	53	105	116	300
Coal	,, tons	723	1,500	1,500	3,000
Natural gas	million cubic feet	25,750	100,000	80,600	200,000
Petroleum (crude)	ooo imperial gals.	92,000	n.a.	140,000	200,000

D. Transport and Communications					
Locomotives	no. acquired in 5 yrs.	135	217	209	277
Wagons	,, ,, ,, ,,	7,253	14,451	14,000	15,655
Rail (track) renewals	miles renewed ,, ,,	n.a.	1,261	1,141	1,200
High type roads	miles	10,775	14,520	13,300	15,700
Buses and trucks	number operating	25,000	36,000	52,100	63,900
IWT routes	miles	2,800	4,000	n.a.	n.a.
Handling capacity—ports	ooo tons	7,500	9,300	12,500	17,000
Post and telegraph offices	number	10,890	12,490	12,190	14,200
Telephones	,,	75,000	120,700	135,000	285,000
E. Housing and Settlements					
Development of plots, incl. nucleus houses	ooo plots	n.a.	300	150	350
Government employee housing	ooo houses	n.a.	28	n.a.	n.a.
Tube-wells and hand-pumps	ooo wells	n.a.	110	148	200
F. Education					
Primary schools: Enrolment	ooo pupils	4,706	7,246	7,300	13,100
Secondary schools: Enrolment	ooo ,,	1,099	1,529	1,040	2,000
Primary teachers	annual intake cap.	n.a.	9,600	19,000	40,000
Vocational training	,, ,,	n.a.	n.a.	8,300	50,000
Technicians	,, ,,	500	3,900	4,100	14,000
Engineers	,, ,,	400	1,405	1,630	3,300
G. Health and Medical Services					
Doctors	number at end of Plan	9,200	13,000	15,600	19,800
Nurses	,, ,, ,, ,,	2,000	3,500	3,600	5,400
Hospital beds	,, ,, ,, ,,	28,000	36,000	33,000	45,800
Rural health centres	,, ,, ,, ,,	nil	300	200	810

[1] Base period is 1959–60 except in agricultural crops and fish output where a preceding three-year period has been adopted.
[2] Refers to increase in five-year period.
[3] Bench-mark production in 1964–5.

Source: The Third Plan, Chapter 4, Annexure Table: and Second Five Year Plan, Table 3, Chapter 19.

Agricultural Development Corporation in West Pakistan. About 3·5 million acres are expected to be protected against floods and another 1·5 million acres against the ingress of saline waters through construction of coastal embankments in the eastern wing. In the West, about 2 million acres are to be provided with drainage by the sinking of 2,000 tubewells, the laying of 350 miles of open drains, etc. Progress in the installation of electric power capacity has been substantial. About 1,435,000 kw. will be in service by the end of the Plan, although actual generation will be only 39 units per capita against the target of 50 units because of delays in distribution.

In transport, railway and port expansion programmes have proceeded on schedule. For the first time, an effective organization has been created for dealing with the problems of inland water transportation, and while progress may not come up to targets a good beginning has been made for accelerating programmes in subsequent years. In education and health, results have generally tended to fall behind targets, which is in contrast to the almost complete implementation of financial targets; this suggests that project costs may have risen substantially.

A major test of the success of the development process we have been discussing is the improvement in living standards which flows from it. Per capita consumption of food-grains has risen by 17 per cent. in the seven years ending 1961–2, of cotton fabrics by 20 per cent., of raw sugar by 22 per cent., of tea by 64 per cent. and of paper by about 200 per cent. But there is a long way to go. The average consumption of food remains below minimum nutrition requirements. Cloth consumption is about 14 yards per capita. Housing is deficient—with a shortage estimated at roughly a million dwellings in the urban areas alone. No more than 15 per cent. of the population is literate; potable water-supply is available to about 6 per cent. and only 45 per cent. of primary school age children are in school. The backlog of unemployment has mounted over the years. The balance of payments gap is far from being bridged. The rate of gross savings is no more than half of investment and net savings must be in the range of 6 to 7 per cent. Expectations of 'take-off into self-sustaining growth' have little meaning at the end of the Second or even the next few Plan periods.

These problems are most meaningfully examined within the

framework of a 'perspective plan' having a time-horizon as long as twenty years. The preparation of the Third Plan has proceeded within such a framework. At the time of writing (early 1965) it is not possible to comment on the Third Plan as its content is not yet firm.[21] It may be viewed as the first step in an exercise (*see* Table 51), which is predicated on the proposition that the level of national income is quadrupled over the expected 1965 level by the end of the Sixth Plan period (i.e., by 1985). In order to achieve these targets, the annual rate of growth would have to rise from 5·2 per cent. during the Second Plan period to 6·5 per cent. during the Third Plan period and $7\frac{1}{2}$ per cent. in the Sixth Plan period. If the growth of population can be slowed to an average of 2·1 per cent. per annum, per capita income at the end of the Sixth Plan could be two and a half times the 1965 level.

Adherence to this growth pattern would require that gross investment increase from 18 per cent. of GNP in 1965 to about 23 per cent. by 1985. In absolute terms, this means that the level of investment in the Sixth Plan period would have to be five times higher than in the Second. Since it is unrealistic to expect foreign assistance to continue at a proportionately high level, and since a major objective is to become self-reliant these investment targets imply that the country must save from one-fourth to one-third of all additions to output in the future.

To reach a stage wherein the country's own foreign exchange resources would be sufficient to meet its developmental and other needs, exports would have to grow by about 7–8 per cent. a year and the import component of investment would have to be reduced to 20 per cent. by 1985 (from a current level of about 47 per cent.). Fundamental changes in economic policies and social institutions are inevitable if the targets are to be reached. Increased incentives to export must be devised.. Reductions in the import component of investment can only be brought about by developing basic and heavy industries, especially in metallurgy. On this foundation, capital goods industries like machine tools, transport equipment, machinery for consumer goods plants, heavy chemicals and the like can be erected. Whether this can be done on Pakistan's existing resource-base remains to be seen. A

[21] There is some impression of euphoria in targets set for agriculture, exports, savings and employment as also expectations of foreign aid; these are based on experience in the latter years of the Second Plan which may not be wholly sustainable.

TABLE 51

TENTATIVE PROJECTIONS FOR THE PERSPECTIVE PLAN, 1965–85
(In millions of rupees 1964–5 prices)

	1965	1970	1975	1980	1985
Gross national product (market prices)	45,540	62,765	89,815	129,690	187,300
GNP growth rate (%)	(5·2)	(6·5)	(7·3)	(7·5)	(7·2)
Population (million)	112	128	147	168	187
Per capita income (Rs.)	407	490	611	772	1,002
Gross investment	8,400	12,700	19,180	28,650	42,800
Investment as a % of GNP	(18·5)	(20·2)	(21·4)	(22·1)	(22·9)
Gross domestic savings	4,710	8,515	15,180	26,150	40,800
Savings as a % of GNP	(10·3)	(13·6)	(16·9)	(20·2)	(21·8)
External resources	3,690	4,185	4,000	2,500	2,000
External resources as % of GNP	(8·1)	(6·7)	(4·5)	(1·9)	(1·1)
Exports and other receipts	3,050	4,800	7,300	11,000	14,000
Exports growth rate(%)	(7·2)	(9·5)	(8·8)	(8·5)	(5·0)
Imports and other payments	6,990	8,985	11,300	13,500	16,000
Imports growth rate (%)	14·6	(5·1)	(4·7)	(3·7)	(3·5)
Labour force (million man-years)	37·25	41·45	46·75	54·00	62·30
Employment (million man-years)	29·70	36·20	44·30	51·40	59·70
Unemployment as a % of labour force	(20)	(13)	(5)	(5)	(4)
Assumptions:					
Capital/output ratio (gross)	2·8	2·9	2·9	2·9	3·0
Marginal rate of saving (%)	22	22	25	28	25
Marginal propensity to import %)	15·5	12·1	9·0	6·0	4·0
Population growth rate (%)	2·6	2·7	2·8	2·6	2·1

Notes: 1. Percentage growth refers to compounded annual rates over five years.
2. Assumptions relate to preceding five year periods.
3. Capital/output ratio assumes no time-lag between investment and output.

Source: The Third Five Year Plan, Chapter 2.

vast programme of geological prospecting and revolutions in product-technology may open avenues that can be only dimly perceived at present.

Given reasonable internal stability and international co-operation, Pakistan has a chance of reaching its objectives. The ability to organize large enterprises efficiently, and to integrate them with other aspects of the economy is now gradually being acquired. New forms of social organizations, new habits and attitudes are developing. Most important perhaps is the conviction that Pakistan's leaders can and will administer the development effort with efficiency and determination, while persuading their fellow citizens to work together towards the common end of alleviating the poverty that is the lot of so many millions of Pakistanis.

BIBLIOGRAPHY

Ahmed, Ziauddin, *Central Banking in South and East Asia* (ed. G. Davies), Hong Kong, 1962.

Ahrensdorf, Joachim, 'Central Bank Policies and Inflation', *Staff Papers*, International Monetary Fund, Vol. VII, No. 2, Washington, 1959.

Baqai, Moinuddin, 'The National Bank of Pakistan, its origin and Development', Selected Papers in Pakistan Economy, Vol. 2, State Bank of Pakistan, Karachi, 1955.

Bell, David E., 'Allocating Development Resources: Some Observations Based on the Pakistan Experience', *Public Policy*, Vol. IX, Harvard, 1959.

Bose, S. R., 'Labour Force and Employment in Pakistan 1961–86: a preliminary analysis', *Pakistan Development Review*, Vol. III, No. 3, 1963.

Bruton, H. J. and Bose, S. R., 'Export Bonus Scheme: a Preliminary Report', *Pakistan Development Review*, Vol. II, No. 2, 1962.

Central Jute Committee, *Report on Cost of Production of Jute*, Karachi, 1962.

Central Statistical Office, *Monthly Bulletin*, Karachi.

Central Statistical Office, *Wholesale Price Index*, Karachi.

Comptroller General of the United States, *Economic and Technical Assistance Program for Pakistan*, Washington, 1959.

Credit Enquiry Commission, *Report*, Karachi, 1959.

Dacca University Socio-Economic Research Board, *Marketing of Jute in East Pakistan*, Dacca, 1961.

Darling, Sir Malcolm, *Punjab Peasant in Prosperity and Debt*, Bombay, 1947.

Finance and Revenue Department, Government of East Pakistan, *Economic Survey*, 1961–62.

Food and Agriculture Commission, *Report*, Karachi, 1960.

Food and Agricultural Organization, 'Jute: A Survey of Markets, Manufacturing, and Production', *Bulletin No. 28*, Rome, 1957.

George, G. M., Report to the Government of Pakistan on the Agricultural Bank of Pakistan, *Report No. 1321*, Food and Agricultural Organization, Rome, 1961.

Haq, Mahbub ul, *Strategy of Economic Planning*, Karachi, 1962.

Haq, Mahbub ul, and Khanam, Khadija, *Deficit Financing in Pakistan, 1951–60*, Institute of Development Economics, Karachi, 1961.

Hasan, Parvez, 'Balance of Payments Problems of Pakistan', *Pakistan Development Review*, Vol. I, No. 2, 1961.

Hasan, Parvez, *Deficit Financing and Capital Formation—the Pakistan Experience, 1951–59*, Institute of Development Economics, Karachi, 1962.

Husain, A. F. A., 'Pakistan's Commercial Policy in the Recession', *Pakistan Economic Journal*, Vol. 4, 1954.

Husain, Zahid, *Report of the Economic Appraisal and Development Enquiry Committee*, Karachi, 1953.

International Bank for Reconstruction and Development, *Annual Reports*, Washington.

Islam, N., 'Some Aspects of Inter-Wing Trade and Terms of Trade in Pakistan', *Pakistan Development Review*, Vol. III, No. 1, 1963.

Jute Enquiry Commission, *Report*, Government of Pakistan, Karachi, 1961.

Khan, A. R., 'Import Substitution, Export Expansion and Consumption Liberalization, a Preliminary Report', *Pakistan Development Review*, Vol. III, No. 2, 1963.

Khan, S. U., 'A Measure of Inflation in Pakistan—a Summary', *Pakistan Development Review*, Vol. I, No. 1, 1961.

Khan, S. U. and Khan, R. A., 'A note on the Wholesale Price Index in 1961', *Pakistan Development Review*, Vol I, No. 3, 1961.

Krotki, K. J., 'Population Growth, Size and Age Distribution; Fourth Release from the 1961 Census of Pakistan', *Pakistan Development Review*, Vol. III, No. 2, 1963.

Mason, Edward S., 'Economic Planning in Underdeveloped Areas', *Government and Business*, New York, 1958.

Ministry of Finance, *Annual Budgets*, Karachi and Rawalpindi.

Ministry of Finance, *Annual Financial Statements*, Karachi and Rawalpindi.

Ministry of Finance, *Explanatory Memorandum, Budget of the Central Government*, Rawalpindi, 1964–65.

Ministry of Finance, *Financial Institutions*, Office of the Economic Adviser, Rawalpindi, 1964.

Mohammad, A. F., *Some Aspects of the Impact of Foreign Aid on an Underdeveloped Country*, Unpublished Ph.D. Thesis, The George Washington University, Washington, 1958.

Mohammed, A. F., 'A Note on the Foreign Exchange Limitation,' *Pakistan Economic Journal*, Vol. IX, Nos. 2 and 3, 1959.

Pakistan Development Review, Karachi, quarterly.

Pakistan Economic Journal, Dacca, quarterly.

Pakistan Insurance Yearbook, 1961, Karachi.

Papanek, Gustav F. and Qureshi, Moin A., *The Use of Accounting*

Prices in Planning Organization and Programming for Economic Development, Geneva, 1963.

Planning Commission, *The Second Five Year Plan 1960–65*, Karachi, 1960.

Planning Commission, *Preliminary Evaluation of Progress during the Second Five Year Plan*, Karachi, 1965.

Planning Commission, *Mid-Plan Review*, Karachi, 1964.

Planning Commission, *Outline of the Third Five Year Plan*, Karachi, 1964.

Planning Commission, *The Third Five Year Plan 1965–70*, Karachi, 1965.

Porter, R. C., 'Income-Velocity and Pakistan's Second Plan', *Pakistan Development Review*, Vol. I., No. 1, 1961.

Power, John H., 'Industry in Pakistan: A Case of Frustrated Take-off', *Pakistan Development Review*, Vol. III, No. 2, 1963.

Power, John H., 'Two Years of Pakistan's Second Plan', *Pakistan Development Review*, Vol. III, No. 1, 1963.

Sadeque, A., 'Economic Emergence of Pakistan', *Dacca Economic Publications*, Series No. 1, Dacca, 1956.

Shonfield, Andrew, *The Attack on World Poverty*, London, 1960.

State Bank of Pakistan, *Action Plan for East Pakistan*, Karachi, 1962.

State Bank of Pakistan, *Agricultural Credit in Pakistan*, Karachi, 1962.

State Bank of Pakistan, *Balance of Payments*, Karachi, 1963.

State Bank of Pakistan, *Index Numbers of Stock Exchange Securities*, Karachi.

State Bank of Pakistan, *Marketing and Finance of Cotton in Pakistan*, Karachi, 1953.

Taxation Enquiry Committee, *Report Vol. I*, Karachi, 1961.

Waterston, Albert, *Planning in Pakistan*, Baltimore, 1963.

Wilcox, Clair, Pakistan (Chapter 3), *Planning Economic Development* (ed. Hagen), Homewood, Illinois, 1963.

INDEX